THE FIRE AND THE ROSE

BY THE SAME AUTHOR

The Story of England
*Makers of the Realm (B.C.–1272)
†The Age of Chivalry (1272–1381)

The Seventeenth Century
King Charles II (1630–1685)
Restoration England (1660–1688)
Samuel Pepys: The Man in the Making (1633–1669)
Samuel Pepys: The Years of Peril (1670–1683)
Samuel Pepys: The Saviour of the Navy (1683–1689)

The Napoleonic Wars
The Years of Endurance (1793–1802)
Years of Victory (1802–1812)
The Age of Elegance (1812–1822)
*Nelson (1758–1805)
The Great Duke (1769–1815)

The Victorian Age
English Saga (1840–1940)

Selected from above
*The Fire and the Rose

Social History selected from above
The Medieval Foundation
Protestant Island

The Alanbrooke Diaries
The Turn of the Tide (1939–1943)
Triumph in the West (1943–1946)

Autobiographical
The Lion and the Unicorn
Jimmy: The Dog in My Life

*available in Fontana
†to be published in Fontana

THE FIRE
AND THE ROSE

Dramatic Moments in British History

Arthur Bryant

Revised Edition

COLLINS/FONTANA

First published by Collins 1965
First issued as revised edition in Fontana Books 1972
© Introduction, Sir Arthur Bryant, 1972
© Text, in this edition, Sir Arthur Bryant, 1972

Printed in Great Britain
Love & Malcomson Ltd
Redhill, Surrey

*To Dick O'Connor
who in
the Western Desert,
when Britain stood alone,
took Time by the forelock*

CONTENTS

REFERENCES

The original works from which the chapters in this book are drawn and adapted are listed below.

THE BATTLE OF CRECY	*The Age of Chivalry*
THE PEASANTS' REVOLT	*The Age of Chivalry*
CHARLES II'S ESCAPE	*King Charles II*
THE FIRE OF LONDON	*Samuel Pepys: The Man in the Making*
THE RETREAT TO CORUNNA	*Years of Victory*
WATERLOO	*The Great Duke*
THE RISING IN THE NORTH	*English Saga*
THE SUMMER OF DUNKIRK	*The Lion and the Unicorn*

Why should we celebrate
These dead men more than the dying?
It is not to ring the bell backward
Nor is it an incantation
To summon the spectre of a Rose.
We cannot revive old factions
We cannot restore old policies
Or follow an antique drum.
These men, and those who opposed them
And those whom they opposed
Accept the constitution of silence
And are folded in a single party.
Whatever we inherit from the fortunate
We have taken from the defeated
What they had to leave us—a symbol:
A symbol perfected in death.
And all shall be well and . . .
All manner of thing shall be well
When the tongues of flames are in-folded
Into the crowned knot of fire
And the fire and the rose are one.

T. S. Eliot

INTRODUCTION
TO THE REVISED EDITION

My old friend and master, G. M. Trevelyan, always held that narrative was the essential basis of a historian's craft. For though, apart from his initial task of research, a writer of history has other and, perhaps, more important functions—of analysis, interpretation and judgment—man is a creature of time, and history is the record of what time does to him and of what he does with time. There are moments—T. S. Eliot called them 'timeless moments'—when the history of a nation, and sometimes of mankind itself, turned on what, in a few hours, days or weeks, men make of the time given them. Such a moment occurred over England during the summer of 1940; another 'in the hundred days that changed the world' at Petrograd in 1917. And the historian of such moments has, first and foremost, to use the instrument of narrative; to practise the chronicler's art.

Having at times essayed that art, in 1965 I took from the detailed mass of political, military, economic, social, legal, religious, literary and architectural history in which they are embedded in my books, eight accounts of decisive events in which men were pitted against time and one another. To give them unity and set them in a wider context of time, I partly adapted and re-wrote them. For the purpose of this edition I have replaced several of my original chapters in order to avoid duplication of episodes described in *Makers of the Realm* and *Nelson* which are being issued simultaneously in paperback. Nevertheless I have followed precisely the same principles as before in arranging the passages selected. Most were contests of will in which the contenders were ready to stake their all. Two occurred in the Middle Ages—the miraculous victory of an outnumbered army at Crécy, and the rising of a despairing peasantry who, turning against their rulers the weapon which had enabled them to triumph on the battlefields of

France, were only stayed by the courage of a young king from destroying the realm of which they were part. Two more are taken from my writings on the Seventeenth century, the one describing how another king, Charles II, was saved—and with him the English monarchy—by the loyalty and devotion of a handful of his poorest subjects, and the other how Samuel Pepys, diarist and naval administrator, fared in the Fire of London.

The next two narratives are taken from my account of the struggle between Britain and Revolutionary and Napoleon's France : the near-disastrous retreat of a British army to Corunna and the victory of another at Waterloo— 'the nearest run thing you ever saw in your life', as its commander, Wellington, called it. My last two examples, one from the Victorian age and the other from our own, record the despairing revolutionary attempt in 1842 of the mine and factory workers of the industrial North and Midlands to better their conditions, and the salvationary summer of 1940 when an isolated and apparently doomed Britain saved herself—and, by her example, the world—from the triumph of Nazi tyranny.

Through these widely diversified chronicles runs a common thread—of the greatness of the human spirit and its capacity to transcend disaster. Someone said of the British people that their spiritual home was the last ditch. It was certainly there that the protagonists in these contests found themselves. Their common theme is how men, who had reached the point of no return, faced death for something they felt to be greater than themselves. And because victors and vanquished are now, in T. S. Eliot's words, 'folded in a single party'—that of the grave and history—I have chosen my title from his poem, *Little Gidding*, which I quote on a previous page. For it is not the victor's triumph over their adversaries that matters today but their victory over themselves.

CHAPTER ONE

THE BATTLE OF CRÉCY 1346
The Grey Goose Feather

'No warring guns were then in use,
They dreamed of no such thing;
Our Englishmen in fight did use
The gallant grey-goose wing.

And with the gallant grey-goose wing
They shew'd to them such play
That made their horses kick and fling,
And down their riders lay.''

Old Ballad

The long-bow first appeared in England at the end of the thirteenth century, among the yeomen of the Cheshire and Midland forests who had learnt its use from the Welsh hillmen during the wars of Edward I. Under that king's statute of Winchester, and by the old Anglo-Saxon rule under which every free man between the ages of fifteen and sixty was expected to turn out with his personal arms in the shire levy to defend the realm and maintain the peace, the English countryman was trained to arms, unlike his counterpart on the continent where fighting was the preserve of heavily armoured mounted nobles and knights.

His chief arms were a long-bow and a sheaf of arrows. By the time of Edward III, after half a century of almost continuous campaigning against the Welsh and Scots, skill at archery in the woodland areas of England had become widespread. Practice at the village butts after service on Sundays was enjoined by law, and archery competitions were a favourite recreation on feast-days and holidays, when rustic bowmen

'showéd such brave archery
By cleaving sticks and wands.'

According to the Robin Hood ballads, which became

current about this time, there were occasions when they did
so in the presence of their warlike lords and princes. 'Bend
all your bows,' Robin bade his men,

> 'and with the grey-goose wing
> Such sport now show as you would do
> In the presence of the king.'

The legendary hero of these ballads—the North Country
outlaw who lived with his merry men in the greenwood and
robbed the rich to right the poor—was himself a wonderful marksman. Thrice, we are told, at the sheriff's archery
competitions at Nottingham,

> 'Robin shot about
> And always sliced the wand.'

And when he and his followers switched their aim from
the butts to the sheriff's men, the latter had to run for their
lives under a hail of arrows.

Originally in its native Wales made of rough, unpolished
wild elm, in England the long-bow was usually of yew. It
was drawn not by strength of arm but of the whole frame.
Bishop Latimer in a later century was taught as a boy to
lay his body to the bow and was given weapons of increas-
ing size as he grew bigger, 'for men shall never shoot well
unless they be brought up in it.' The arrows, a cloth-yard
long, were plumed with the feathers of the geese that had
fed on the village greens and commons:

> 'Their arrows finely pared, for timber and for feather,
> With birch and brazil pierc'd to fly in any weather,
> And shot they with the round, the square or forkéd pile,
> The loose gave such a twang as might be heard a mile.'

Even before the outbreak of the Hundred Years War with
France the long-bow had become the English weapon *par
excellence*—one which no other people could use and
which seemed designed for the Englishman's physique. A
century later a foreign visitor noted that the bows employed
by the island commonalty were 'thicker and longer than
those used by other nations, just as their bodies are stronger

than other people's.' In the hands of such masters as the Sherwood and Cheshire foresters the long-bow was a more deadly and accurate instrument of destruction than any hitherto known.

The first to feel its power were the Scots. Nineteen years after Robert Bruce's great victory over England's chivalry at Bannockburn, a Scottish army was attempting to relieve Berwick, then besieged by the young English king, Edward III. When on July 19th, 1333, it came within sight of the town, it found the English barring its path on the northern slopes of Halidon Hill. They were drawn up in a long thin line from which projected four triangular salients formed by archers, one on either flank and two in the centre. The three gradually narrowing funnels formed by these salients were closed at the top of the hill by three brigades of dismounted but armour-clad knights and men-at-arms with banners and pennons fluttering above the sheen of their swords and lances. Behind was a reserve brigade to deal with any attempt to drive in the archers on the wings, while in the rear, encircled by baggage-wagons, were laagers packed with horses awaiting a summons from their riders in the battle-line and guarded by the pages who looked after their masters' steeds and armour.

The trap set by the English king for the Scots was even more deadly than the Bannockburn bogs and the pits which Bruce had dug on the road to Stirling. For in the hands of English archers the long-bow of Gwent had come of age, and Edward and his lords had found a way to turn it into a military arm of startling mobility and killing-power. One of them, the crusader Henry of Grosmont—son of the king's cousin, the earl of Lancaster—had fought at Bannockburn, and it may have been this brilliant, imaginative commander who first saw how the long-bow could be used to revolutionise the art of war. What seems certain is that during those waiting weeks while the English army was blockading Berwick the archers, whom Edward's commissioners of array had gathered from the northern and midland counties, were trained to manœuvre and exercise their art under orders, just as Bruce's pikesmen before

Bannockburn had been trained to fight the battle he had
foreseen. Brigaded with men-at-arms from their native
shires and disciplined by veterans who had learnt war the
hard way on the Welsh and Scottish hills, they were taught
to operate, not only as individual marksmen, but in massed
phalanxes from which, at the word of command, rhythmic
volleys of arrows, travelling at incredible speed, could be
directed first at one part of an attacking force, then at another, until every living thing in the target area had been
killed or maimed. In their metal helmets and padded
deerskin jackets these light, active men could manœuvre in
extended order, enfilade a column from flank or even rear
and, combining fire and movement, at a bugle call or other
signal, reform, under cover of their comrades' volleys, in
massed ranks in which, so long as their ammunition lasted,
they were virtually unassailable.

As the Scottish pikesmen moved forward in dense schil-
trons across the marshy ground at the foot of the hill, they
suddenly came into range of the archers. Though hundreds
fell as the showers of steel-tipped arrows struck home, they
pressed stubbornly on. Lowering their heads against the
blinding hail and closing their ranks, they instinctively
edged away from the salients of archers on either side of
them and started to climb. Packed together till they were
almost suffocated, riven and tormented by the shooting of
the marksmen and the massed volleys from the formations
into which the archers withdrew at every attempt to attack
them, they stumbled up the slope towards the waiting line
of English armour and the one place on the battlefield
where no arrows were falling. When, breathless from the
ascent, the survivors reached that hedge of levelled lances,
the knights and men-at-arms started to hack at them with
great swords and battle axes, forcing them down the slope
where they came once more into that enfilading hail. The
regent of Scotland was mortally wounded, and six earls
were left dead on the field. Altogether the seventy Scots
lords and five hundred knights and squires fell, and almost
the entire infantry. The defenders lost one knight, one
man-at-arms and twelve archers.

Four years after this battle—which attracted little notice outside the British Isles—England became involved in a long, inconclusive war with France, originally caused by French attempts to whittle away the hereditary rights and domains of the English king in Gascony. During its course, in order to forestall charges of treason against his allies, the Flemish weavers—vassals of the French king and the chief buyers of English wool—Edward III advanced a dubious dynastic claim to the throne of France. In its pursuit, in the summer of 1346 he crossed the Channel with a small, well-equipped army, raised, unlike the feudal hosts of the continent, by indenture—a system under which fighting lords recruited, at agreed rates of pay, the numbers and types of fighting men required by the Crown. Such retinues comprised both armoured and mounted knights and men-at-arms and large numbers of bowmen. The latter, who were paid at the then high rate of sixpence a day, carried, in addition to their bows and sheaves of arrows, short swords, knives and steel-tipped stakes for building protective hedges against cavalry.

The English landed on July 12th at St. Vaast in Normandy almost without opposition. Once ashore, the king wasted no time. On the 18th, after knighting the sixteen-year-old Prince of Wales, he began his march on Rouen with the intention of joining hands with the Flemings in the north. Crossing the marshes at the south-eastern foot of the Cotentin peninsula, where his pioneers and carpenters repaired the demolished bridges over the Vire, he reached St. Lô on the 22nd. By keeping abreast with the army's left flank the fleet provided a moveable base, while the troops lived on the countryside, avenging the raids of Norman seamen on the English south-coast towns by burning their harbours and ships. After a few days of this atrocious business—the usual accompaniment of fourteenth-century warfare—the king, as claimant to the French throne, issued an order threatening death to any soldier who should 'set on fire towns or manors, . . . rob churches or holy places, do harm to the aged, the children or women of his realm.'

Edward's French subjects showed no enthusiasm for their would-be sovereign. The peasants fled in terror from his march and, when on July 25th he summonsed Caen, the Bishop of Bayeux tore up the summons and imprisoned his messenger. Yet, though a formidable town—larger, a chronicler wrote, than any English city save London—the invaders carried it in a day after the archers had out-shot the cross-bowmen defending the Orne crossings, and the

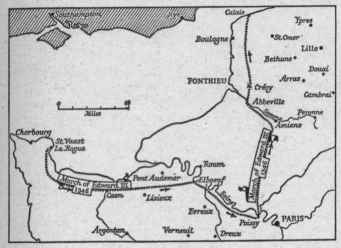

The Campaign of 1346

fleet, sailing up the river from Ouistreham, had joined in the fight. They took a rich haul of prisoners and a copy of a treaty made eight years before by King Philip of France with the Normen authorities for an invasion of England. This Edward sent home to be read in parliament.

On the last day of July the march to the Seine was resumed. On August 2nd the army reached Lisieux. But on the same day the French king entered Rouen forty miles ahead, interposing his force between the English and their Flemish allies who, two hundred miles to the north, were just setting out from Ypres. As soon as news had reached him of Edward's landing he had raised the oriflamme at St. Denis and, recalling his son, who was attacking the English in Gascony, hurried to the Norman capital, gathering troops as he marched. The Seine here was three hundred yards wide and, with the city held in force, the English could not hope to cross.

Instead, on reaching the river at Elboeuf, twelve miles above Rouen, they turned upstream to seek a narrower crossing. By doing so they abandoned their communications with England but threatened Paris. For the next six days the rival armies marched south-eastwards along opposite sides of the Seine. Everywhere the English found the bridges demolished or strongly held. But on the 13th, when they were only a dozen miles from the capital, Edward allowed the French to outmarch him and, by a sudden feint, turned back to Poissy where the bridge, only partially destroyed, was lightly guarded. Crossing by a single sixty-foot beam only a foot wide, Northampton, the constable, got a detachment to the far side. For the next two days, while skirmishing parties set fire to St. Cloud and other villages under the western walls of Paris to deceive the enemy, the carpenters worked feverishly to repair the bridge. Meanwhile, though by now in far superior strength, King Philip remained in a frenzy of indecision, marching first to one side of his capital and then the other, uncertain whether the English were about to assault it or move south to Gascony.

On August 15th the carpenters finished their work, and during that night and next morning the army and its baggage train crossed the Seine. In the next five days it marched seventy miles due north, hoping to cross the Somme between Amiens and Abbeville and join hands with the Flemings who were besieging Bethune, fifty miles beyond that river. But though he had been temporarily outwitted, when he found that his foe had crossed the Seine King Philip acted with equal speed. Realising at last Edward's weakness, he covered the seventy-three miles from Paris to Amiens in three days, ordering the feudal levies of the north to join him there. With him were the flower of France's chivalry, together with King John of Bohemia and his son, Charles of Moravia—titular King of the Romans.

The position of the English was grave in the extreme. Between them and their Flemish allies in Artois lay the marshy valley of the Somme, with the French king at Amiens only a day's march away and every bridge over the river in his hands. All contact had been lost with the fleet, whose seamen had returned to England in the wake of the ships that had taken home the sick and the spoils of Caen. The army's food supplies were almost exhausted and in the closing stages of their march the troops had been living on unripe fruit. After covering nearly three hundred miles their boots were worn out and the horses dying for lack of forage.

Edward had been far too bold. But he showed no sign of his anxiety; 'he was so great hearted,' a contemporary wrote, 'that he never blanched or changed countenance at any illhap or trouble soever.' On August 23rd he started westwards in the hope of finding a crossing above Abbeville, but, as the estuary here widened to two miles, the prospect was unpromising. Scarcely had he set out when news arrived that Philip had left Amiens and, moving up the south bank of the river to attack, was already within a mile of Airaines where the English had spent the previous night.

Cut off in a strange land and without maps—a military commodity then unknown—the king ordered the prisoners to be brought before him and offered a huge reward for anyone who would reveal a crossing place. A native of the district told him of a concealed causeway across the estuary at Blanchetaque, midway between Abbeville and the sea, where at low tide a man could cross waist-deep. Without hesitation Edward decided to take the risk.

It was a hundred and thirty years since his great-great-grandfather, John, had lost his baggage and treasure in the Wash in a similar crossing. Before dawn on the 24th, marching the six miles to the ford in single column his advance-guard reached the river. The far bank was held

by a French force of between three and four thousand men.
As soon as the tide was low enough for a man to stand
without being swept away, the troops started to cross, led
by Hugh Despenser, whose father had been hanged on a
fifty-foot gallows by Edward's mother. Carrying their bows
above their heads to keep them dry, the archers struggled
through a mile and a half of water, while the knights followed on horseback. A few hundred yards from the
northern bank they came within range of the enemy's
cross-bowmen but continued to advance until they were in
killing distance. Then, standing ten abreast on the causeway and shooting over one another's heads, they loosed
their usual devastating hail. When their arrows were
exhausted they stepped into the deeper water on either side
and let the mounted armour splash past them into the
shallows where, after a brisk skirmish, it put the French
cavalry to flight.

Meanwhile on the south bank Edward's rear-guard had
been holding off the advance echelons of Philip's host until
the baggage wagons, with their precious load of arrows
and cannon, had passed through the water, now starting
rapidly to rise. Save for a few stragglers who were caught
by the tide the whole army passed over in safety. The
enemy, barred by the rising flood, could only watch in
amazement.[1]

After crossing the Somme the English fanned out. The
constable pursued the enemy towards Abbeville, while
Hugh Despenser pushed down the estuary as far as the
little port of Crotoy where he seized some wine-ships. By
nightfall the whole army was encamped in the forest of
Crécy, a few miles north of the ford. Though the troops
were still short of rations, their morale was high, for in a
deeply religious age the passage of the river seemed a
miracle. The king therefore decided to stand and give
battle. The odds against him were immense, but with so
cautious an adversary such an opportunity might never
recur.

All day on Friday the 25th, while the French were re-
crossing the Somme, he searched for a defensive position.

He found it on a low ridge facing south-west, between the villages of Crécy and Wadicourt. Behind lay a wood—the Bois de Crécy-Grange—into which and the forest of Crécy on his right his woodland-trained archers could withdraw in case of need.

.　　　.　　　.

On the morning of August 26th, 1346, having attended Mass and 'committed his cause to God and the Blessed Virgin,' Edward marched his army to its position. Allowing for losses he had now about 13,000 men, of whom more than half were archers, and, at the outside, some three thousand knights and men-at-arms. Under his directions the marshals deployed the latter in three divisions or 'battles,' two of them a little way down the forward slope of the ridge, which was about a mile long, and the third under his personal command in reserve. He himself took up his station in a windmill in the centre, with an extensive view of the valley which the French would have to cross. The right-hand division was under the earls of Warwick and Oxford with the Prince of Wales in titular command, and the other commanded by the constable. As usual, the knights and men-at-arms were dismounted in single line, their horses being taken by the pages to the wagon-laager in the rear.

Forming four projecting salients on the flanks of each of the forward divisions were the archers, with Welsh spearmen in support. Before retiring to their laager, the baggage-wagons unloaded a supply of arrows along their lines. In front, to protect themselves from the cavalry, they hammered in iron-pointed stakes and dug pot-holes as the Scots had taught their predecessors to do. Such a formation, like that at Halidon Hill, was calculated to force the attackers into two narrowing gulleys where they would have to contend with the English armour while raked by arrows from the flanks.

When the troops were all posted, the king rode along the ranks on a small palfrey, carrying a white wand and wearing a crimson surcoat of golden leopards. To each contingent he spoke a few words. Beside him was Sir Guy de Brian,[2] bearing the dragon banner of Wessex—the standard under which the English had fought at Hastings. It was a symbol of the national character Edward had given his army—so different from that of the feudal hosts of the past.

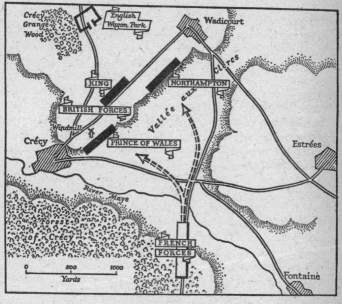

Crécy

'Next to God,' it was said of him, 'he reposed his confidence in the valour of his subjects.'

After the king's inspection the army dispersed for the midday meal, which the cooks had been preparing in the baggage-laager, the men-at-arms leaving their helmets to mark their stations and the archers their bows and arrows. It had been arranged that the trumpets should recall them at the first sign of the enemy, who were now believed to be moving up from Abbeville. During the afternoon there was

a heavy shower, which brought the archers scurrying back
to their lines to guard their bowstrings, each man unstring-
ing his and placing it in a coil under his helmet. Afterwards the sun came out and the men sat down in their
lines with their weapons in front of them. There was still
no sign of the French, and it was felt that there would be
no battle that day.

But a little before four o'clock the trumpets sounded
and everyone stood to arms. Coming out of the woods
three miles to the south-east along the track still known as
le chemin d'armée was the French vanguard. For a whole
hour the English watched as Philip's immense host moved
into view, 'the fresh shining armour, the banners waving in
the wind, the companies in good order, riding a soft pace.'
According to the lowest estimate which has come down from
the fourteenth century, they were 40,000 strong, of whom
more than 12,000 were mounted knights and men-at-arms.
They rode forward in eight successive divisions, so that
there seemed no end. The advance-guard was commanded
by the blind King John of Bohemia—a romantic figure
and world-famous warrior—who was accompanied by the
French king's brother, the Count of Alençon, and the
Count of Flanders whom Edward's allies, the burghers of
Ghent, had driven from his country. The centre was under
the Duke of Lorraine with Philip's nephew, the Count of
Blois, as lieutenant.

The king—'Philip Valois tyrant of the French,' as the
English chroniclers called him—followed with the rearguard, together with the German King of the Romans,
Charles of Moravia, and the exiled King of Majorca.
There were nearly a score of ruling counts, French, German,
Luxemburger and Spanish. It was not so much a national
army as the embodiment of the international chivalry
which for three centuries had dominated the battlefields of
the continent, commanded by the greatest monarch in
Christendom. Above him waved the oriflamme—the sacred
banner flown when no quarter was to be given to France's
enemies. For there had been disputes on the previous night
about the allocation and ransom of the prisoners, and to

prevent quarrelling the king had given orders to slay them all.

In addition to this array of chivalry there marched among the vanguard six or seven thousand Genoese cross-bowmen, the best trained troops on the continent and the only professionals in the host. The rest of the army was composed of peasant levies—the 'communes' as they were called—low-spirited serfs considered incapable of standing up to gentlemen, but useful to follow in the wake of their mounted superiors and help crush the foe by sheer weight of numbers. In the French army infantry were despised; it was knights—'the crested helmets'—who counted.

Goliath was pitted against David, but David had a sling. David, too, had discipline which Goliath lacked. When the French vanguard reached the valley in front of the English position the sun was already starting to sink, and Philip's advisers urged him to halt for the night and deploy for battle in the morning. To this, the only sane course, the king, who had not expected to find the English barring his path, agreed. But his vassals had other views. Seeing the English with their banners on the ridge, the young knights—arrogant and inexperienced—pressed forward, impatiently confident that they were at their mercy. Before even a blow had been struck the French army was out of control and committed to an attack undeployed.

The vanguard, therefore, came straight on, halting only to let the Genoese bowmen open the attack. With trumpets and clarions sounding they started to climb the ridge. The setting sun was in their eyes and it was hard to focus their target, waiting motionless and ready.

At this point, wrote Froissart, 'when the Genoese began to approach, they made a great leap and cry to abash the Englishmen. But they stood still and stirred not for all that. Then the Genoese again the second time made another leap and a fell cry and stept forward a little, and the English removed not one foot. Thirdly again they leapt and cried and went forward till they came within shot; then they shot fiercely with their cross-bows. Then the English archers stept forth one pace and let fly their arrows so wholly together and so thick that it seemed snow.' Firing four or five times faster than the cross-bowmen, they shot them out of the field. To add to the Italians' confusion and terror, two or three English cannons—a novelty from the Tower armoury which had been dragged round France and concealed among the archers—opened fire, sending their balls of iron and stone rolling through the densely packed ranks amid flames and smoke.

As the Genoese broke, the French knights, with a cry of, 'Ride down the rascals,' charged through their ranks, trampling down the wounded and dying. They rode in a dense, glittering line of solid armour, waving plumes and levelled lances. Everyone expected them to crush the thin, defending line of the Prince of Wales's division before them. But they never reached it. For once again the English archers stepped forward.

As their arrows, aimed at the chargers, struck home, the stately advance dissolved into disorderly heaps and clusters of dead and wounded horses and of dismounted knights weighed down by their armour. Those who went forward on foot or succeeded in driving their terrified beasts through the hail of arrows came up against a solid line of English men-at-arms, as steady as the archers who continued shooting down each new batch of attackers as they struggled up the hill through the fading light.

The fight had now become general, with the second French wave assailing the constable's division. But everywhere the result was the same; the mounted knights struggling to reach and break the line of the English armour above them and the archers continuing to massacre their horses. There was no-one to give the former orders and no-one to co-ordinate the attack. For five hours, though darkness had fallen, the mêlée continued, wave after wave of knights entering the fight only to meet the same fate. At one moment it seemed as if the Prince of Wales's slender force would be overwhelmed, and Godfrey de Harcourt hurried across to the nearest unit of the constable's division to beg its commander, Lord Arundel, to make a flanking attack to relieve the pressure. But when a similar appeal reached the king, he only remarked, 'Let the boy win his spurs.' For he knew that the moment to throw in his reserves had not yet come. When the messenger returned he found the prince and his companions leaning quietly on their swords, taking breath as, amid mounds of French corpses, they waited for the next attack.

Soon after midnight, after fifteen or sixteen assaults had failed, the French army began to dissolve. The dead were now piled in walls before the English lines. Among them was the blind King of Bohemia, the reins of his bridle tied to those of the knights with whom he had charged. Two archbishops, the royal Count of Alençon, the Duke of Lorraine and the counts of Blois and Flanders had all fallen. King Philip himself, his horse shot under him, was led from the field as Edward II had been from Bannockburn. There was no pursuit, for the English king, who had never once lost his grip on the battle, had forbidden his men to break rank.

As the French melted away into the darkness and no more attacks came, the exhausted victors lay down, supperless and waterless, to sleep where they had fought. When, on the misty morrow they counted the dead they found the bodies of more than 1,500 knights and 10,000 common soldiers. The French army had ceased to exist. Edward himself with his son attended the burial of John of Bohemia—a paladin after his own heart, who had long predicted that he would die in battle against the bravest knights in the world.

A new phenomenon had appeared in the western world: the military power of England. 'The might of the realm,' wrote the astonished Froissart, 'most standeth upon archers which are not rich men.' The English had shown that on their own ground they could conquer against any odds and almost without cost. Their losses at Crécy were forty dead, only three of them men-at-arms.

CHAPTER TWO

THE PEASANTS' REVOLT, 1381
The Hurling Time

'Englishmen suffer indeed for a season, but in
the end they repay so cruelly that it may stand
as a great warning. . . . There is no people
under the sun so perilous in the matter of its
common folk as they are in England.'

Froissart

Two years after Crécy, England suffered the greatest social
disaster in her history. The Black Death or bubonic plague
carried off a third of her people, and, in three further out-
breaks during the next quarter of a century, the population
fell to about half its pre-1348 figure. One result was a grave
labour shortage and a spectacular rise in wages, which the
Council and successive parliaments of landowners tried
to prevent by punitive ordinances and legislation. These
statutes of Labourers aroused bitter class-feeling.

Yet for a century before the Black Death the position of
the English peasant had been slowly improving, whether
he was a well-to-do yardlander farming two or three
hundred acres or a landless cottar earning his daily bread
by wages. Compared with the wretched peasantry of the
continent, he was not too badly off except when the harvest
failed; the bowmen of Crécy had not been drawn from an
oppressed populace. It was a commonplace to contrast the
lot of the stalwart English husbandman with that of the
French serf, wrapped in sacking and living on apples and
bitter rye-bread.

Yet probably somewhere near half the English people
were not legally free but tied by inheritance to the soil
they cultivated. Described as villeins and subject to the
discipline of the lord's manorial court—on whose juries
and inquests they served—they could not claim a free
man's rights under the Common Law, let alone representa-

tion in parliament. Like the feudalism of which it was part, the servile manorial system of the open field villages of central and southern England had long been in decline and was gradually giving way to an economy based on paid labour and rented farms. But it was still the basis of life for nearly a million men and women who, though not technically slaves, were bound by birth to the soil and compelled to perform unpaid menial services for its lord. They could only gain release by a formal grant of manu-mission or by flight from their homes and fields to some chartered borough where servile status had been abolished and residence for a year and a day gave a man his freedom.

The extent of the services the villein had to perform for his lord varied with the size of his holding and the custom of the manor. But wherever the open-field system operated, as it did in most parts of England except the pastoral north and west and in Kent, the peasant was confronted by uncertain demands on his time and galling restrictions on his freedom of action. Among these were the obligations to grind his corn, bake his bread and brew his ale at the lord's mill, oven and brewery—'suit of mill' and 'suit of oven,' as they were called—which not only enriched the lord, but offered opportunities for every kind of chicanery and oppression by those to whom the latter leased his rights. An equally resented monopoly was the lord's dove-cot and 'free warren' from which hordes of pigeons and rabbits descended on the peasant's crops, while if he retaliated by trapping such pests he faced a heavy fine in the manorial court. If he wished to sell a beast, if he wished to reside outside the manor, if he wished to marry his son or daughter, even if the latter became pregnant—for this depreciated her value—he was fined. And on his death his widow or heir was forced to pay a heriot—the value of the best beast and chattel—and an entry-fine equivalent to a year's rent as the price of taking over the family holding.

All this had come to be intensely resented. Villeinage was seen by the bondsman as an economic imposition and a degrading distinction. It was no longer taken for granted, and every opportunity was taken to escape or evade its

burdens. Those who resented them most were the richer
villagers who occupied the traditional yardlands—holdings
of thirty acres or more in the arable fields, with correspond-
ing rights in the manorial meadowland, waste and woodland. A yardlander had to perform for his holding, in
person or by proxy, not only a full half-day's labour on the
lord's land for three or four days a week throughout the
year but additional services called 'love-boons'—given, in
theory, out of love for his feudal protector—at the very
seasons, haymaking and harvest, harrowing and sowing
times, when he needed all the labour he could command
to wrest a living from his own soil.

Those who could afford it, therefore, seized every opportunity to commute as many of such services as possible for
money payments. In the expanding agricultural economy
of the thirteenth and early fourteenth century many
peasants were able to free themselves from the more
onerous burdens, for progressive landowners often found
it paid them to hire labour rather than depend on the
unwilling services of disgruntled serfs. The halving of the
national labour-force by the Black Death halted this
gradual emancipation. Labour suddenly became the most
precious commodity in the kingdom. A landowner who had
made no concessions to his serfs found himself able to
cultivate his depopulated estates far more cheaply than
one who had commuted his villeins' services for a cash
payment. Bound by agreements to let their serfs enjoy their
holdings at rents which now bore no relation to what they
themselves had to pay for hired labour, and desperate for
lack of workers, many lords tried to enforce rights that had
lapsed or to stretch those that remained.

If the Black Death made lords more conscious of the
value of compulsory services, it made every serf more eager
to evade them. Shaking off their ancestral shackles, bondsmen fled from their homes and took service for wages with
distant employers who asked no questions. It was the poorer
members of the village community who had no land to
lose who were able to seize such opportunities—the young
and those with no possessions but their tools and skill as

husbandmen or craftsmen. The attempts of the Commons
and local justices to keep down wages by branding,
imprisonment and the stocks drove them to make common
cause with their richer neighbours, who were confronted
by demands from their lords for services which they regarded as unjust and oppressive.

It was against the lord's officers and agents that the
peasant's indignation was, in particular, directed. From the
receivers and bailiffs who wrung from him the services and
rents on which the landowner lived, from the steward who
presided at his manorial court and the lawyers who made
extreme claims on his behalf, he received little mercy.
Times were bad, money hard to come by for a luxurious
ruling class in need of the income it could no longer obtain
from victories abroad. The business of its agents was to
exact the uttermost service and payment obtainable. In the
process they often took—and even more often were suspected of taking—more than was due or than the lord
himself received.

Some of the hardest task-masters were the monasteries
who, hit by the economic recession and the plague, had
never enjoyed, like the secular lords, the opportunity of
making good their losses by the plunder and ransoms of
war. Intensely conservative and, like all corporations, impersonal in business relationships, they had the justification
that their exactions were for the service of God. More
easily than most they were able to prove rights to long-
lapsed services by the charters which every religious house
preserved, added to by cultivating the friendship of the
great and sometimes, if their critics are to be believed,
improved by a little pious and skilled forgery. Nor, conscious of the sanctity of their claims, were they always very
tactful with those whose labour they exploited; the abbot
of Burton told his tenants that they owned nothing but
their bellies.

Of all who enforced the lord's rights the lawyer was the
most hated. To the peasant the purpose of the law seemed
to be to keep him down and enforce the servile status that
deprived him of liberty and opportunity. In the thirty years

after the first post-Black Death statute against what Council and parliament called 'the malice of labourers,' nearly nine thousand cases of wage enforcement were tried by the courts and in nearly all judgment was given in the employer's favour. The peasant's indignation at those who put such restraints on him was increased by the spectacle of expanding freedom in the chartered towns which had sprung up in every part of England and to which so many of the younger men of his village had fled to better their conditions. Some of these, who had survived the harsh conditions and competition of the medieval town, had grown rich and famous.

Because of this, and for other reasons, there was a captious, bitter, disillusioned spirit abroad. The strain and cost of the long war with France, which after its resumption in 1369 turned against England, tended like the successive visitations of the Black Death to shake men's faith in society. The pestilence which had driven weak natures to a hectic pursuit of pleasure, elevating the self-indulgence of the moment above duty and morality, had left only half the labour formerly available to do the nation's work and supply the luxuries of the rich. For a generation the burden of war debts and taxes had borne with what seemed insupportable severity on the survivors. The result was a widespread sense of frustration, of loss of familiar standards, of resentment between employer and employed, landowner and husbandman, government and taxpayer. Everyone tended to blame someone else for his sufferings.

Deep down the malaise of England after the Black Death was spiritual. It was the sickness of soul of a people who felt that justice was being outraged. The old static feudalism, in which every man knew and accepted his place, was disintegrating; the more fluid society which was replacing it was on the make and given to lavish and ostentatious luxury. The reign of Edward III had witnessed a steady rise in the standards of comfort, not only of the aristocracy but of new classes—financiers, merchants, woolmasters, franklins, master-craftsmen. Hearths with chimneys had taken the place in rich men's houses of sooty open fires; Flemish glass had appeared in traceried windows; dovecots, fishponds and nut-alleys were laid out in parks and gardens; manor-houses and fine merchants' dwellings, with private bedrooms and plastered walls, were rising in place of the old gloomy fortresses where men and beasts had slept together on filthy, rush-strewn floors in draughty halls, full of smoke and stink. Yet such signs of progress struck moralists like the poet, William Langland, as symptoms of a diseased society :

> 'Ailing is the hall   each day in the week
> Where the lord nor the lady   liketh not to sit.
> Now hath each rich man a rule   to eaten by himself
> In a privy parlour,   for poor men's sake,
> Or in a chamber with a chimney,   and leave the chief hall
> That was made for meals   and men to eaten in.'

With the advance in civilization, arts and sciences, exchange of goods and merchandise had thrown the career open to the talents. In every city a race of men had arisen who pursued money-making as an end in itself, who bought and sold not primarily to supply the consumer with goods but to increase their stock of money and use it for making more. Usury, forestalling, regrating, making a corner in commodities and artificially lowering market-prices in order to buy and raising them in order to sell—all the practices which the Church had taught were unchristian and unneighbourly—were pursued as a profession by men who made fortunes by doing so and put ordinary folk out of countenance by extravagant living and the grandeur of their ways. Merchants whose grandfathers or even fathers had been simple craftsmen or serfs were addressed by their fellow townsmen as worshipful or sire, wore scarlet robes and costly furs as masters and liverymen of monopolistic merchant companies founded originally to protect and foster honest craftsmanship. By their own standards most of them were worthy, if self-important, men whose bond could be trusted by their fellows; they could hardly have continued to succeed otherwise. Yet there was a widespread

feeling that vintners diluted wine, that woolmongers
cheated wool-growers, that grocers and corn-merchants
sold false measure, that those who lent money to the
Crown cheated the tax-payer, and that if a man had
grown rich by trade he must be a rogue. And some of those
who had made money out of the French war were vulgar
upstarts with extravagant standards of display and
notorious for jobbery and corruption. 'Soapmongers and
their sons for silver,' wrote the indignant Langland, 'are
made knights.' 'Covetise hath dominion over all things,'
complained his fellow poet, Gower; 'there is no city or
good town where Trick does not rob to enrich himself.
Trick at Bordeaux, Trick at Sevile, Trick at Paris buys and
sells; Trick has his ships and servants, and of the noblest
riches, Trick has ten times more than other folk.'

Running through society, including the Church, was this
sense of division, strife and covetousness. 'Avarice,' a
preacher said, 'makes men fight one another like dogs over
a bone.' By its side went 'the foul sin of pride.' Both the
old ruling class and the new vied in the extravagance of
their clothes, feasts and entertainments; 'in such manner
they spent and wasted their riches with abuses and ludicrous wantonness that the common voice of the people
exclaimed.' Contrasted with 'the gay robes, the soft sheets,
the small shirts' of the rich was the peasant, with his gar-
ment of hodden grey, living on cold cabbage, bacon and
penny ale; his wattle-and-log hut full of holes; the poor
Norfolk deerstalker whose feet were so putrefied by the
dungeons of Norwich castle that he could not walk at his
trial, and his eight fellow-prisoners who died in Northampton gaol from hunger, thirst and want. 'I have no penny,'
declared Langland's Piers Plowman,

> 'pullets for to buy
> Neither geese nor gris but two green cheeses,
> A few curds and cream and a cake of oats,
> And two loaves of beans and bran to bake for my
> bairns.'

To him it seemed a denial of Christianity that the honest

poor should be defrauded. His heart was stirred and his indignation roused for 'prisoners in pits' and poor folk in cottages 'charged with children and chief lord's rent,' and country women 'rising with rue in winter nights to rock the cradle,'

'To card and to comb to clout and to wash; . . .
Many the children and nought but a man's hands
. To clothe and feed them and few pennies taken.'

Out of the air of fourteenth-century England, with all its glaring inequalities, arose the conviction—so strangely contrasted with the assumptions of the warrior and prelate class—that 'the peasant maintained the state of the world' and was receiving less than justice. It was put in its highest form by Langland, who in his *Vision of Piers Plowman* voiced the recurring English reaction to the contrast between ill-used wealth and undeserved destitution, with its characteristic resolve, not to destroy society, but to redress the balance. Though it never seems to have attained the dignity of an illuminated manuscript—the *imprimatur* of fashionable esteem in that intensely aristocratic age—his poem had an astonishing success; some sixty copies have survived and, since it circulated among the poor and lowly, far more must have perished. Overlooked by the rich like the *Pilgrim's Progress* of a later age, its readers and copyists were probably parish priests and it may have been through them and their sermons that the name of its humble peasant hero and his identification with the crucified Christ became so widely known. At the end of the fourteenth and the beginning of the fifteenth century there appeared on the nave walls of parish churches in southern England a number of paintings, crude and almost certainly executed by local hands, of Christ naked, lacerated and bleeding, with a carpenter's tools—mallet, hammer, knife, axe, pincers, horn and wheel—haloed round his head. This figure of 'Christ of the Trades,' is to be found in churches as far apart as Pembrokeshire and Suffolk. Many more probably disappeared during the Reformation; among the best preserved are those at Ampney St. Mary in the Cots-

wolds—not far from the hillside on which Langland saw
silhouetted the tower of Truth—at Hessett in Suffolk and
at Stedham in Sussex. In the first, the labouring Christ
faces a painting of the hero of knightly chivalry, St. George
slaying the dragon; in the last, of the Virgin sheltering
the congregation under her cloak.

.   .   .

There was a wide gap between the patient, Christ-like
craftsman and peasant of the wall-paintings and of Langland's dream, and the angry labourer refusing service for
his lord, cursing landlords, monks and lawyers and finger-
ing his bow. It was not hard to inflame uneducated men
with a sense of injury, and it was not the selfless side of
human nature that was inflamed. The poet himself was
well aware of it. 'Then,' he wrote,

'would Wastour not work   but wandren about. . . .
Labourers that have no land   to live on but their hands,
Deigned not to dine today   on yesterday's cabbage,
No penny ale may please them   nor no piece of bacon,
But if it be fresh flesh or fish   fried or baked.'

He depicted the runagate villein, demanding ever higher
wages, who, when refused,

'would wail the time   that ever he was workman born;
Then curseth he the king   and all his Council with him
That lay down such laws   the labourers to grieve.'

Parliament was being flouted and the Statute of Labourers
made a dead letter by surly villeins standing idle in the
fields or tramping in angry companies to the nearest town
to sell their labour to those who would pay highest for it.
Phrases like 'stand together!', 'make a good end of what
hath been begun!' passed from shire to shire, and wandering agitators preached incendiary sermons on village
greens. 'Things will never go well in England,' proclaimed
the defrocked hedge-priest and demagogue, John Ball, 'so
long as goods be not in common and so long as there be

villeins and gentlemen. By what right are they whom we call lords greater than we?' 'We are formed,' he declared, 'in Christ's likeness and they treat us like beasts.'

It was an age of war and violence; war always breeds violence. Resentment amongst the labouring classes against their oppressors was not confined to England. In the middle of the century the Roman mob had risen under the demagogue Cola di Rienzo; a decade later occurred the terrifying Jacquerie or peasants' revolt in northern France. Wherever men were brought together in large numbers to serve masters who catered for the luxuries of the rich, the spirit of rebellion was present. In 1378 the oppressed wool-carders of Florence revolted against the merchant oligarchs of the city, stormed the palazzo of the Commune and installed one of their members as Gonfalonier of Justice. A year later the weavers of Ghent and Bruges and the Flemish cloth towns had risen and were still defying their count and the French king.

In England unrest so far had mainly taken the form of mass withdrawals of labour-services, particularly in places where the lord was an impersonal ecclesiastical corporation. When the jurymen of Harmsworth, Middlesex—the property of a Norman abbey—defied the lord's steward by returning a false verdict in favour of their fellow villeins who had absented themselves from the previous year's haymaking, the villagers deliberately opened the river sluices to flood the hay. There were mob rescues of fugitive bondsmen as they were being haled back to their 'villein nests,' and armed assemblies by night to poach the lord's woods and slay his game. The labour laws, too, help to explain the passion and vehemence of some of these sudden explosions of rustic wrath, often on seemingly trivial pretexts. Englishmen were not prepared to suffer the indignity of being branded on the forehead with an 'F' for 'falsehood' because they took day-hire or demanded more than the inadequate statutory wage allowed by parliament. A year or two after the first Statute of Labourers, when feeling against this form of class legislation was running particularly strong, the peasants from the villages round

Oxford joined the townsmen in a murderous attack on the university—later known as St. Scholastica's Day—distinguishing themselves by their savagery and furious cries of 'Havak, havoc, smygt faste, gyf good knok.'

During the opening years of Richard II's reign such riots had grown ominously in number. They were fomented by the egalitarian sermons of friars and wandering priests like John Ball, who for the past twenty years had been tramping the country preaching, in defiance of the ecclesiastical authorities, against the rich 'possessioners' of Church and State. In the words of the monastic chronicler Walsingham, he preached 'those things which he knew would be pleasing to the common people, speaking evil both of ecclesiastical and temporal lords, and won the goodwill of the common people rather than merit in the sight of God. For he taught that tithes ought not to be paid unless he who gave them was richer than the person who received them. He also taught that tithes and oblations should be withheld if the parishioner was known to be a better man than the priest.' Forbidden to preach in church, he continued to do so in streets, villages and fields until he got himself excommunicated. Nothing, however, stopped him, and, though he several times suffered imprisonment, as soon as he got out he started again. He also took to circulating inflammatory letters full of dark riddles and rhymes calling on the virtuous poor to prepare for the day when they could fall on their oppressors. 'John Ball, St. Mary's priest,' ran one, 'greeteth well all manner of men and biddeth them in the name of the Trinity, Father, Son and Holy Ghost, stand manlike together in truth, and help truth, and truth shall help you.

> 'Now reigneth price in price,
> Covetise is holden wise,
> Lechery without shame,
> Gluttony without blame,
> Envy reigneth with reason
> And sloth is taken in season
> God amend, for now is time.'

On top of this strained situation came the demand for a new and crushing tax. Like all medieval peoples the English tended to regard taxes as a form of robbery and injustice. The evolution of their government had turned largely on their rulers' recognition that the consent of the taxed to new imposts could only be won by allowing them a share in their imposition. When, Magna Carta having placed limitations on the feudal taxation of land, imposts had been levied on personal wealth and merchandise—moveables, as they were called—the same rule had been adopted.

Superseding the feudal lord's right to tallage at will, the principle that the subject should be party to the fiscal burdens imposed on him had been applied at every stage of the tax-structure. Whenever parliament agreed that a fifth, tenth or fifteenth should be levied on moveables, justices had been sent into every county to assess the local proportion payable with representative knights from every hundred, who, in turn, met the representatives of every vill, where a jury of inquest swore to the number, quantity and value of taxable goods in the township. Shortly before Crécy, as a result of an agreement between Exchequer officials and representatives of the localities, a fixed proportion of the subsidy rate voted by parliament had been allocated to every county, hundred and township. During Edward III's reign, which lasted fifty years, vast sums were raised by this method for the war with France, which, after the victorious 'forties and 'fifties, ceased to finance itself and forced Government and parliament to seek ever new ways of raising money.

In 1371 the latter adopted the novel device of a tax on every parish in England at a standard rate. Six years later a still more revolutionary innovation was adopted by the aged king's last parliament. This was a poll-tax of fourpence a head on the entire lay adult population except beggars. This 'tallage of groats,' as it was called, mulcting the poorest at the same rate as the richest, proved intensely unpopular and very hard to collect. But it appealed to a parliament of landowners and employers, since for the first time it imposed a direct fiscal burden on the peasant and unpropertied wage-earner.

Three years after Richard II's accession, faced by the Government's now desperate need, a new parliament, meeting at Northampton in the autumn of 1380, imposed the tax for a third time, trebling the rate per head. For a poor rustic householder with a large family who might have to defray the tax of several aged or female relatives, this was a crushing burden. Reflecting the belief of the rich that the labour-shortage caused by the Black Death had placed 'the wealth of the kingdom in the hands of artisans and labourers,' it not only showed astonishing ignorance of the circumstances of 'common folk whose occupations standeth in grobbying about the earth'; it ignored the principle for which parliament had long contended : that there should be no taxation without representation and consent. The peasantry and town-artisans on whom the tax bore so hardly were completely unrepresented in a parliament of magnates, prelates, landowners, merchants and lawyers.

The consequence of the shilling poll-tax was a wholesale falsification by the villages of southern England of their tax-returns. When these reached the commissioners appointed to collect the money, it seemed as though the population had shrunk by a third since the last poll-tax of two years before. The amount brought in fell far below what was expected, and the Government was furious. On March 16th 1381 the Council found that the local collectors had been guilty of gross negligence and favouritism and appointed a new commission to scrutinize the lists and enforce payment from evaders.

The decision was received with universal execration. It was spoken of as a corrupt job engineered for the private profit of the head of the commission of revision, John Legge, a serjeant-at-law, and of the treasurer, Sir Robert Hales—'Hob the robber,' as he was called. When news of a further descent of tax assessors reached the villages, the ignorant supposed that a new tax was to be levied on top of that already paid. Everywhere in the populous counties of the south-east, rustic opinion was at boiling point against tax-collectors, escheators, jurymen, lawyers and royal officials in general and against the chancellor and treasurer in particular and, illogically enough, for he was no longer actively engaged in government but absent on a mission in Scotland, the young king's uncle, John of Gaunt, Duke of Lancaster.

No-one in authority treated the dissatisfaction of the peasantry very seriously. But when at the end of May the new poll-tax commissioner of Essex, Thomas Brampton, appeared at Brentwood with two serjeants-at-arms to open enquiries into the returns for the hundred of Barstaple, he was met by the representatives of the defaulting townships with a sullen refusal to pay. They possessed, they said, their receipt for the subsidy and would not pay a penny more. But it was the fishermen and fowlers of the Thames estuary —the men of the sea and salt-water creeks—who provided the spark that fired the revolution of working-class England. Summoning to their aid their neighbours from Corringham and Standford-le-Hope, the men of Fobbing-by-Tilbury met Brampton's threats of arrest with open violence, and with sticks and stones drove him and his men out of the town.

This was more than the Government could ignore. On Sunday, June 2nd, the chief justice of the Common Pleas, Sir Robert Belknap, descended on Brentwood with a commission of trailbaston and an escort of pikesmen. His business was to punish the rioters and hang the ringleaders. He found the place in a ferment. For by now the rebellious fishermen had prevailed on the entire neighbourhood to rise. Armed with staves, pitchforks and bows, a mob surrounded the judge, seized and burnt his papers and made him swear on his knees never to hold another commission. They then murdered his three clerks and three local tax-assessors or jurymen whose names they had made him reveal. Sticking their heads on poles they bore them in triumph round the villages of south-east Essex, while the terrified Belknap fled back to London.

On the same day trouble began on the other side of the Thames. At Erith in Kent a band of rioters broke into the monastery of Lesnes and made the abbot swear to support them. The ringleaders then crossed the river to take counsel of the men of Essex. During the next few days rebellion spread northwards across the county as rioters carried their messages from parish to parish. Everywhere government agents were attacked, their houses plundered and their records and papers thrown into courtyard or street and burnt. The admiral of the Essex coast, Edmund de la Mare of Peldon, and the sheriff, John Sewall of Coggeshall, had their homes sacked, the former's papers being carried on a pitchfork at the head of the triumphant fishermen. At every manor visited, a bonfire was made of all charters and manorial rolls.

It was as though the whole system of law and government, built up over centuries, was being repudiated by the common people. Yet though damage to property was widespread, there was comparatively little loss of life, most of the local lords managing to escape. The chief escheator of the county was murdered as well as a number of Flemish merchants in Colchester where the mob rose at the approach of the peasantry. Had the treasurer been at his home at Temple Cressing instead of in London, he would certainly have been torn to pieces; as it was, his 'very beautiful and delectable manor,' as a chronicler described it, was burnt to the ground after the populace had eaten the fine fare and broached 'the three tuns of good wine' which he had laid in for an impending meeting of the chapter-general of the Order of St. John of Jerusalem of which he was master.

Meanwhile trouble was growing in Kent. On the day after the assault on the chief justice at Brentwood two serjeants-at-arms acting for Sir Simon Burley, the boy-king's tutor, arrested a respected burgess of Gravesend on the ground that he was a runaway serf. When the townsfolk declined to pay £300 for his manumission—at least £15,000 in to-day's purchasing-power—the poor man was sent to the dungeons of Rochester castle. Two days later, on Wednesday, June 5th, heartened by the arrival of a hundred insurgents from Essex, the people of all the towns and

villages on the south bank of the river between Erith and
Gravesend rose in rebellion. They were careful, however, to
stress in a proclamation listing the crimes of their young
sovereign's ministers that, though there were 'more kings
than one in the land,' they wished for none but Richard.
Patriotically they added, that 'none dwelling within twelve
miles of the sea should go with them but should keep the
coast of the sea from enemies.'

Next day, June 6th, decided the fate of Kent. At one
end of the county the men of Gravesend and Dartford
marched on Rochester. At the other end a commission of
trailbaston, directed against tax-evaders and accompanied
by the hated John Legge, was prevented from entering
Canterbury. Rochester Castle, though strong enough to
withstand a siege for weeks, was surrendered by its constable that afternoon after several ineffective attempts to
storm it. Probably it was under-garrisoned, but, like almost
everyone else, the defenders were bemused by the fury and
turbulence of the mob. For the rustic population of
England to behave in such a way seemed something outside nature : it was as though the animals had rebelled.

Certainly the Government seemed unable to grasp the
situation. Like the local authorities it remained inert
throughout that critical first week of June, helplessly watching the course of events. The chancellor, its head, was the
gentle primate, Simon Thebaud of Sudbury—the son of a
Suffolk trader whose family had grown rich supplying
the local gentry with luxury goods and developing the new
rural cloth industry. He was utterly without martial instinct
or experience. The king's uncles were far away; John of
Gaunt was in Edinburgh negotiating a truce with the
Scots, Thomas of Woodstock was in the Welsh marches
and Edmund of Cambridge had just sailed for Portugal.
On news of the outbreak a messenger had been sent to
Plymouth to countermand the expedition but arrived too
late. Owing to the needs of the English garrisons in Gascony
and Brittany the country was almost denuded of troops
except on the remote Scottish and Welsh borders. In the
capital and the crucial south-east there were only a few

hundred men-at-arms and archers guarding the king, and a small force which the old condottiere, Sir Robert Knollys, had started to collect in his London house to reinforce Brittany. Nothing was done to call out the country gentry and their retainers who in the insurgent counties to the east and north of London were paralysed with fear.

But if the Government was without an active head, the insurgents had found one. On Friday, June 7th, the men of Kent marched up the Medway valley from Rochester to Maidstone, where they were welcomed by the populace who rose and plundered the richer inhabitants, murdering one of them. Here they chose as their captain one Wat Tyler. Little is known of his past, but according to Froissart he had seen service in the French wars and, it subsequently transpired, like many old soldiers, had since been earning a livelihood by highway robbery. He was clearly a mob orator of genius, for he immediately reduced to discipline the motley throng of excited peasants and artisans. And he quickly showed himself a man of action and exceptional military talent.

On the day he assumed command Tyler issued a proclamation setting out the insurgents' aims. They would admit, he said, no allegiance except to 'King Richard and the true commons'—in other words, themselves—and have no king named John, a reference to the Duke of Lancaster. No tax should be levied 'save the fifteenths which their fathers and forebears knew and accepted,' and everyone should hold himself in readiness to march, when called upon, to remove the traitors around the king and root out and destroy the lawyers and officials who had corrupted the realm.

The rebels not only found a military leader. They acquired a spiritual one. Among the prisoners released from Maidstone gaol was John Ball. Only a few weeks before, the long-suffering archbishop had clapped him in again, describing how he had 'slunk back to our diocese like the fox that evaded the hunter, and feared not to preach and argue both in the churches and churchyards and in markets and other profane places, there beguiling the ears of the laity by his invective and putting about such scandals concerning our person and those of other prelates and clergy and—what is worse—using concerning the holy father himself language such as shamed the ears of good Christians.' The irrepressible preacher now found himself free again and with a ready-made congregation of twenty thousand ragged enthusiasts after his own heart. According to Froissart, who, though often an unreliable witness, visited England soon after the rising and was clearly fascinated by the whole affair, he addressed them in these terms :

'My good friends, matters cannot go well in England until all things be held in common; when there shall be neither vassals nor lords; when the lords shall be no more masters than ourselves. How ill they behave to us ! For what reason do they thus hold us in bondage? Are we not all descended from the same parents, Adam and Eve? And what can they show, or what reason can they give, why they should be more masters than ourselves? They are clothed in velvet and rich stuffs, ornamented with ermine and other furs, while we are forced to wear poor clothing. They have wines, spices and fine bread, while we have only rye and the refuse of the straw; and when we drink, it must be water. They have handsome seats and manors, while we must brave the wind and rain in our labours in the field; and it is by our labours that they have wherewith to support their pomp. We are called slaves and, if we do not perform our service we are beaten, and we have no sovereign to whom we can complain or would be willing to hear us. Let us go to the king and remonstrate with him. He is young and from him we may obtain a favourable answer, and, if not, we must ourselves seek to amend our conditions.'

At the same time the preacher sent out to the villages of Kent and Essex more of his inflammatory missives :

> 'John Ball
> Greeteth you all,
> And doth you to understand
> He hath rung your bell.

Now with right and might,
Will and skill,
God speed every dell!'

Another, written under a pseudonym and addressed to the
men of Essex, was subsequently found in the pocket of a
rioter condemned to be hanged.

'John Schep, sometime Saint Mary's priest of York and
now of Colchester, greets well John Nameless and John
the Miller and John Carter and bids them that they
beware of guile in the town, and stand together in God's
name, and bids Piers Plowman go to his work and
chastise well Hob the Robber. And take with you John
Trueman and all his fellows and more, and look sharp
you to your own head and no more.

John the Miller hath ground small, small, small.
The King's Son of Heaven shall pay for all.
Beware or you will be in woe,
Know your true friend from your foe,
Have enough and say "Hello!"
And do well and better and flee from sin,
And seek true peace and hold therein.
And so bids John Trueman and all his fellows.'

Tyler and Ball—brigand and hedgerow preacher—were
the leaders 'the true commons' needed. While Ball addressed
himself to his sympathizers, Tyler acted. Sending emissaries
to urge the surrounding villages to rise and join him at
Maidstone, he set out with several thousand followers for
Canterbury. By midday on the 10th he had reached the
city, where he was greeted with enthusiasm by the inhabitants, all those, that is who had nothing to lose. On
enquiring whether there were any traitors in the town, he
was directed to the houses of the local notables, three of
whom he had executed on the spot. Then, having burnt
the judicial and financial records of the shire, beaten up
the sheriff and sacked the castle, letting out the prisoners
from the gaols, he and his followers poured, a vast tumultuous multitude, into the cathedral during Mass. Here with

one voice they cried out to the monks to elect a new archbishop of Canterbury in place of Sudbury whom they
declared to be a traitor and 'about to be beheaded for his
iniquity.' They also extracted an oath of fealty to the king
and true commons from the mayor and corporation and—
for the summer pilgrimage season was at its height—
recruited their ranks by a number of pilgrims. At the same
time they dispatched agitators to the towns and villages of
East Kent.

Early on Tuesday, June 11th, having spent less than
twenty-four hours in Canterbury and set the eastern weald
and coast from Sandwich to Appledore aflame, Tyler set
off again. Reinforcements poured in as he marched. By
nightfall he was back in Maidstone, having covered eighty
miles in two days. Then, pausing only for the night, he
marched with his entire host before dawn on the 12th for
the capital, sending messengers into Sussex and the western
counties to summon the commons to join him and 'close
London round about.' Simultaneously on the other side of
the Thames the Essex insurgents, who by now had won
complete control of the county, began a parallel march
under Thomas Farringdon, an aggrieved Londoner.

While the two hosts converged on the capital, terror
reigned on either side of their march as village mobs
smoked out royal and manorial officials, lawyers and unpopular landlords, breaking into their houses and burning
every record they could find. They would have, they
declared, 'no bondsmen in England.' Many of the gentry
took to the woods, among them the poet John Gower, who
afterwards recalled in his long Latin epic, *Vox Clamantis,*
the pangs of hunger he suffered while living on acorns and
trembling for his life in wet coppices. Others, less fearful or
unpopular, made timely contributions to the 'cause' and
took the oath of fidelity to the 'king and true commons.' A
few, but only a few, were murdered, while others, being
persons of distinction who had not done anything to make
themselves unpopular, were carried off as hostages to grace
Wat Tyler's entourage, including Sir Thomas Cobham and
Sir Thomas Tryvet, a hero of the wars.

Meanwhile the authorities had at last resolved to act. On either the Tuesday or Wednesday Tyler's men, pouring towards the capital, were met by messengers from the king at Windsor to ask why they were raising rebellion and what they sought. Their answer was that they were coming to deliver him from traitors. They also presented a petition asking for the heads of the Duke of Lancaster and fourteen other notables, including the chancellor, treasurer and every leading member of the Government. On receipt of this the fourteen-year-old king and his advisers left hastily for London and the Tower to form a focus of resistance round which the forces of order could rally. The king's mother and her ladies, who had been on a summer pilgrimage to the Kentish shrines, also set out for the same place of refuge. On the way they encountered the rebel vanguard. Yet, though greatly frightened, they were subjected to nothing worse than a little ribald jesting and were allowed to continue their journey to the capital. Here the mayor, William Walworth, after escorting his sovereign to the Tower, was extremely busy putting the city into a state of defence.

That evening the Kentish host encamped on the Blackheath heights, looking down across the Thames to the distant city. On the opposite bank the Essex men took up their station in the Mile End fields outside the suburb of Whitechapel and about a mile to the east of the walls and the Aldgate. Some of the less exhausted Kentish rebels continued as far as Southwark, where, welcomed by the local mob, they burnt a bawdy house rented by some Flemish women from Mayor Walworth and let out the prisoners from the Marshalsea and King's Bench. Finding the drawbridge in the centre of London Bridge raised against them, they went on to Lambeth where they sacked the archbishop's palace and the house of John Imworth, the warden of the Marshalsea.

It was not only the proletariat of Southwark who sympathized with the insurgents. There were thousands of journeymen, apprentices and labourers inside the city walls who did so too. On the mayor's orders the gates had been closed and entrusted to the aldermen and watch of the adjacent wards. But there were bitter rivalries among the city's rulers. The victualling interests were at daggers drawn with the older merchants, drapers and mercers, who, employing labour on a large scale, favoured a policy of free trade and low-priced food in order to keep down wages and feed their journeymen and apprentices cheaply—a matter of vital importance to them since the labour shortage caused by the Black Death. Both were monopolists, but, to overthrow their rivals, the victuallers had formed an alliance with the discontented city proletariat—wage-earners and small craftsmen—who regarded their employers and the capitalists who controlled the market for their handiwork in much the same light as the villeins regarded their lords. Among three aldermen whom the mayor dispatched to urge the insurgents to keep the peace was a certain John Horne, a fishmonger, who, separating himself from his companions, sought a private interview with Tyler and secretly promised his support. When he returned to London he not only assured the mayor that the marchers were honest patriots who would do the city no harm but, under cover of darkness, smuggled three agitators across the river to stir up the mob.

Earlier that evening an emissary from the rebel camp had travelled by boat from Greenwich to London to seek an interview with the king and Council. This was the constable of Rochester castle, Sir John Newton, who for the past week had been a prisoner of the insurgents. Brought into the presence and given leave to speak, he explained that, though his captors would do the king no harm, they were determined to meet him face to face to communicate certain matters of which he had no charge to speak. Since they held his children as hostages and would slay them if he failed to return, he begged for an answer that would appease them and show that he had delivered his message.

To this after some hesitation the Council agreed. Next morning at prime the king and his lords embarked in five barges for Greenwich. Here, on the shore below Blackheath the Kentish men, after a hungry and sleepless night, were assembled in battle array under two great banners of St. George. While they waited, Mass was celebrated, it being Corpus Christi day, and afterwards John Ball preached, taking as his text the old popular rhyme :

> 'When Adam delved and Eve span
> Who was then the gentleman?'

According to the St. Albans chronicler, 'he strove to prove that from the beginning all men were created equal by nature, and that servitude had been introduced by the unjust oppression of wicked men against God's will, for if it had pleased Him to create serfs, surely in the beginning of the world He would have decreed who was to be a serf and who a lord. . . . Wherefore they should be prudent men, and, with the love of a good husbandman tilling his fields and uprooting and destroying the tares which choke the grain, they should hasten to do the following things. First, they should kill the great lords of the kingdom; second, they should slay lawyers, judges and jurors; finally they should root out all those whom they knew to be likely to be harmful to the commonwealth in future. Thus they would obtain peace and security, for, when the great ones had been removed, there would be equal liberty and nobility and dignity and power for all.' 'When he had preached this and much other madness,' wrote the disgusted chronicler, 'the commons held him in such high favour that they acclaimed him the future archbishop and chancellor of the realm.'[1]

Whether it was this sermon or the presence of the archbishop in the royal barge or the fact that the Kentishmen had not breakfasted, they greeted the king's arrival with such a tumult of shouting that he was unable to make himself heard. 'Sirs,' he kept calling across the water as the rowers rested on their oars just out of reach of the frantic multitude, 'what do you want? Tell me now that I have come to talk to you.' But as the crowd steadily grew more threatening, fearing lest some of the bowmen might start to shoot, the Earl of Salisbury—by far the most experienced soldier present—ordered the boats to put out into mid-stream and return to the Tower.

At that both the Kentist host and the Essex men who had been watching from the other shore set up a great shout of 'Treason' and, with their banners and pennants, moved off towards London. Access to the city's markets and provision shops had by now become essential if they were not to have to disperse through hunger—a fact on which the authorities were counting. Within the city, processions of clergy were marching through the streets praying for peace, while crowds of sympathizers with the insurgents were gathering in the poorer lanes and alleys. For, though the city gates were still barred against them, the agitators whom Horne had slipped into the town had not been idle. As Wat Tyler's men neared the southern approaches to the bridge they were again met by this liberal-minded fishmonger waving a royal standard which he had procured by a trick from the town clerk. And as, headed by this emblem of loyalty and respectability, they surged on to the bridge, the drawbridge in the midst of its shops and houses was lowered to them by the alderman of the Billingsgate ward. About the same time another alderman of the opposition faction let in the Essex men through the Aldgate.

Once the head of the rebel columns was in possession of the southern and eastern entrances the whole multitude poured into the city, while the apprentices and journeymen and the labouring poor of the slums flocked into the streets to greet them. For a time the newcomers were too busy eating, drinking and gaping at the city sights to do much harm. But presently, refreshed by several huge barrels of ale which some rash philanthropists had broached in the streets and incited by the apprentices who had old scores to pay off against John of Gaunt, they set up a cry of 'To the Savoy!' The Duke of Lancaster might be in Edin-burgh, but the superb palace he had furnished from the plunder of France—and, as many supposed, of England—stood a mile outside the western walls where the fields and gardens sloped down to the riverside from the Strand that linked London to Westminster. Thither the men of Kent, with thousands of excited apprentices—a great company with torches—made their way in an angry tumult, breaking into the Fleet prison on the way and letting out the criminals, while the duke's servants fled as the shouting came nearer.

No time was wasted. In the general desire for justice or revenge even plundering was forbidden. Everything in the great house was hurled out of the windows—tapestry, sheets, coverlets, beds—and hacked or torn to pieces. Then the building was set on fire and burnt to the ground. At the height of the fire there was an explosion caused by three barrels of gunpowder, which were thrown into the flames in the belief that they contained specie. Some of the rioters afterwards continued towards Westminster where they destroyed the house of the under-sheriff of Middlesex and let the prisoners out of the gaol. Others, on their way back to the city, broke into the lawyers' home in the Temple, tore the tiles off the roof and took all the books, rolls and remembrances from the students' cupboards to make a bonfire. They also fired some shops and houses which had recently been built in Fleet street, declaring that never again should any house deface the beauty of that favourite country walk of the Londoners. Those who had gone on to Westminster returned by way of Holborn, setting light to the houses of several 'traitors' pointed out to them by their London comrades and breaking open Newgate still further to enlarge their company. Meanwhile the men of Essex descended on the priory of St. John's, Clerkenwell, the headquarters of the Knights Hospitallers just outside the city's northern wall. Here they burnt the priory and hospital—'a great and horrible piece of damage for all time to come'—and murdered seven Flemings who had taken sanctuary in the church.

That night, while the insurgents camped round the royal fortress in the open spaces of Tower Hill and St. Catherine's wharf and while their leaders drew up lists of persons to be liquidated, the king and Council debated long and anxiously what was to be done. Since the morning their position had changed dramatically for the worse; instead of waiting behind London's walls while the rebels starved outside, they themselves were hemmed in the Tower, and the city it was supposed to dominate was in possession of a fanatic, uncontrollable mob. From a garret in one of the turrets into which he climbed the boy king could see twenty or thirty fires burning in different parts of the town. Beyond, the whole of the home counties to south and east were in revolt, while, unknown as yet to the beleaguered Council, the revolutionary ferment had spread that afternoon into Hertfordshire and Suffolk, where burgesses and bondsmen had risen together against the rich monks of England's two most famous abbeys, St. Albans and Bury.

The key to the situation lay, however, in the capital. If the mob who had taken possession of it could be defeated, the flames of revolt might be put out elsewhere. But, with London lost and the court imprisoned inside it, there was nothing round which the forces of order could rally. Mayor Walworth, a bluff and vigorous man, urged an immediate sally against the insurgents while they were sleeping off the effects of their evening's debauch. There were six hundred armed men-at-arms and archers in the Tower and a hundred or so more in Sir Robert Knollys's house and garden; with a bold front they would probably be joined by all the law-abiding in London. Only a small minority of the insurgents wore armour; if the loyal forces struck at once, thousands might be slain as they slept. But the Earl of Salisbury, who had fought with the king's grandfather and father at Crécy and Poitiers, thought otherwise. Once fighting began in the narrow streets and lanes, the rebels' immense superiority in numbers would tell and total disaster might ensue. 'If we should begin a thing which we cannot achieve,' he said, 'we should never recover and we and our heirs would be disinherited and England would become a desert.' Instead, he offered the Ulysses-like counsel that an attempt should be made to induce the rebels to disperse by fair words and promises, which could afterwards be repudiated as obtained under duress.

An earlier attempt that evening to persuade them to do so by putting up the king to address them from the ramparts and offer a free pardon to all who should go home had been shouted down in derision. Some more signal mark of royal trust was needed if the populace was to be appeased. It was, therefore, proposed that the king should offer to confer with the rebels in the Mile End fields and to ride out there next morning through their midst with such of his lords as were not expressly marked down for execution. While under cover of this bold move the crowds were drawn away from the Tower, the archbishop and treasurer and John of Gaunt's son and heir, young Henry Bolingbroke, earl of Derby, could be smuggled out to safety by water.

The plan depended on the king's readiness to take the risk. But, though he appeared a little pensive, the boy was ready and even eager. He was now fourteen, and it was something to find that at last all the great lords and counsellors around him looked to him for leadership. As soon as it was light a proclamation was made from the walls and soon afterwards, surrounded by an immense multitude of excited country folk, the royal cortège set out along the Brentwood road for Mile End. But many of the Londoners stayed behind to watch the Tower, for the rebels' leaders were not so easily fooled. When the boat by which their intended victims attempted to escape appeared, it was forced to put back as soon as it emerged from the water-gate.

Nor did the royal ride to Mile End prove easy or pleasant. At one moment the Essex leader, Thomas Farringdon, a highly excitable man, seized the king's bridle, demanding to be avenged on that false traitor Prior Hales, the treasurer, who he said had deprived him of his property by fraud. So threatening was the crowd that the king's half-brothers, the Earl of Kent and Sir John Holland, finding themselves at the edge of the throng, seized the opportunity to gallop away and escape to open country to the north. When, however, the royal party arrived in the Mile End fields the simple country folk who were waiting there knelt before the king crying, 'Welcome, our lord King Richard, if it pleases you we will have no other king but you.' It was like the scene in the ballads when the sovereign whom Robin Hood and his men had captured revealed his identity and promised to restore every honest man to his own.

It must have seemed to many present that such a golden time had come when their young king—the son of England's dead hero, the Black Prince—announced he would grant all their demands. He promised the abolition of serfdom, of villein services and seigneurial market monopolies, and that all holders of land in villeinage should henceforth become free tenants at the modest rent of 4d. an acre a year. Nor did he only promise them all free pardons and an amnesty if they would return quietly to their villages, but offered to give a royal banner to the men of every county and place them under his special protection and patronage. His words, as Froissart put it, 'appeased well the common people, such as were simple and good plain men.' They rather took the wind, however, out of their leaders' sails. The latter, therefore, returned to the charge. 'The commons,' Tyler told the king, 'will that you suffer them to take and deal with all the traitors who have sinned against you and the law.' To which the king replied that all should have due punishment as could be proved by process of law to be traitors.

This, however, was scarcely what Tyler and his fellow-leaders wanted. While the king, surrounded by the better disposed of his humbler subjects, was helping to set them on their way to their distant villages, the two captains of the commons of Kent and Essex hurried back with a band of picked followers to the Tower where a large crowd was still waiting outside the gates, clamouring for the archbishop's and treasurer's blood. Pushing through them they succeeded in bluffing their way into the fortress itself either through the treachery of the guards or, more probably, because, with the king and his lords expected back at any moment, the portcullis was up and no one knew what to do. Fraternizing with the soldiers, shaking their hands and stroking their beards, the crowd pressed after their leaders into the royal apartments, shouting for the traitors' blood. In their search the king's bed was hacked to pieces and his mother, the Princess of Wales, subjected to such rude treatment that she was borne off in a dead faint by her pages and put into a boat on the river. John Legge, the serjeant-at-law who had drawn up the poll-tax commission, and three of his clerks, the Duke of Lancaster's physician, a Franciscan friar named Appleton, and several others were found. The duke's son, Henry Bolingbroke— who eighteen years later was to become king—was more fortunate, being saved by the resources of one of his father's retainers. The archbishop and treasurer were taken in the chapel, where, expecting death, the former had just received the confession of the latter and administered the last rites. Dragged by the mob into the courtyard and across the cobbles to Tower hill, they were summarily be- headed across a log of wood. It was the third time in the country's history that an archbishop of Canterbury had been assaulted at the altar and brutally done to death.

After that, all pretence of moderation and order vanished. While the primate's head, stuck on a pike and crowned with his mitre, was being borne round the city before being set over the gateway to London Bridge—the traditional place for traitors—and the king, shunning the desecrated Tower, made his way with his escort to the royal wardrobe at Baynard's Castle near St. Paul's, where his mother had taken refuge, the riff-raff of the capital and the peasants' army ran riot in the streets, forcing passers-by to cry, 'With King Richard and the true commons' and putting everyone to death who refused. By nightfall 'there was hardly a street in the city in which there were not bodies lying of those who had been slain.' The chief victims were the Flemish merchants who were hunted through the streets and killed wherever found; more than a hundred and fifty are said to have perished, including thirty-five who had taken shelter in St. Martin-in-the-Vintry and who were dragged from the altar and beheaded outside on a single block. Every disorderly person who had

old grudges to pay off or property he coveted seized his
opportunity; Alderman Horne, with a mob at his heels,
paraded the streets bidding anyone who wanted justice
against a neighbour to apply to him. Tyler himself hunted
down and cut off the head of the great monopolist, Richard
Lyons, whose servant he was at one time said to have
been, while his lieutenant, Jack Straw, led a gang to burn
the home of the murdered Sir Robert Hales, the treasurer,
at Highbury. Far away in Suffolk at about the same hour
the head of Sir John Cavendish, chief justice of the King's
Bench, was being carried on a pike through the rejoicing
streets of Bury St. Edmunds,[2] while his friend and neighbour, the prior of the great abbey, who had been hunted
all day on the Mildenhall heaths, cowered before his
captors, awaiting the trial that was to lead to his death
next morning. Later, on the Saturday, when his head, too,
was borne back on a pike to Bury, the crowd carried the
heads of the two friends round the town together, making
them converse and kiss one another.

Dawn on Saturday, June 15th, saw the nadir of the once
proud kingdom whose princes a quarter of a century before had led the French king captive after Poitiers through
the streets of London. From Lincolnshire, Leicester and
Northampton to the coasts of Kent and Sussex its richest
and most populous counties were aflame, while, as the
news spread of London's capture and the king and
Council's humiliation, other shires as far as Cornwall and
Yorkshire crackled with rumours of impending rebellion.
The greatest officers of state—the primate and chancellor,
treasurer, and chief justice—had all been brutally done to
death, and everywhere magnates and gentry were flying
to the woods or, isolated and helpless in their homes, awaiting the sound of mobs and the light of torches. In London
riot, plunder, arson and murder had continued all night
and, though thousands of law-abiding peasants had returned to their homes on receiving the king's promise,
thousands more, including their leaders and all the more
violent and criminal elements, were in control both of the
capital and what remained of the government.

The king spent the night at the wardrobe in Baynard's Castle comforting his mother. His surrender at Mile End seemed to have achieved nothing, and, though thirty royal clerks had been employed all the previous afternoon copying out pardons and charters, the hard core of the insurgents remained both unsatisfied and seemingly insatiable. Yet, since there was no other way of loosening their stranglehold, Richard resolved, regardless of the risks involved, to try again. Accordingly on the morning of Saturday the 15th he proposed a further meeting with the commons and their leaders. This time the rendezvous was to be the cattle market at Smithfield, just outside the city's north-western walls close to the church of St. Bartholomew the Great and the smoking ruins of the priory of St. John's, Clerkenwell.

Before proceeding there the king rode to Westminster Abbey to pray at the shrine of his ancestor, St. Edward the Confessor. Murder and sacrilege had been there that morning before him, a mob having broken into the sanctuary, tearing from the pillars of the shrine, to which he had clung in terror, the warden of the Marshalsea—a man hated by the populace as being 'without pity as a torturer.' The monks of Westminster and the canons of St. Stephen's met the king at the abbey gates, barefooted and carrying their cross. For a while all knelt before the desecrated shrine while the young king confessed to the abbey's anchorite and received absolution, afterwards repairing to the little oratory in the royal closet of St. Stephen's chapel to pray before a golden image of the Virgin which had been a treasured possession of his family since the days of Henry III and was believed to have special protective powers. It is possible that it is this deeply moving incident in the king's life, rather than his coronation four years earlier, that is depicted in the Wilton Diptych—the young Plantagenet, robed and crowned, kneeling before the figures of St. Edward, King Edmund the Martyr and St. John the Baptist whose hand rests on the boy's shoulder and all three of whom seem to be gazing fixedly and sternly as at some threatening force, while a winged galaxy of guardian angels, wearing Richard's badge of the hart, gather round the Virgin and her child beneath the banner of St. George.

The king and his retainers, about two hundred strong, now mounted and rode on to Smithfield. Because of their peril they wore armour under their robes. They were joined at St. Bartholomew's church by Mayor Walworth and a small party, while on the opposite side of the market-place the entire insurgent army awaited in battle order. It must by now have been about five o'clock of the afternoon and the weather very hot.

Tyler now felt himself to be master of the kingdom. He was at the head of a host which outnumbered by many times the little royal band, and all day news had been coming in from every quarter of new risings. On the previous evening he had boasted that he would shave the beards—by which he meant slice off the heads—of all who opposed him and that in a few days there would be no laws in England save those which proceeded from his mouth. 'He came to the king,' wrote the Anonimalle chronicler, 'in a haughty fashion, mounted on a little horse so that he could be seen by the commons and carrying in his hand a dagger which he had taken from another man. When he had dismounted he half bent his knee and took the king by the hand and shook his arm forcibly and roughly, saying to him, "Brother, be of good comfort and joyful, for you shall have within the next fortnight 40,000 more of the commons than you have now and we shall be good companions."

'When the king asked Tyler, "Why will you not go back to your own country?", the insurgent chief replied with a great oath that neither he nor his fellows would depart until they had their charter such as they wished to have, and such points rehearsed in their charter as they chose to demand, threatening that the lords of the realm would rue it badly if the points were not settled to their satisfaction. The king asked him what were the points that he wanted, and he should have them freely without contradiction written down and sealed. He then rehearsed points which were to be demanded. He asked that there should be no law except the law of Winchester, and that there should be henceforth no outlawry on any process of law, and that no lord should have any lordship . . . and that the only lordship should be that of the king; that the goods of Holy Church should not remain in the hands of the religious nor of the parsons and vicars and other churchmen; but those who were in possession should have their sustenance from the endowments, and the remainder of their goods should be divided amongst their parishioners; and no bishop should remain in England save one, and that all the lands and tenements now held by them should be confiscated and shared amongst the commons, saving to them a reasonable substance. And he demanded that there should be no more bondsmen in England, no serfdom nor villeinage, but that all should be free and of one condition. And to this the king gave an easy answer, and said that he should have all that could fairly be granted, saving to himself the regality of the Crown. And then he commanded him to go back to his home without further delay. And all this time that the king was speaking no lord nor any other of his council dared nor wished to give any answer to the commons in any place except the king himself.'

'After that Tyler, in the king's presence, called for a flagon of water to rinse his mouth because he was in such a heat, and when it was brought he rinsed his mouth in a very rude and disgusting fashion before the king; and then he made them bring him a flagon of ale of which he drank a great deal, and in the king's presence mounted his horse. At this time a yeoman of Kent, who was among the king's retinue, asked to see the said Wat, the leader of the commons; and when Wat was pointed out to him, he said openly that he was the greatest thief and robber in all Kent. Wat heard these words and commanded him to come out to him, shaking his head at him in sign of malice; but the yeoman refused to go to him for fear of the mob. At last the lords made him go out to Wat to see what he would do in the king's presence; and, when Wat saw him, he ordered one of his followers, who was riding on a horse carrying his banner displayed, to dismount and cut off the yeoman's head. But the yeoman answered that he had done nothing worthy of death, for what he had said was true and he would not deny it, but in the presence of his liege lord he could not lawfully make debate without leave, except in his own defence. . . . For these words Wat would have run him through with his dagger and killed him in the king's presence, and because of this, the mayor of London, William Walworth by name, reasoned with the said Wat for his violent behaviour and contempt done in the king's presence and arrested him. And because he arrested him, the said Wat struck the mayor with his dagger in the stomach with great anger; but, as God would have it, the mayor was wearing armour and took no harm. But like a hardy and vigorous man the mayor drew his cutlass and struck back at Wat and gave him a deep cut on the neck and then a great cut on the head. And in this scuffle a yeoman of the king's household drew his sword and ran Wat two or three times through the body, mortally wounding him. And the said Wat spurred his horse, crying to the commons to avenge him, and the horse carried him some four score paces, and there he fell to the ground half dead. And when the commons saw him fall and did not know for certain how it was, they began to bend their bows to shoot.'[3]

It was thirty-five years since Crécy and a quarter of a century since Poitiers, and even the youngest who had shared in these masterpieces of the bowman's art were now, by the standards of the fourteenth century, old men. Even Najera was fourteen years away, and few of the English archers who had wrought that Pyrrhic victory can ever have returned to England. Yet there must have been at least several hundreds in the insurgent host who had served in the French and Breton wars and many thousands more who had learnt to use the long-bow at the butts after church on Sundays and were armed with the terrifying weapon— the most formidable in the world—which the Plantagenet kings had given the yeomanry of England. It seemed, as hundreds of bows were drawn in the rebel ranks, that it was going to cost the last of them his life and throne.

At that moment Richard clapped spurs into his horse and rode straight across the square towards the massed insurgents. 'Sirs,' he cried as he reined in before them, 'will you shoot your king? I am your captain. I will be your leader. Let him who loves me follow me!' The effect was electric; the expected flight of arrows never came. Instead, as the young king slowly wheeled his horse northwards towards the open country, the peasants in ordered companies followed him like the children after the piper of Hamelin.

As they did so, the mayor galloped back into the city to rouse the loyalists and call them to rescue their sovereign. His chief adversary—Alderman Sibley who had lowered the river drawbridge two days before—arrived just before him, spreading the rumour that the whole royal party had been killed. But Walworth's appearance gave him the lie and sickened by the plunder, murder and arson of the last forty-eight hours, the shopkeepers and wealthier citizens flocked with their arms into the streets as the sole hope of saving their homes and possessions. Mustered by the aldermen and officers of their wards and led by old Sir Robert Knollys with his archers and men-at-arms, they hurried in thousands out of the Aldersgate in pursuit of the imperilled king and his rabble following. They found them in the Clerkenwell cornfields with the boy, still unharmed, sitting on his horse in their midst, arguing with the insurgents, now leaderless and confused in the absence of Tyler who had been borne dying into St. Bartholomew's hospital. While they were so occupied, Knollys quietly deployed his men, outflanking and surrounding the multitude, while a band of heavily armoured knights pushed through the crowd to the king's side.

The threat to the Crown and capital was over. The insurgents made no resistance; it was the end of a long hot day and they must have been parched and exhausted. Encircled by armed men and appeased by the king's promises, even the extremists had no more fight in them and were ready to return home. He refused to listen to the proposal of some of his rescuers that, as his former captors were now at his mercy, he should order them to be massacred; 'Three-fourths of them,' he is said to have replied, 'have been brought here by force and threats; I will not let the innocent suffer with the guilty.' Knollys, who was himself of yeoman birth, strongly counselled the course of mercy and helped to organize the march of the Kentish men through London to their homes.

The whole multitude now dispersed. When Richard returned to the Wardrobe amid the rejoicings of the Londoners whose mayor he had just knighted in the Clerkenwell fields, he said to his anxious mother, 'Rejoice and praise God, for today I have recovered my heritage that was lost and the realm of England also.'

.   .   .

Had the king fallen at Mile End or Smithfield there would have been no authority but that of the rebellious peasantry left from Yorkshire to Kent and from Suffolk to Devon. When he and Walworth so unexpectedly, and at the eleventh hour, turned the tables on Tyler, the revolution was on the point of complete success. For on the very afternoon that Richard, preparing for death, confessed and received absolution in the desecrated abbey, the fires of rebellion, fanned by the news of the previous day's massacre in the Tower and the insurgents' triumph, spread from St. Albans to Cambridge and Ipswich and into Bedfordshire, the Fens and Norfolk. At St. Albans, led by a local tradesman called William Grindcobbe—a brave man with a burning love of freedom—the townsfolk invaded the abbey, seized its charters and burnt them in the market place, ripping up the confiscated millstones—symbols of the abbey's monopolistic privileges—with which the abbot had paved his chamber, while the countryfolk drained the fishponds and trampled down the fences enclosing the monastic woods and pastures. At Cambridge, as during that Saturday village after village rose in the Fenland, the bell of Great St. Mary's brought out the mob in a riotous crusade against the university and the adjacent priory of Barnwell. Corpus Christi College, the chief owner of house-property in the town, was gutted, and the university charters, archives and library were burnt next day in the Market Square while an old woman shouted, as she flung parchment after parchment into the flames, 'Away with the learning of the clerks! away with it!' During the weekend other risings occurred in hundreds of villages in East Anglia, the Fenland and east Midlands. In all of them justices of the peace, tax commissioners, lawyers and unpopular landlords, particularly monastic ones, were attacked, their houses sacked or burnt and their charters and court-rolls destroyed.

The most formidable of all the risings outside the capital occurred in Norfolk, the richest and most populous as well as most independent-minded county in England. In West Norfolk, where it broke out during the weekend of the king's triumph and lasted for ten days, it was without a leader and apparently quite purposeless, the one common denominator being robbery under threats of violence. In the eastern half of the country, where a leader of Tyler's calibre appeared, rebellion took a political course, though a different one from that of the home counties. Its aim, natural in so remote an area, was not the reform and control of the Government, but the setting up of an independent East Anglia. But though for a week its leader, a dyer named Geoffrey Litster, kept regal state in Norwich, with the king and Council in possession of the capital the revolution collapsed as suddenly as it had begun. It disintegrated piecemeal. By the end of June all resistance was over.

Except for the summary execution of a few ring-leaders like Tyler's lieutenant, Jack Straw, and John Starling—the Essex rioter who had decapitated Archbishop Sudbury and who was taken still carrying the sword that had done the deed—the insurgents were tried and punished by the normal processes of law. Though a large number of persons were charged with treason or crimes of violence, only about a hundred and fifty[4] suffered the death penalty, nearly all of them after being found guilty by a local jury.

Most of the ring-leaders perished including John Ball, who was found in hiding at Coventry, and John Wraw, another priest who had led the Suffolk insurgents and who tried to save his life by turning king's evidence. The noblest of all— the leader of the St. Albans townsmen against the tyranny of the great abbey that held them in bondage—died with sublime courage, protesting the righteousness of his cause. 'If I die for the liberty we have won,' he said, 'I shall think myself happy to end my life as a martyr for such a cause.'

Before the end of the summer the king put a stop to further arrests and executions, and in December a general amnesty was declared. The peasants' revolt and its repression were over. Only the smouldering ashes of anger and resentment remained; that and fear of its recurrence. But for two circumstances the king would have perished with his ministers. One was his courage, the other the deep-seated loyalty to the throne which transcended the sense of injustice and desire for revenge of the peasant multitude. Fierce as were the passions aroused during the 'hurling time,' and cruel and atrocious some of the deeds done during it, the majority of those who had marched under the banner of 'King Richard and the true commons' sincerely believed that they were restoring the realm to justice and honest government and rescuing their young sovereign from traitors and extortioners. They did not seek to destroy either him or his kingdom, and, even at the height of the rebellion, provided for the defence of the country. And, though they released the criminals from the jails and allowed the more savage of their companions to wreak their will on those whom they regarded as oppressors, they made no attempt to massacre their social superiors like the French Jacquerie of a generation before. When in their wretchedness after their ruler's defeat in war the French peasants had risen, they had loosed their vengeance on the entire ruling class, murdering, raping, torturing and mutilating every man, woman and child within their reach. In the contemporary accounts of the English peasants' revolt no instance is recorded of violence

to a woman, though for three days the capital and for
several weeks the richest parts of England lay at their
mercy.

Yet they and their leaders came very near to over-
throwing the government of their country, far nearer than
the rebellious peasants of France, Flanders and Italy had
ever come. They had done so because their cause was
based, not on mere desperation or unthinking anger, but on
certain principles of justice on which, when they could free
their minds from class prejudice, all Englishmen were
agreed. And though they seemed to have been defeated and
to have been reduced once more to bondage, they had, in
fact, as time was to show, achieved their object. When, a
week after the Smithfield meeting, a delegation of peasants
waited on the king at Waltham to ask for a ratification of
the charters, he replied that his pledges, having been
extorted by force, counted for nothing. 'Villeins you are
still,' he told them, 'and villeins ye shall remain!' He was
wrong. For the present the lords might enforce their
rights; they could not do so permanently. The magic of
their old invincibility was gone. Given arms by the Statute
of Winchester and taught to use them on the battlefields
of France, the peasants had tested them on the manor itself and knew their strength. They would no longer brook
servitude.

As an economic means of cultivating the soil for profit,
villeinage was doomed. With such surly and mutinous
labour and no police to enforce it, it proved impossible to
make it pay. Faced by the growing competition of the
towns the lord had to make concessions to keep his villeins
on the land. And as the population began to rise again
after the first waves of Black Death, the process of com-
muting services for money payments was resumed and paid
labour increasingly took the place of servile. In other
places, lords found their demesnes so hard to work that to
maintain their incomes they were forced to let them to the
wealthier and more industrious peasants. Within half a
century of the revolt, even in the open-field villages of the
Midlands, tenant-farming with hired labour had become

the norm, and hereditary servile status had ceased to have any practical significance. It was only a question of time, before the common law, with its bias in favour of freedom, had transformed villein tenure into copyhold. The property-less bondsman became the copyholder enjoying, by virtue of his copy from the manorial rolls, the same protection from the king's courts and the same right to enjoy or dispose of his hereditary holding as a freeholder.

CHAPTER THREE

CHARLES II'S ESCAPE, 1651
The Miraculous Providence

'It being so rare, so excellent, that aged Time out of all the archives of antiquity can hardly produce a parallel.'

As the last streaks of daylight, September 3rd, 1651, fell on the Worcestershire landscape, a tall dark fugitive drew in his horse on a lonely heath. About him clustered some sixty lords and officers, whose looks told a tale of peril and defeat.

At that moment the young king of England had touched a lower point than any to which his twenty-one chequered and poverty-stricken years had yet brought him. A few weeks before he had ridden at the head of a Scottish army along the moorland road by Shap Fell, watching, across the unclouded atmosphere of summer, the distant Derbyshire heights beckoning him on to London and a golden crown. Now his gallant gamble had ended in dust. All day he had fought at the head of outnumbered and despairing men as Cromwell's net closed in on Worcester. Only at evening, as the shattered Scots poured out through St. Martin's Gate, had King Charles the Second, protesting that he would rather die than see the consequences of so fatal a day, been swept by the rout from the doomed city.

At Barbourne Bridge, where the grass highway to the north was crowded with flying men, there had been a hasty consultation. The king himself had wished to ride alone to London, trusting to arrive before news of the battle and so take ship to France. But the day was already waning, and his companions had dissuaded him from this desperate course. Leaving the main line of fugitives to the west, they rode with him across a land of wooded valleys and little hills, until at nightfall they reached Kinver Heath. Here the scout, who was leading, admitted that he was lost.

In the confusion that followed, the Earl of Derby brought forward a Catholic gentleman, Charles Giffard, owner of a remote house in Shropshire, near which he had found shelter a few days before. To Giffard and his servant, Yates, a poor rustic skilful in the ways of that country, the fugitives entrusted themselves. So guided they came down into the hidden lands below. As complete darkness fell, romance spread her cloak over the king and hid him from the thousand eyes that sought him.

Nobody suspected the little party of Cavaliers who walked their horses through the streets of sleeping Stourbridge. At an inn near Wordsley the king stopped for a hasty tankard of ale : then rode on through the night, a crust of bread in one hand and meat in the other. Giffard rode at his side, telling him of the secret hiding-places of Whiteladies and Boscobel, while the broken lords and officers trotted behind. For some hours they followed a maze of winding lanes till they came to the edge of Brewood Forest. Here, fifty miles from the battlefield, and a little before dawn, the tired king saw the dark outlines of the ruined monastery of Whiteladies.

The clatter of hooves and the whispered calls of Giffard brought down the Penderels, the poor Catholic woodcutters who tenanted the house. To these humble folk the great personages, crowding into the hall, turned for help and advice. While a hasty message was sent to bring William, the eldest of the five Penderel brothers, from Boscobel, the king, in an inner chamber, broke his fast on sack and biscuits. A few minutes later Lord Derby brought in William and Richard Penderel to him, telling them that they must have a care of him and preserve him. To this they proudly and gladly assented. Richard went out to fetch some country clothes, while the king stripped and put on a rough noggen shirt. The first lines of dawn were appearing when Richard returned with an old sweaty doublet, a green, threadbare coat and a greasy steeple hat without band or lining. Lord Wilmot, the stoutest and merriest of the fugitives, began to cut the royal locks with a knife, but did the job so badly that Richard was commanded to finish it, which he did in great pride with a basin and a pair of shears. Placing his hands up the chimney, Charles, who, despite peril and weariness, could not refrain from laughing, completed his make-up by blacking his face. Then, while his companions rode off to join the flying Scots, he went out into the dawn with Richard Penderel and a bill-hook.

It was raining. All day the king crouched in the damp undergrowth of a little wood, called Spring Coppice. About midday Penderel's sister-in-law, Elizabeth Yates, brought him a blanket to sit on and a mess of milk, butter and eggs. She told him news of the world outside the woods—of long streams of Scottish fugitives and pursuing Roundheads and of search-parties already at Whiteladies. Afterwards he fell into a broken slumber.

Charles had changed much since Vandyke had painted him amid the silken dresses, the flowing hair, the lace, the pearls, the roses of his father's court. Before his twelfth year he had seen the lights of Whitehall darken into tragedy, while a blind mob, which cared for none of these things, bawled out for reform and liberty. While still a child he had become a wanderer on the face of the earth. For three years he had followed his ill-fated father; seen the royal standard raised and blown down one tempestuous autumn evening at Nottingham, seen Rupert's men charge across the Warwickshire plain, and played where gown and sword mingled in Christ Church meadow. Sent at fifteen to preside over the king's ruined fortunes in the west, he had spent a last year of boyhood on English soil, amid the squabbles and debaucheries of a broken army, driven back week by week towards the sunset until the royal banner floated in solitary loyalty above Pendennis castle. Thence, on a March night in 1646, he had passed out of England.

Three years later, after his father's execution, he had become king at eighteen—of an estate of broken men and women, dangers, debts and beggary. Nor had he had anywhere to lay his head, for the rulers of Europe, overawed by the 'powerful devils at Westminster,' had little wish to shelter him. Then the tempter had appeared in the homely guise of an elder of the Presbyterian Kirk and offered him the Scottish Crown in return for the renunciation of the Anglican cause for which his father had died. After many pitiful evasions, to find bread for himself and his followers he had taken the Covenant and sailed for Scotland. In the year that followed, he had learnt many things. He had been humiliated and catechised; subjected to an infinity of dull, tedious sermons, made to do penance for the sins of his father and the idolatry of his Roman Catholic mother, and threatened with betrayal to his iron foes. Yet by patience and a certain gentle persuasiveness he had at last overthrown the supremacy of Argyll and the Kirk, and at the eleventh hour rallied a united Scotland behind him. But his triumph had come too late; half the country was in Cromwell's hands, and the sequel had been that bold, desperate march into England. Now an adventure, which had begun in shame, degradation and the sorrow of honest men, was ending in a little wet wood in a corner of the and he had come to conquer. But it was pleasanter to sleep under a hedge in England than in a palace in Scotland: even the rain and the weariness were better than that.

In the intervals of sleep the king talked to Penderel. He had still hopes of reaching London and there taking ship for France, but his companion knew of no one on that road who could assist him. It was therefore decided that he should make for Wales, where he had many friends, and that Penderel should escort him that night to Madeley, ten miles to the west, where a Catholic gentleman of his acquaintance might secure them a passage across the Severn.

A little before dusk the two left the wood and made their way across a heath to Hobbal Grange, the cottage where Richard lived with his widowed mother. The old peasant came out to welcome her king, blessing God that she had raised up children to succour him in his time of need. She gave him bread, cheese and a fricassee of bacon and eggs, and wondered to see his appetite, half regal and wholly boyish. While she waited at the table, her son-in-law, Francis Yates—who not long after was hanged at Oxford for his share in the affair—came in with thirty pieces of silver, his all, which he offered to the king. The latter, who —though he perhaps did not realise the full grandeur of the sacrifice—was not unacquainted with poverty, accepted ten of them in his necessity.

The night was pitch black, and Charles, after two days of continuous action and exposure, was tired out. He and Penderel made their way across country, avoiding the haunts of men and clambering the wet fences and pales of remote enclosures. After a few miles the trackway they were following dipped down to bridge a stream, beside which stood a mill. The miller, hearing footsteps, appeared at the door and called on them to stop. Instead of obeying, they ran blindly past him. The lane beyond the river was muddy and steep, and the darkness was such that Charles had nothing to guide him but the rustling of Penderel's breeches ahead and the miller's footsteps behind. When his breath and courage could carry him no longer he flung himself into the hedge and waited for the end. Here Penderel joined him, and the two lay listening for their pursuer. But all was quiet, and after a time they resumed their journey through the briary, dripping night. Poor Charles was now in despair. His ill-made country shoes so racked his feet that he threw them away and walked in his slashed stockings. His nose began to bleed, his head throbbed and his limbs trembled with cold and weariness. 'Many times he cast himself upon the ground with a desperate and obstinate resolution to rest there till the morning, that he might shift with less torment, what hazard so ever he ran. But his stout guide still prevailed with him to make a new attempt, sometimes promising him that the way should be better, sometimes assuring him that he had but a little farther to go.' Shortly after midnight they came to Madeley.

At the edge of the village Penderel left the king in hiding and made his way to Francis Wolfe's house. The old gentleman—he was sixty-nine and lived to see the Restoration—

came to the door. Penderel asked him if he would help a royalist fugitive of rank to cross the Severn. Wolfe replied that the town was full of troops, and all the passages across the river guarded, and that he would not undertake so perilous a task for anyone but the king himself. But when Penderel blurted out the truth he expressed his readiness to venture his life and all that he had.

As the priest-holes in the house were known, the Wolfes and their daughter, Anne, sheltered the king all that day in a hayloft. In the evening they brought him food and money and new shoes and stockings. Then, as the passage of the Severn was judged impossible, the two travellers started on the return journey for Boscobel. At Evelith Mill, fearing their challenger of the previous night, they left the roadway, intending to ford the river above the bridge. Here Penderel's courage, for the first and last time, failed him. The heavy rain had swollen the little stream, and, child of the Midlands that he was, he confided that he could not swim and that it was a scurvy river. Thirty years afterwards Charles dictated the story of that passage to Pepys. 'So I told him that the river, being but a little one, I would undertake to help him over. Upon which we went over some closes to the river side, and I, entering the river first to see whether I could myself go over, who knew how to swim, found it was but a little above my middle, and, thereupon, taking Richard Penderel by the hand, I helped him over.' At about three o'clock that morning they passed the gateway of Whiteladies and came into the woods between that place and Boscobel.

Leaving the king in the wood, Penderel went on to Boscobel to consult his brother as to the next step in their desperate enterprise. Here news awaited him. Lord Wilmot had found a refuge at the house of a neighbouring Catholic gentleman, Mr. Whitgreave of Moseley Hall, through the offices of Father Huddleston, a priest, who lived there. The other piece of news was that Colonel Careless, who two days before had led the last charge over the cobblestones of Worcester, was in hiding at Boscobel.

Careless accompanied Penderel back to the wood. He

found the king, at the first stroke of dawn, sitting forlorn on a tree-stump, and could not refrain from weeping at the sight. The three then walked together across the high ground towards Boscobel, looking back, as the sun touched the Wrekin, on the far Welsh mountains beyond the Severn.

At Boscobel, a black and white hunting-lodge amid a a jumble of barns and hayricks, the king breakfasted off bread, cheese and small beer. Joan Penderel, William's wife, washed and dressed his feet, cutting the blisters and inserting pads of paper between his toes. Then, as it was probable that the house would be searched by one of the numerous companies of soldiers in the neighbourhood, Charles and Careless went out again into the wood.

At the edge of the copse, overlooking the highway, was an old hollow oak. Into this, at Careless's suggestion, they climbed. The road below was soon busy with passers-by, and through the veil of leaves that concealed them they could see a party of soldiers searching the woods, where the Penderels, to allay suspicion, were 'peaking up and down' with their nut-hooks. After a time Charles, worn out, fell asleep with his head in Careless's lap. As the hours passed and the king's fitful slumber continued, Careless's supporting arm became completely numbed. With infinite difficulty he awoke him, motioning him to silence lest the troopers below should hear.

At nightfall, when the seekers had gone home to prepare for the Sabbath, the Penderels brought a ladder to the tree, and Charles and Careless, tired, cramped and hungry, returned to Boscobel. They passed through the big parlour of the house—it still stands—and up the stairs to a long attic gallery, used for storing cheeses. Here Mrs. Penderel, whom Charles christened Dame Joan, brought them a supper of chickens. Afterwards, as the night was fine, Charles sat for a while drinking wine in the garden, where Humphrey Penderel, the miller, came with news. While in the town that day he had been questioned by a republican officer, who suspected that he knew of the king's whereabouts. Humphrey had stoutly denied all knowledge, whereupon the officer showed him a proclamation, threatening death to all who should aid 'Charles Stuart, a long dark man above two yards high,' and offering a reward of £1,000 to anyone who should betray him. On hearing this Charles could not help reflecting on the temptation to which the poor men who sheltered him were exposed, but Careless, divining his thoughts, assured him that had the reward been a thousand times as great it could not have shaken their fidelity.

Before the king retired to rest, Careless asked him what he would like for breakfast. Charles suggested mutton—a reply which caused the Penderels to exchange glances, for suspicion might be aroused should they attempt to obtain so unusual a luxury from their neighbours. He then made his way upstairs to a hiding-hole beneath the attic floor, where he spent the night on a straw pallet in a space little bigger than his own body.

He awoke early on Sunday morning, and the first sounds he heard were the church bells of Tong. Careless had been up before him and brought home his breakfast from Father Staunton's sheepcote. Together they fried the mutton collops before the fire.

Charles spent the greater part of the day reading in a 'pretty arbour' in the garden, where there was a stone seat and table. 'He commended the place for its retiredness,' and so rested. Here, as in other places, there is a touch of the *Pilgrim's Progress* in the narrative : one is reminded of the shepherd's boy in the Valley of Humiliation. The king's state was indeed very low. He was surrounded by his enemies, a price was set on his head, and his poor protectors were hard put to it to know where to turn for food for another day.

While the king spent that Sabbath in the garden John Penderel made his way to Moseley to consult Lord Wilmot and ask his help. He found Whitgreave and Father Huddleston, who informed him that Wilmot had left Moseley for Colonel Lane's house, Bentley, beyond Wolverhampton, intending thence to travel to the coast. As every hope of Charles's escape now depended on Wilmot,

Penderel persuaded the others to take him to Bentley. Here Wilmot was found. In consultation with this cheerful, self-confident fugitive, who himself scorned any disguise but a hawk on his sleeve, it was decided that Charles should be brought that night from Boscobel to Moseley and that Wilmot should meet him there. On the way back Penderel revealed the identity of their intending guest to Whitgreave and Huddleston. Having fixed a rendezvous at the foot of the garden, he returned with the news to Boscobel.

From Boscobel to Moseley was eight miles : the night was dark and stormy. Charles was still too lame to walk, and Humphrey Penderel's aged mill-horse, with a 'pitiful old saddle and rough bridle,' was requisitioned for him. He bade farewell to Careless and set out, surrounded by the five Penderel brothers and Yates who marched beside him armed with bill-hooks and pistols, ready to sell their lives in his defence. With this curious and devoted army the king crossed Chillington Park and the dark Staffordshire woods. At Pendeford old mill, two miles from his destination, he dismounted, leaving the horse with William, Humphrey and George Penderel. He had gone a few paces on his way when he turned back and, begging their pardon that his troubles had made him forgetful of his friends, gave them his hand to kiss. The peasant brothers kneeling before the king in the storm are the epitome of this night. It was the supreme moment of their simple and pious lives.

In a little grove of trees in the corner of a field called the Moor, Father Huddleston was waiting for the king. He led him down a long walk of trees, through a gateway and across a garden. At the darkened door of the house Whitgreave did not know before which of the eight shadowy figures, all habited alike, he should kneel, until the light of the hall fell on the pale, kingly boy with his cropped hair and shabby clothes, and Wilmot said : 'This is my master, your master, and the master of us all.'

While Whitgreave fed the Penderels, Wilmot led the king through the hall and up the broad staircase to a panelled chamber. Here Charles, sitting on the bed, asked questions about the fate of his companions. Presently Whitgreave and Huddleston joined them with sack and biscuits and a change of shirt. Refreshed, Charles expressed himself fit for a new march and ready, should God bless him with an army of resolute men, to drive all the rogues out of his kingdom.

Next morning, Monday, September 8th, the king awoke after the first night of comfort he had enjoyed since the battle. At breakfast he saluted old Mrs. Whitgreave, his host's mother, and made her sit with him at table while Huddleston and Whitgreave waited. The latter had sent all his servants to work in the fields, except a Catholic cook, who could be trusted with the half truth that the house sheltered a fugitive from Worcester. Charles spent most of this day sitting in a room over the porch, watching the high road that ran past the house. Three boys, who were living at Moseley as pupils of Huddleston's, were released from their lessons and told to keep guard, a task which they thoroughly enjoyed. That night at supper the eldest of them called to his companions, 'Eat hard, boys, for we have been on the life-guard this day,' an observation, as Whitgreave remarked, 'more truly spoken than he was aware.'

On Tuesday a message arrived that Colonel Lane would ride over that night to escort the king to Bentley, where he had arranged for him to start next day for the coast, disguised as a servant of his sister Jane, who had obtained a pass to visit a pregnant friend near Bristol. That morning Charles was in good spirits. He joined Huddleston and Whitgreave in the latter's study and amused them by stories of his usage by the Scots. Seeing a volume of Catholic devotions on the table, he picked it up and read for a time, commending several passages to Huddleston's great joy and edification. In the afternoon there was an adventure. A servant arrived with news that a company of militia was on its way to search the house and arrest Whitgreave on a charge of having been present at Worcester. The latter at once hid Charles in the priest-hole, and, leaving all doors open to avert suspicion, went downstairs to meet the soldiers. A long and angry altercation took place in the doorway; in the end Whitgreave's neighbours were able to persuade the search-party that he had never left Moseley during the battle. When at last he was free to let Charles out of his narrow hiding-place, he found him in some fear that he had been abandoned for ever.

That evening the king asked Huddleston to show him his master's oratory, saying 'he knew he was a priest, and he needed not fear to own it, for if it pleased God to restore him to his kingdom, they should never more need privacies.' The priest led him to the little secret oratory. Charles looked with respect on this plain, decent room with its crucifix and candles, and with regard at the man, who, without fear or cant, faced poverty and death in order to minister to his flock. Brought face to face with the same poverty and peril, Charles was perhaps nearer the inner truth of religion at that moment than at any other in his life. He stood there before the altar, no longer boy or king, but man in his simple dignity, humble in the presence of God.

At midnight Lane arrived from Bentley with two horses and waited in an orchard at the foot of the garden. At the top of the stairs old Mrs. Whitgreave was waiting to bid farewell to her king. Pressing sweetmeats into his hands, the old lady knelt down before him, and in this posture she, her son and Huddleston prayed God to preserve him. Charles, deeply touched, gave them his hand to kiss, thanking them for their love and care and telling them that, if ever it pleased God to restore him, he would not be unmindful. After that he went into the garden. In the orchard the horses were waiting. The night was cold, and Huddleston lent the king his cloak; once more squire and priest knelt : then Charles and Lane rode off into the darkness.

They made their way eastwards across a wilderness of heaths and wide fields. On the high land between Willenhall and Walsall, where now the night sky is lit by blast furnaces, they came to Bentley Park. Wilmot was waiting for them in the hall, and the three sat down to supper. It

was arranged that Charles was to start for Bristol at dawn,
riding pillion with Jane Lane and disguised as William
Jackson, a tenant's son in attendance, while the pair were
to be escorted by Henry Lassels, a young cousin of the
house. Wilmot, who still refused to compromise his nobility
by a disguise, was to travel with Colonel Lane at a short
distance from the main party. Charles retired to bed for
the remainder of the night in the servants' quarters.

A little before dawn Lane called the king and gave him
£20, a suit and cloak of country grey and a high black hat.
When Charles had dressed himself like a sober farmer's
son on holiday and received the final instructions as to his
part, he fetched the horses from the stables and waited,
with his hat under his arm, before the house for his
mistress.

Jane mounted and took her seat behind the king. Her
mother stood at the door to see her go, ignorant of the
honour done her daughter. But the girl knew her prince
and trembled as she touched his shoulder. For the next
week she carried the crown of England in her hands, and
never was trust more bravely or delicately performed.

For the greater part of the first day's journey the travel-
lers were accompanied by a self-opiniated brother-in-law
of the Lanes, John Petre, who was taking his wife to
Buckinghamshire and knew nothing of the identity of
Jane's servant. All morning they rode through the broad,
undulating country which now marks the western fringe of
Birmingham, but which was then rural enough. At Broms-
grove, 'a poor scattering village,' Charles's mare cast a shoe.
While he worked, the smith discoursed of current politics.
No, he replied to the king's inquiry, he had heard no news
since that of the victory of Worcester, nor had he heard
that the chief rogue, Charles Stuart, had yet been captured. The king remarked that if that rascal were taken he
deserved to be hanged for bringing in the Scots, on which
the smith replied with an oath that he spoke like an honest
man.

In the afternoon they skirted the Forest of Arden. A
little beyond Wootton-Wawen an old woman, gleaning by

the wayside, called out to them to have a care of the soldiers on the main Stratford road. Charles was for riding on, but Petre, who had once been beaten by a band of drunken troopers, insisted on turning out of the way. Passing through Snittersfield, Shakespeare's paternal home, they came to Stratford by another route, only to meet the soldiers entering the town. Their foes, however, merely opened their ranks to let them pass, duly returning Charles's respectful salute. Here the Petres turned towards Banbury, while Charles, Jane and Lassels pursued their way southwards towards the Cotswolds. At Long Marston, having ridden fifty miles that day, they halted for the night at the house of John Tomes, a cousin of the Lanes. Charles supped in the kitchen, and, when the maid asked him to wind the jack, the well-nourished Cotswold servants gathered round, wondering what kind of a countryman he might be who could not perform so simple a task. But Charles knew his Staffordshire. 'We seldom,' he replied, 'have meat, and when we do we rarely use a jack.'

Next day, September 11th, the travellers were abroad early, and the view from the Cotswold edge across western England was their recompense. As they crossed the hills by Chipping Campden, Charles could see a dark patch in the north, Worcester of fatal memory, westwards wooded Bredon and the Malverns, and far off the hills of Wales. For the next few hours, in all that busy, seeking kingdom, the pure winds and the tinkling sheep-bells were their only companions. They rode through Stow-on-the-Wold and Northleach, coming at dusk to Cirencester. Here Charles and Lassels slept together in the low upper room of an inn. After the chamberlain had taken away the candles, they changed beds, Lassels taking the little truckle mattress on the floor and resigning his bed to his king.

On Friday they reached Bristol. They entered the city at Lawford's Gate and crossed the Avon at Rownham Ferry. Charles remembered Bristol well; he insisted on riding about the town, inspecting the site of the former Royalist fortifications and noting with surprise the many changes and improvements. Then, skirting the left bank of the Avon, they climbed the upland to Abbots Leigh, the home of Jane's friend, Mrs. Norton, and her husband. As they reached the summit, the sun was sinking over the Bristol Channel. Below them in the dusk was a gabled

The Escape from Worcester

Elizabethan house, and from its trees and lawns arose the sound of rooks and of men playing bowls.

As they rode past the little group of players, Charles saw to his dismay a former chaplain of his, Dr. George—a most loquacious man—leaning against the railings watching the game. He took the horses to the stable, and Jane Lane, on entering the house, told Pope, the butler—an old Royalist soldier—that her servant was sick of an ague and not fit to be below stairs. Accordingly Charles, who must have been feeling lonely on his separation from his charming fellow-traveller, found himself accorded a private room and a fire away from the other servants. At supper Miss Lane filled a little dish of broth and asked Pope to carry it to her retainer, telling him that he should have some more presently. Pope took it with a napkin, spoon and bread, and spoke kindly to the young man, who he found was very willing to eat. Meanwhile in the dining-hall, Dr. George, 'being a man of a cheerful conversation, asked Mistress Lane many questions concerning William of whom he saw she was so careful by sending up meat to him, how long his ague had been gone and whether he had purged since it left him and the like.' To these embarrassing questions poor Jane gave what answers she could. After supper Dr. George, who much fancied himself as a physician, paid a call on the invalid. He felt his pulse, asked many questions, and wondered why he shrank from him. His patient was not a little relieved when he heard that he was leaving Abbots Leigh next day.

In the morning the king rose early and, having an excellent appetite, went downstairs to get his breakfast at the buttery-hatch. Here he found Pope and two or three other men. While they ate bread and butter, washed down by the butler's ale, one of the men started to give a detailed account of the battle of Worcester. Charles, asking him how he came to know so much of the engagement, was not a little alarmed to learn that he had actually been a trooper in his own guards. Hoping to allay suspicion he asked him to describe the king's clothes and appearance, which the other did most accurately, looking hard at him and explaining that the king was at least three inches taller than he. 'Upon which,' Charles afterwards related, 'I made what haste I could out of the buttery, for fear he should indeed know me.'

The surprises of that morning were not yet over. As

Charles stood by Pope's side, bare-headed at the hall door, to let Mrs. Norton pass, he noticed that his companion was staring at him very earnestly. Worried by this attention, he went out into the fields for half an hour. On his return to his chambers Lassels came to him and told him that he thought Pope had recognised him. Charles asked what kind of a man he was, and, on being assured of his proven loyalty, decided to place his safety in his hands. He accordingly sent for Pope, who, looking upon him, fell upon his knees with tears in his eyes.

The good butler, hearing that Wilmot, who was lodging at a neighbouring house, was proposing to pay a visit to Abbots Leigh that afternoon, warned Charles that the servants were not to be trusted and that Wilmot would certainly be recognised. He contrived, therefore, to delay the latter and to bring him that night secretly to the royal chamber. Here a consultation was held, and it was agreed that Pope should try to find a ship at Bristol to carry the king to France.

Charles spent that week-end resting quietly at Abbots Leigh, mostly sitting alone in the chimney corner and feigning illness. Miss Lane continued to express her anxiety for her servant in public, saying, 'the boy will never recover—he'll ne'er be good again,' while Margaret Rider, a maid of Mrs. Norton's, conceiving a romantic passion for the lonely young man, made him a carduus-posset and waited on him tenderly.

Pope's efforts to charter a vessel were fruitless. On Monday it was decided to remove Charles to Trent, near Sherborne, the home of an enthusiastic royalist, Colonel Frank Wyndham, a brother-in-law of Charles's old nurse. Wilmot went on at once to warn Wyndham, while the others prepared to set out next morning. Just before announcing their intentions to the household, a disaster occurred. Their hostess miscarried, and poor Jane was at her wits' end to know what excuse to make to enable her to leave her friend at such a moment. The butler's resource saved them. He concocted a letter from Bentley, announcing the sudden illness of Jane's father, and handed it to her at supper: the girl's skilful acting did the rest.

Early on Tuesday Charles, Jane and Lassels set out for Trent. They travelled eastwards for a few miles, as though heading for Bentley, and then turned south. Following the old Roman trackway past Shepton Mallet, they reached Castle Cary, where they were met by Lord Hertford's steward, who found them accommodation for the night. Next morning, a fortnight after the battle, they came at about ten o'clock to the retired and beautiful village of Trent, where Wyndham and his young wife were awaiting them. Charles, who was in good spirits, called out, 'Frank, Frank, how dost thou?' He was escorted to the house, where a suite of black panelled rooms had been set apart for him. Here he was to make his longest stay during the period of his flight, and here, in a household of twenty persons, his presence remained unknown to all but his host and hostess, their little cousin, Juliana Coningsby, and two loyal maids. Their names, Eleanor Withers and Joan Halsenoth, are worthy of remembrance; they waited upon him, passing the food, cooked in the kitchen below, to his room by means of a rope in the chimney.

On the king's arrival a conference was held. Wyndham related a strange tale of his father, who, on his death-bed fifteen years before, had called his sons about him, telling them that they had seen serene and quiet times, but must now prepare themselves for cloudy and troublesome ones. 'I command you,' he had said with his last breath, 'to honour and obey your sovereign, and though the crown should hang upon a bush, I charge you forsake it not.' In these dying words Wyndham perceived a prophecy, now nearing fulfilment.

The next day Jane and Lassels set out for Staffordshire, and Wyndham paid a visit to his neighbour, Giles Strangways, about finding a boat. The latter sent him on to Lyme Regis, where, after some delay, a royalist merchant, called Ellesdon, succeeded in chartering a coasting vessel, the master agreeing for a substantial sum to convey two royalist gentlemen to France. It was arranged that on the night of the following Monday, September 22nd, Limbry, the master, should bring his ship to the little coastal village of Charmouth, where Charles and Wilmot were to be in waiting. A room was booked in the inn at Charmouth, and, to avert suspicion, the landlady was informed 'that there was a young man to come thither the next Monday that had stolen a gentlewoman to marry her.' Having completed these romantic arrangements, Wyndham returned to Trent.

On the Monday morning Charles set out on his travels once more, riding pillion, this time in front of pretty Juliana Coningsby, with Wyndham as guide and chaperon. The undisguised Wilmot and Wyndham's servant, Peters, followed them at a safe distance. They went by Over Compton and Berwick, crossing the high Dorset downlands at Pilsdon Pen. At a house among the hills a few miles above Charmouth, they met Ellesdon, who was able to assure them that all was ready. An hour later, as dusk fell, they rode down the steep hill into Charmouth and put up at the Queen's Arms. The wind was blowing for France and the auspices were kindly.

It had been a fair day at Lyme, and the little inn was packed with horse-dealers. After supper Wyndham and Peters went to the beach to await Limbry's long boat, leaving Wilmot and Juliana, with Charles to wait on them, to masquerade, before an extremely interested household, as lovers. Hour followed hour, the disappointed company retired to bed, and still the three waited. At dawn, after what seemed an eternal night, Wyndham returned with news that the tide had gone out and no boat come.

As the people of Charmouth were obviously intrigued by their visitors, it was decided that Charles, Miss Coningsby and Wyndham should set out for Bridport, where Wilmot and Peters, after ascertaining the cause of Limbry's failure, should join them later in the day. Peters accordingly went to Lyme, while Wilmot sent his horse, which had cast a shoe, to be shod. The blacksmith noticed that the remaining shoes were of Midland make, which tallied ill with the couple's tale that they came from Exeter, and confided his suspicions to the ostler, who confirmed them by recounting the strange behaviour of these supposed lovers. Having finished his task, the smith therefore made his way to the house of the local minister to seek advice. Finding the latter engaged in his morning devotions—a somewhat lengthy affair[1]— the honest craftsman, fearing to lose the hire of his labour, returned to the inn. But when he had been paid and had seen the fat and jovial Wilmot ride away, his suspicions revived. There was something, he reflected, very peculiar about that man. Was not Charles Stuart at large in England, seeking to escape, and was there not a reward of £1,000 upon his head? Once more he sought the house of the minister. He told his tale, confided his fears and hopes, and was rewarded when he saw the good man's eyes light with zeal. Together they hastened to the inn, where they wasted five minutes in upbraiding the indignant landlady. Then they sought a Justice of the Peace. But the latter was a true Englishman, with all an Englishman's love of deliberation and fear of rendering himself foolish in the eyes of his neighbours, and flatly refused to issue a warrant for a king's arrest upon such slender evidence. In despair the two sleuth-hounds left him and made their way to Captain Massey, who commanded a troop of Roundhead militia. He proved to be the man they were seeking, called out his soldiers and at once set out in hot pursuit along the Bridport road.

While these events were happening at Charmouth the king's party had reached Bridport. Here the town was full of red-coats on the point of embarking for the conquest of Jersey. While Wyndham and Juliana ordered a meal at 'The George,' Charles, with the horses, pushed boldly through the troopers in the yard. At that moment an ostler approached him and said he was sure he knew his face. Charles, after discovering that this would-be friend had been in service at a house in Exeter at which he had formerly lodged, claimed to have been a fellow-servant with him there. This satisfied the ostler, who asked him to drink, but the king begged to be excused, explaining that he had to wait on his master and mistress. He found them in an upper room, with a meal set before them, of which they made him eat before he returned to the horses. At this moment Juliana's sharp eyes caught sight of Peters in the street below. From him she learned that Wilmot was in Bridport and was urging an immediate departure; the imperturbable nobleman had at last sensed peril. Accordingly they set out at once along the London road, joining Wilmot and Peters just outside the town. About a mile out of Bridport they decided to turn up a lane northwards and work back across country in the hope of tidings of the lost vessel. It was well that they did so. A minute later Massey's pursuing troopers galloped past the turning towards Dorchester. Meanwhile the travellers continued their rambling journey, unconscious that a whole countryside was seeking them. They lost their way and rode all afternoon in a wilderness of downs and lonely valleys. 'Providence directed these strangers,' leading them at nightfall to the little village of Broad Windsor, a few miles north of Bridport.

Here, in the heart of the bleak Dorset uplands, they put up at a poor little inn, the best harbourage the place could afford. Happily the landlord was an old servant of Wyndham's family, and he and his wife were both staunch Royalists, having 'according to their condition undergone their share of troubles.' Though they did not know the full extent of the greatness they were entertaining, they bustled about to make their guests comfortable. But the latter's perils were not yet over. At midnight a company of soldiers arrived, on march for the coast, and demanded quarters. They swarmed all over the lower part of the house, completely cutting off the attic in which the king was trying to sleep. One of their doxies who accompanied them was unexpectedly brought to bed of a child on the kitchen table; the clamour of this event and the furious dispute as to the babe's future upkeep, which it occasioned between the military and the parish overseers, made sleep impossible. Fortunately the soldiers resumed their march at daybreak, and the fugitives were able to breathe again. During the morning Peters, who had been sent to Lyme to interview Ellesdon, returned with the explanation of Monday night's fiasco. Apparently Limbry had confided to his wife that he was about to carry a dangerous cargo to France, and the latter, much alarmed, had locked him up in his room and kept him there till he gave his word that he would not sail. Further attempts to embark from Lyme were plainly out of the question, and the little party returned to Trent.

Here the king remained for nearly another week. The two maids and his pretty hostess waited on him, and he passed his days cooking his own food and boring holes in coins as keepsakes for them. On one occasion, hearing the church bells pealing, he looked out of the window to see a crowd of villagers dancing round a bonfire in celebration of his own supposed capture and death. On another Mrs. Wyndham was put to great fear for her guest—she had none for herself—by the arrival of a mysterious troop of horse at Sherborne, but Charles, who was growing used to dangers, only laughed.

Meanwhile further attempts were being made to secure a ship. Through the suggestion of a neighbour, Wyndham had got into touch with a little group of royalists at Salisbury. One of these, Colonel Robin Phelipps, a younger son of the house of Montacute, undertook to find and charter a vessel from a Hampshire or Sussex port. His first attempt at Southampton was unsuccessful, but he transferred his efforts to Chichester. To be nearer the scene of action, it was decided to move the king from Trent to Heale, near Salisbury, the residence of Mrs. Hyde, a widow.

On the evening of Sunday, October 5th, Phelipps arrived at Trent to act as guide. Next morning the king took leave of his kind hosts. That day Phelipps and Charles rode fifty miles, the latter once more in front of Juliana, while Peters followed them in attendance. They passed, by Sandford Orcas and Wincanton, through a little frequented and lovely corner of England. At Mere, eighteen miles on their way, they stopped for a drink at the George Inn, where Phelipps knew the host, a good royalist. They drank in the cellar, where the landlord turned to Charles with a 'Thou lookest like an honest fellow. Here's a health to the king!' The subject of this loyal toast naturally hesitated, and mine host turned to Phelipps in disgust and asked him what kind of a Roundhead fellow he had brought.

In the afternoon the travellers, passing through Hindon, Chilmark and Teffont, skirted Salisbury Plain and came to Wilton. Here Juliana and Peters said good-bye, and Charles and Phelipps, leaving the main road, made their way across the plain towards the Avon valley. At nightfall they found the welcoming lights of Heale House.

Mrs. Hyde was waiting for them, and a cheerful little party of loyalists from Salisbury sat down together to supper, though the identity of the newcomer was not known to all. Mrs. Hyde recognised him at once and, though she tried to hide her feelings, could not refrain from showing her loyalty by helping him to two larks instead of one. Among the guests was Dr. Henchman, a canon of Salisbury Cathedral, one of the chief agents in the search for a boat. After supper this wise and brave old churchman had a long talk with his king.[2]

It was not thought safe that Charles, who had been seen by all the servants at supper, should remain publicly at Heale, and it was decided that on the next day he should pretend to depart, returning secretly in the evening. Accordingly in the morning he rode off with Robin Phelipps. The pair spent the day pleasantly enough on Salisbury Plain, where there was no one to observe or disturb them. They galloped on the soft down turf, started hares and paid a visit to Stonehenge. Here Charles stood looking upon the stones for some time and proved to his companion the fallacy of the popular belief that they could not be counted twice alike. At dusk Henchman met them in a meadow near Heale, where Phelipps took his leave. The king then re-entered the house by a back way and was escorted to a secret hiding-hole. Here he spent the next five days, waited upon by Mrs. Hyde and her sister, who alone knew of his presence. His quarters were cramped, but he was probably safer at this period of his wandering than at any other. The Government had lost all trace of him.

Meanwhile his faithful friends were seeking a boat. Wilmot and Phelipps, stopping at Hinton-Daubnay, near Hambledon, had recruited George Gounter of Racton, a Sussex royalist. A much persecuted man, he had just returned from London, where he had been borrowing the wherewithal to pay the heavy fines laid on his estates. Without hesitation he undertook a new burden in the cause for which he had already given so much. His poor wife, struggling to make both ends meet, wept when she heard of the new danger he had accepted, but encouraged him in his resolve. On Saturday, October 11th, this gallant gentleman found what he was seeking at Chichester, where, with the help of Francis Mansel, a loyal merchant, he negotiated a treaty with Nicholas Tattersall, the master of a Brighthelmstone coal-brig, who, for sixty pounds down, agreed to carry two fugitives from Shoreham to France.

On Sunday, October 12th, Charles made ready for his departure from Heale. At three o'clock that night, Phelipps, with a led horse for the king, arrived at the appointed rendezvous. The led horse broke its bridle and ran up the river; with great difficulty Phelipps recaptured it. The two horsemen then rode through the night, past Clarendon Park corner and Old Sarum. Dawn found them crossing the high and lonely hills to the east of Salisbury. All that morning they rode through Hampshire, by Tytherley and through the woods of the Test Valley, and so, by Mottisfont and Hursley, to Twyford. Here, leaving Winchester and the gleaming Itchen behind them, they trotted across the sweet, wind-swept open downs.

On a hill called Old Winchester, the highest in those parts, above the little village of Warnford, Wilmot and his servant, Swan, Gounter and his brother-in-law were waiting for the king. They had left home early, calling at the house of Gounter's sister, Mrs. Symonds, at Hambledon, to borrow a brace of greyhounds on the pretence of coursing; they warned her that they might seek her hospitality that night. When the hour fixed for the rendezvous passed without any sign, Gounter rode down to Warnford. There, at the town's end, he encountered Charles and Phelipps

Pretending not to have recognised them, he continued his way into the village, drank a glass of ale and purchased some tobacco, and then rode back, catching up the travellers as they reached the summit of the hill.

On that high October afternoon, with half England—rolling down and far woodland—spread around them, they held a council of war, deciding to spend the night in some quiet neighbouring house. 'I know,' said Gounter, 'divers yeomanry men, where for a night we may be very welcome, and there is one who married my sister and whose house stands privately and out of the way.' 'Let us go thither,' replied the king.

As evening fell on the Hampshire landscape they rode over Broadhalfpenny Down, where men already played a quaint game with stump and ball, towards the valley. Below them lay Hambledon, on the edge of the forest. At about candle lighting they came to Mrs. Symonds's house; though all unconscious of her honour, she welcomed them and led them into a little fire-lit parlour setting biscuits and wine before them.

That night was the pleasantest in all the king's travels. They sat down to supper at a round table, and, when the meal was almost over, the master of the house joined them. He, like an honest Cavalier, had been drinking in a tavern, and was filled with an hospitable desire to see all about him as merry as he. He settled down among his wife's guests, taking a stool by Charles, whose cropped hair and solemn aspect marked him out as a suitable object for conversion. Then, shaking his hand and mixing a bottle of strong waters in a tankard of beer, he called him Brother Roundhead and bade him drink deep. The scene is a delicious one—the wainscotted room, the firelight and the candles on the table, the faces of the hunted fugitives lit by the glow and the wine, and the hiccoughing host, half scared by the king's puritanical appearance and wholly jovial. Whenever a bibulous oath escaped him, Charles was ready with the appropriate rebuke : 'Oh, dear brother, this is a scape : swear not, I beseech you.' But the other was incorrigible. At ten o'clock, in order to let Charles escape to bed, Gounter suggested to his host that the Roundhead would be better away. Symonds gladly assented.

It is not improbable that Charles awoke with a headache. That day, the 14th of October, was the last of his pilgrimage. Before he left Hambledon a message arrived from Lord Southampton, who had somehow learnt of his presence in the neighbourhood, offering his services and hospitality. Charles, having the promise of a ship, would not allow him to run the risk, but ever afterwards gratefully acknowledged his obligation to a nobleman, who, having great possessions, was ready to sacrifice them all for his sake.

Phelipps went to London to make arrangements for a supply of money to await the fugitives in France, and the king, Gounter, Wilmot and Swan set out alone. For thirty miles they rode eastwards through the forest. On the fringe of Arundel Park they saw the Governor of the castle and his men riding out to hunt; they did not like the look of his 'starched moustaches,' so turned aside and led their horses up the slope of the high woods. Beyond the downs they crossed the Arun at Houghton Bridge. In the quiet village street they halted before the ale-house door and while they drank, Gounter pulled out a couple of Mrs. Symonds' neats' tongues from his pocket.

East of the Arun they climbed, and for eleven miles rode along the downs. The thrill of the upland air caught their hearts and, as the king gazed northwards from Chanctonbury over the Weald, England seemed to him a country worth fighting for. In Bramber, where they came down to cross the Adur, the street was full of soldiers, and in the narrow lanes beyond they heard horse-hooves close behind them. Boldly they slackened pace, and the troopers, on some military errand, pushed by unregarding.

Near Beeding they parted company, preferring to approach Brighthelmstone by different routes. Charles and Wilmot climbed Edburton Hill and cantered over the nine miles of down which divided them from the sea. At Brighthelmstone, then only a cluster of fishermen's cottages, they pulled up at the George. When Gounter and Swan arrived they could hear the king's voice in the parlour, toasting Wilmot : 'Here, Mr. Barlow, I drink to you!'

At the inn Mansel and Tattersall, who as yet only knew of Charles as a royalist fugitive, met them. They all sat down together to supper. Though there was some anxiety about the wind, the king was in excellent spirits.

That evening witnessed two last touching pieces of loyalty. After supper Tattersall, who had looked much at Charles during the meal, drew Mansel aside and told him that he had not dealt fairly with him, 'for, though he had given him a very good price for the carrying over of that gentleman, yet he had not been clear with him; for he was the king, and he very well knew him to be so. But, said he, be not troubled at it, for I think I do God and my country good service in preserving the king, and, by the grace of God, I will venture my life and all for him and set him safely on shore if I can in France.' To such simple men it was given to see further than the politicians in their wisdom.

There was a further incident. As the king was standing alone by the fireside after supper, with his hand leaning on his chair, the innkeeper, an old guardsman, came in and started to talk. Suddenly he raised the king's hand and kissed it, saying, 'God bless you wheresoever you go; I do not doubt before I die to be a lord and my wife a lady.' Charles laughed and hastily left the room, but he had no cause to fear the old soldier's loyalty.

For a long time they sat up drinking and smoking, Charles desiring to keep Tattersall with him, lest he should decline the venture at the last moment, as Limbry had done. When it became known that the wind had changed and set fair for France, Charles and Wilmot lay down for a brief rest. At two o'clock Gounter called them, showing them the time on his watch. They rose and made their way on horseback through the night to a creek at the mouth of the Adur, where Tattersall's brig, *The Surprise,* was lying. They climbed aboard and lay down in the little cabin, waiting for the tide. Here Gounter bade them farewell.

At about seven o'clock of the morning, being high water, they went out of the port, steering a westward course as though for Poole, the boat's normal destination. At that very hour another fugitive from Worcester, less fortunate than Charles, was waiting for the axe to fall in Bolton market square. A few days before his death Lord Derby had written to his wife: 'Though I be never so close, my heart is my own—free as the best.' It was such a spirit that made the Restoration a certainty.

All that day Gounter followed on the beach with the horses, watching those vanishing sails. On board *The Surprise,* the king, who had learnt to love ships during his first exile in Jersey many years before, suffered a sea change; he walked the deck, happy and at home, talking to Tattersall and winning that loyal sailor's admiration by directing the course. The crew, four men and a boy, stood watching and smoking.

One further subterfuge was necessary. Tattersall had not broken the news of the vessel's unwonted destination to his men. He now approached the king and begged his help. The latter accordingly confided to the crew that he and Wilmot were merchants, who had suffered losses and were in debt, and offered them twenty-five shillings to drink if they would second his endeavours to persuade the master to set them in France. This speech made a strong appeal to the thirsty throats and romantic hearts of the English seamen. They at once agreed, and the master was quickly persuaded. About five in the afternoon, while still in sight of the Isle of Wight, the brig stood off with a northerly wind for France.

At dawn on Thursday, October 16th, Charles landed at Fécamp. When his mother's Court rode out to welcome him back to the Louvre his friends could scarcely recognise him. The gentle boy, who had left Paris two years before, was now shorn and bearded, his build was manly and powerful, his features had coarsened, his expression grown reckless. Yet to shrewd observers the long mouth and level eyes told their tale. Young though he was he had met as intimates hunger, weariness and peril; he had shared the companionship of the very poor; he had known courage and fidelity. And, if the Commonwealth's spies noted, beneath his outward cheerfulness, a certain sadness, it was because his heart was still in England with the loyal men and women who had shared his perils and from whom he was now divided.

CHAPTER FOUR

THE FIRE OF LONDON, 1666
The Master Chronicler

'And Paul's is burned, and all Chepside.'

Diary, Sept. 4th, 1666.

On the first day of September, 1666, a Saturday, Samuel Pepys—the 33-year-old Clerk of the Acts of the Navy Board who six years earlier had been one of those who heard, for the first time on the deck of the ship bringing Charles II back to England, the story of his miraculous escape—took the afternoon off from the office and, with his wife, her maid, Mercer, and his colleague, Sir William Penn, went to the playhouse. Then, after a jaunt to the cakes and meadows of Islington, he returned to his fine official residence in Seething Lane near the Tower, his mind dwelling on the thought of gilding the backs of his books in the carved and glazed presses which Sympson, the joiner, made for them that summer. His new closet, he reflected, had been set mighty clean against the morrow, when he was entertaining guests to view it for the first time, and all his worldly affairs prospered. The wind was blowing strongly from the east, after long drought.

About three o'clock on Sunday morning Pepys was called from his bed by his maids, who had sat up late setting things ready against the day's feast, with news of a fire in the City. With his unfailing curiosity, he slipped on his nightgown and went to the window to look; he judged it to be at the backside of Mark Lane and, after watching for a little while, went back to bed.

He was up again by seven, and when he looked out the fire seemed to be further off than it was and smaller. So he went to his closet to see that everything was ready for his party. Here the little maid, Jane Birch (now returned to the household) came to him to tell him that they were saying that over three hundred houses had been burnt in the night and that the fire was now raging along the steep slope of Fish Street above the Bridge.

He made himself ready and went out, walking up to the Tower, where he got Sir John Robinson's little son to take him up one of the turrets whence he could see what was taking place. Half a mile to the west lay London Bridge with its northern houses all in flames and a great fire blazing between Thames Street and the river, where a huddled infinity of timber-built, pitch-coated little houses and warehouses of oil, tallow and spirits provided fuel enough in that dry, windy weather to light all London. His heart misgave him at the sight and was full of trouble for little Betty Howlett—now married to young Michell, the bookseller's son, and living near the 'Old Swan' in the very heart of those flames—and for his old sweetheart Sarah who dwelt upon the Bridge; his loves were being burnt out like wasps.

He went down and spoke to the Lieutenant of the Tower, who confirmed his worst fears : then took boat and went up through the Bridge, seeing as he passed through the steep piers the houses of his friends blazing beside the water. As he watched, unconsciously the great artist that was within him took possession of his being; and for an hour he re-mained as an eye-witness for posterity storing up all he saw —the scorching, untamable, giant flames, the householders crazy to remove their goods, flinging them into lighters alongside or into the very river itself, the 'poor people stay-ing in their houses as long as till the very fire touched them and then running into boats or clambering from one pair of stairs by the waterside to another.' Even the pigeons, the watching eyes of the poet beheld, were loath to leave their houses but hovered about the windows and balconies till their wings were singed and they fell down. The flaming shadow of death, roaring like a giant, was driving the love of home and property from their age-long habitations before his very eyes.

But when he saw that no one in that universal desire of
each man to save his own was making any attempt to stay
the fire, which the wind was driving into the heart of the
City, the administrator took command of the artist, and he
bade the boatmen row him swiftly to Whitehall. Here he
found them all at chapel, but, giving his tidings, he was
brought to the King and the Duke of York, to whom he
told what he had seen, saying that unless his Majesty gave
orders that houses should be pulled down nothing could
stop the fire. They seemed much troubled and commanded
him to go to the Lord Mayor and bid him destroy all in
the path of the flames. With this errand he drove to St.
Paul's and then walked through the narrow panic-stricken
lanes till he found that unhappy magistrate, with a hand-
kerchief about his neck, crying like a fainting woman :
'Lord ! what can I do ? I am spent; people will not obey
me. I have been pulling down houses, but the fire overtakes
us faster than we can do it.' And then walked on. His
useless errand accomplished, Pepys also walked on. Once
more as he did so the artist came out, seeing the flying
distracted crowds and the churches filling with goods borne
thither by people who at this time, had things, he reflected,
been otherwise, should have been quietly praying within.
Then, it being midday, he went home to entertain his
guests. But his dinner party was not a success, for the
hearts of all those who sat down were elsewhere and Pepys'
intention that they should please themselves with the sight
of his fine new closet was not fulfilled. And as soon as they
could, they went away.

Once more Pepys went out into the streets—'full of
nothing but people and horses and carts loaden with goods,
ready to run over one another, and removing goods from
one burned house to another.' He saw familiar friends
passing through that troubled kaleidoscope of driven
humanity, the King and the Duke of York in their barge
going down the river to take command of their kingdom,
the Thames crowded with goods of all sorts—'and there
was hardly,' he noted for the instruction of posterity, 'one
lighter or boat in three . . . but there was a pair of virginalls

in it." Then, as it grew dark, the air filled with flakes of fire, and he and Elizabeth, unable to endure the scorching heat any longer, crossed the river to a little alehouse on Bankside and there watched that terrible spectacle. As night deepened, the fire seemed to grow 'more and more, and in corners and upon steeples, and between churches and houses, as far as we could see up the hill of the City, in a most horrid, malicious bloody flame, not like the fine flame of an ordinary fire. . . . We staid,' he wrote, 'till, it being darkish, we saw the fire as only one entire arch of fire from this to the other side of the bridge, and in a bow up the hill for an arch of above a mile long; it made me weep to see it. The churches, houses and all on fire and flaming at once; and a horrid noise the flames made and the cracking of houses at their ruin.'

When at last they went home, with a bright moon in the sky and fire all over the earth, they found poor Tom Hayter, who was always in trouble, come with a few of his goods which he had saved from his house in Fish Street Hill to take shelter with his master. Pepys gladly offered him a bed and received his goods, but with the fire creeping north and east as well as driving westwards with the wind, he felt that it was time to move his own; the yard was already full of Sir William Batten's carts come up from Walthamstow. So all night long the household tramped up and down the wooden stairs, carrying money in iron chests into the cellar, and bags of gold and boxes of paper into the garden. Hayter trying to sleep in the troubled house, the carts rumbling into the yard from the country, the smell and crackling of fire and the moon looking down serene on the bewildered doings of men, made up the sum of this night. Before it ended, the fire was raging from Queenhithe in the west to Cannon Street on the north, and eastwards beyond the lower end of Botolph Lane.

At about four o'clock on Monday morning, the Clerk of the Acts, riding in a cart of Batten's, packed high with his goods and arrayed only in his nightgown, set out for Bethnal Green. Here at Sir William Rider's, already crowded with the belongings of his friends, he left his

D

most treasured possessions (among them the volumes of his Diary). Then through the crowd of flying people and carts, he fought his way back to the burning City. All that Monday, a glorious summer's day, he and his poor wife, weary and dazed for lack of sleep, packed up their household goods and, bearing them over Tower Hill, loaded them into a lighter at the quay above Tower Dock. Meanwhile the fire burned ever more fiercely, spreading northwards to devour all Lombard Street, the Poultry and Cornhill, and tumbling the Royal Exchange and forty churches in that universal ruin. Beside the river it ran westwards a further half-mile to Baynard's Castle, but its easterly advance was restricted by the wind. Yet even here it crept along Eastcheap and Thames Street, a couple of hundred yards nearer Seething Lane.

In the midst of all this horror Mrs. Pepys, like a woman inspired, contrived to give Mercer notice. That young lady (whose breasts, though she knew it not, her husband had of late taken to fondling as she dressed him of a morning),[1] had without leave, but very naturally, gone to help her mother move her things. Elizabeth, tracking her down, had upbraided her furiously, at which Mrs. Mercer had shouted back that her daughter was no prentice girl to ask leave every time she went abroad. The angry housewives in battle, while the great fire pursued its course less than a quarter of a mile away, was the last scene in Mercer's sojourn. She departed that night, while her erstwhile master and mistress lay down in turn to snatch a few hours' sleep on a little quilt of Will Hewer's in the Office.

Tuesday, the 4th, was the greatest day of the fire. Ranged now far to the north its flaming battalions poured westwards in irresistible strength over the doomed City. Early in the morning it reached St. Paul's, and, while the leaden roof poured in streams of burning lava into the nave below, flames leapt rejoicing across the valley of the Fleet on to the wooden houses of Salisbury Court and St. Bride's, all but encircling the Duke of York and his soldiers, who were gallantly blowing up houses on Ludgate Hill, in an inescapable ring of fire. Eastwards the foe came up both sides of narrow Thames Street with infinite fury, while Batten and Pepys dug a deep pit in the Navy Office garden, in which to lay, one his wine and the other his papers and Parmesan cheese. Threatened with the immediate destruction of his home, Pepys that afternoon received sudden inspiration—to send for the naval dockyard hands from Woolwich and Deptford to pull down houses and save the Office. He communicated these thoughts to Sir William Penn, who was sitting melancholy by his side in the garden. The latter at once went down the river to summon this help, while Pepys (even at this juncture methodically taking a copy) wrote to Coventry for the Duke's permission to pull down houses, there being an ancient rule of the City that whoever destroyed his neighbour's dwelling should be at the expense of rebuilding it.

That night the fire was in Fenchurch Street to the north of the lane and had already reached the 'Dolphin' in Tower Street. Pepys and his wife sat down to a last sad supper in their house with Mr. Turner, the Petty Purveyor, and his wife as their guests. Somehow they contrived to be a little merry. Only when they looked out, the horrid glamour of the sky, 'all in a fire in the night,' terrified them almost out of their wits; it looked as though the whole heaven was in flames. Throughout the night the sound of explosions kept them from sleeping : the authorities, bent on saving the powder store in the Tower, were now blowing up houses all along Tower Street. At two in the morning, after again lying a brief while on Hewer's quilt in the Office, Pepys was called up with news that the fire was at the bottom of Seething Lane. There being now no hope, he took his wife, Will Hewer and Jane, with £2,350 in gold, by boat to Woolwich. Then leaving them at Mr. Sheldon's in the Yard (after charging his wife and Will never to leave the room in which the gold was lodged without one of them to keep watch on it) he returned to London to survey the ruins of his home.

But when he got back at seven in the morning his house and the Navy Office were still standing. The men from the Yards, whom Penn had brought up in the night, had done

their business; and at Barking Church, its porch and dial
already burnt, the fire had been for the moment at least
stopped, though from the north flames still threatened.
Then, the artist overcoming even the man of property,
Pepys climbed to the top of the rescued steeple and surveyed the scene—'the saddest sight of desolation that ever
I saw, everywhere great fires, oil cellars and brimstone . . .
burning . . . the fire being spread as far as I could see it.'

Then, having good hopes that the worst was over—for
everywhere the King and the Duke of York with their
soldiers and volunteers had been opposing its course with
rope and powder—he dined on cold meat at Sir William
Penn's, the first proper meal he had eaten in three days,
and walked abroad to see the town. Over the smouldering
ruins he made his way, as his fellow diarist, Evelyn, did
two days later, clambering over piles of smoking rubbish,
the ground so hot beneath his feet that it scorched the soles
of his shoes. Fenchurch, Gracechurch and Lombard Streets
were all dust, the Exchange a blackened skeleton, and
Moorfields full of poor wretches sitting among their goods.
He noted Anthony Joyce's house still burning, the buckled
glass that had fallen from the windows of the Mercers'
Chapel, and the poor cat, its hair all burned off its body,
which he saw being taken out of a hole in a chimney. So
he went home, and, as the air was still full of flying sparks,
and rumours were abroad of Dutch and French spies
carrying fireballs to spread the flames, he set the dockyard
men to guard the Office all night, giving them beer and
bread and cheese. Then he fell asleep, all sense of time lost.

But that wonderful curiosity did not allow him to sleep
long, and he was up before five. At the gate of the Office
as he went out, he met Gauden, the Victualler, hurrying
to beg the aid of his men to fight a new fire that had
broken out at Bishopsgate. So Pepys went along with his
dockyard men and helped to put it out, which they did in
a little while; it was strange, he reflected, to see how hard
the women worked fetching water and how they would
then scold for a drink and be as drunk as devils. Then, his
work done, and being all in dirt from head to foot, Dapper

Dicky, as some called him, took boat to Westminster to buy a shirt and gloves and get himself trimmed. And as he went up the river he saw the sad sight of the ruined shores, with no house standing from Tower Bank to the Temple. Of the old City within the wall, scarcely a sixth part remained; thirteen thousand houses had been burnt, leaving a hundred thousand people homeless.

Such was the strange and terrible interlude which broke the course of Pepys' life. He for his part had been wonderfully fortunate—'the Lord of Heaven make me thankful and continue me therein!'—his goods, scattered at Woolwich, Deptford and Bethnal Green, were all safe, and when, a week later, the dockyard labourers had ceased to tramp all night through the Office and his house was made clean, he brought them all home by cart and barge (all save two little sea-pictures which were somehow mislaid) and to his infinite joy lay with his wife in his chamber again. Only, he added, 'I do lack Mercer or somebody in the house to sing with.' But though he tried to entice her back, the lady would not return.

For though Pepys might resume the even tenor of his ways—though he might go abroad in fine clothes again[2] or in a single afternoon (less than a week after the fire ceased) visit both Martin's wife and Bagwell's—the background of his life was changed for ever. Around the Navy Office still stood the familiar houses, and at Westminster and at Whitehall there were trees and green grass and the wonted dwellings of men. But between the two lay a vast wilderness of horror. Walking or riding from Whitehall one approached it, as one visitor to London recalled, passing the untouched palaces of the nobility which still lined the south side of the Strand. But once through Temple Bar, a double line of houses ended two hundred yards away in a desolation of blackened rubble and white ashes, stretching as far as the eye could see and broken only by the ruins of old St. Paul's and the tottering towers of churches. Here for many months the stench and smoke of subterranean fires assailed the traveller, nor was it safe at night to pass by for fear of the lawless and homeless men who lurked among the shadows; half a year later when his Majesty's Clerk of the Acts had occasion to pass through the ruins, he sat in the coach with his sword drawn.

But being English, Pepys dwelt as little as possible on all this. From shades and horrors he turned to the normal and familiar; recorded cheerfully, even before the fire was fully burnt out, how house property in his part of the town was soaring in value, how the citizens congregated at the still standing Gresham College to gossip and bargain, and what speedy plans were being made for rebuilding the City. Of that mysterious country, whose horrid landscape he had seen for a brief while, he did not speak; only in dreams, lying (when the memory of it was still fresh) in Penn's naked bed with nothing but his drawers on, or long after beside Elizabeth in his own familiar room, did he revisit it with the fear of fire in his heart.

CHAPTER FIVE

THE RETREAT TO CORUNNA, 1808–9

Twisting Napoleon's Tail

'Slowly and sadly we laid him down,
From the field of his fame fresh and gory;
We carved not a line and we raised not a stone,
But we left him alone with his glory.'

Charles Wolfe

In 1793 Britain went to war with Revolutionary France to defend the frontiers of her European neighbours against lawless aggression. But the Revolutionary armies overran the whole of western Europe and, before long, Britain found herself alone, with most of her former allies aligned by her enemies against her. Yet, though her army was driven from the continent, her fleets held the seas and continued to defy every attempt to destroy her, of the great military genius who, after the short-lived Peace of Amiens, became in 1804 Emperor of the French. Nelson's victory at Trafalgar in 1805 made Britain's mastery of the seas absolute, but in the next two years Napoleon's victories over the Austrians, Prussians and Russians at Austerlitz, Jena and Friedland made his domination of Europe complete and, to all appearance, eternal.

Yet by his very military ascendancy Napoleon was creating a power which one day might help to free the continent. Through sheer necessity the British Army had begun to climb out of the forty years' pit of defeat and neglect into which it had fallen after the great days of Minden and Plassey. The officer who bought his promotion like his uniform in Bond Street and commuted by two hours' daily bullying on the parade ground for a life of drinking bumpers on—and under—the messroom table, was gradually being replaced by the ardent lad who had grown up to hate Bonaparte and view his profession as an opportunity for glory. The crimping house with its sordid tale of mercenary cruelty had yielded to the flashing, devil-may-care recruiting-sergeant, parading in his ribbons and finery before the gaping militiamen and extolling the glories of his corps. By the time Trafalgar had cleared the seas for the free movement of British land forces a new spirit of martial pride was running again through the half-brutalised ranks. The scarlet and gold regiments of England not only looked smart : they felt smart. 'If our commanders are well-chosen,' wrote Lord Paget '(and there are some very good ones), the British Army is in a state that will astonish friend and foe.'

Much of this improvement had been due to the administration of the Duke of York, who since 1795 had re-organised Army training, supervised the appointment of officers and established a Royal Military Academy and a Staff College to promote uniformity of method throughout the Service. Still more was due to bitter experience. The British Army had been driven from the continent by a revolutionary technique of war. The mechanical models of drill and discipline on which it had formed itself had largely failed in action. It had to adapt itself to new methods or accept permanent exclusion from Europe.

But the mainspring of all reform had been the *corps d'élite* of light infantry which had been formed at Shorn-cliffe Camp under the first soldier in the Army, Sir John Moore. Born in November, 1761, the son of a Glasgow doctor, Moore had seen hard fighting in America, Corsica, the West Indies, Ireland, Holland and Egypt, becoming a brigadier at thirty-four, major-general at thirty-six and lieutenant-general at forty-three. Handsome and athletic, with broad shoulders and generous, penetrating eyes, there was something in his glance and bearing that warmed the coldest nature. He seemed made to inspire confidence and courage. 'Every one,' wrote the Duke of York's Military Secretary, 'admires and loves him.'

This great soldier was at once realist and idealist. So clear was his perception of what was wrong and so passionate his resolve to set it right that he sometimes expressed himself with a vehemence that alarmed the timorous. 'My feelings were so strong and my indignation such,' he wrote on one occasion, 'as to bring tears to my eyes and for moments to stop my speech.' When his normal good humour and love of friendly banter were in abeyance, there was a touch of pedantry in his virtue, not uncharacteristic of his uncompromising northern race. Towards corruption and injustice he was merciless. 'Soldiers are flogged for drunkenness,' he once observed, 'I could not look them in the face if I was not to punish it equally in officers.' The chilling contempt with which he turned on those who behaved unworthily was, like the love he inspired, still remembered fifty years after his death.

Yet it was not Moore's frown that made men follow him but his example and inspiration. He expected of others only what he demanded of himself. An ambitious man, he applied to his life, at a time when wire-pulling was the bane of the Service, the unflinching principle that a soldier should not choose his lot but go wherever he was ordered. In the field he shared the lot of the meanest private; at the siege of San Fiorenzo he slept every night in his clothes on a bed of straw. Though a poor man, he on more than one occasion advanced the money to enable a deserving officer to obtain promotion. His simplicity and directness shrivelled up meanness and shabby conduct. Fearless, he shamed fear in others. 'I ordered them to leap over it,' he wrote in his diary after an engagement, 'and upon their hesitating showed them the example of getting over it myself.'

When Moore received his first command the Army was at the lowest point of its history. Its discipline was based on mechanical parades and mass firelock exercises, copied in the letter rather than the spirit from Frederick the Great's Prussia and increasingly divorced from the realities of war and human nature. It was enforced regardless of humanity and common sense; soldiers were treated as automata to be bullied and flogged into an unthinking obedience. Moore, faced by a triumph of the natural courage and enthusiasm of the Revolutionary armies, went

back to nature to defeat them. He did not discard the
traditional discipline of the British Service; he humanised
it. Against the *élan* of the armed *sans-culottes*, so resistless
when confronted only by the 'stiff solidarity' of the old
monarchial armies of the continent, he opposed an equal
enthusiasm based on common-sense discipline and careful
training.

His opportunity to remodel the Army arose out of the
need for light infantry. The French had won their battles
with a horde of highly individualised skirmishers and
sharpshooters going ahead of their dense, half-disciplined
columns and firing from every side into the rigid Teuton
lines whose only reply were machine-like volleys, imposing
on the parade ground but ineffective against such invisible
and fast-moving targets. By the time the columns came into
range or the cavalry charged, the defenders were already
demoralised, and the rather sketchy discipline of the former
—strengthened by successive victories—was seldom tested.
An antidote for the *tirailleur* had had to be found. At the
outset the British, being almost without light infantry, had
relied on hired German Jägers who were little more than
armed gamekeepers and foresters. The exigencies of West
Indian warfare, like those of American warfare two decades
before, caused General Grey and his successors, Aber-
cromby and Moore, to train special companies as protective and reconnaissance screens. The need for more of these
being acutely felt during the brief invasion of Holland in
1799, the Duke of York had ordered the formation of an
experimental rifle corps at Horsham to which fifteen regiments were ordered to send officers and men for courses of
instruction. Trained in Windsor Forest by two brilliant
leaders, Colonel Coote Manningham and Lieutenant-
Colonel William Stewart, these were formed in the spring
of 1801 into the 95th Regiment of the Line—a rifle corps
with distinctive green uniform and dark buttons and
accoutrements. Disbanded at the end of the Revolutionary
War, they were re-formed when the war clouds gathered,
armed with the new Baker rifle—a weapon of high precision compared with the smooth-bore musket of the heavy

infantry—and in October, 1802, consigned to Shorncliffe Camp for special training under Sir John Moore. Here, facing across the Channel towards Napoleon's cantonments, they formed with the 14th Light Dragoons and the 52nd and 43rd Regiments—both reconstituted as light infantry— the spearhead of the force designed to repel invasion. For the next three years, until they passed overseas, they were trained by Moore in an amalgam of disciplined team-work and individual initiative unmatched even among Napoleon's finest veterans. With the archers of Crécy and Agincourt and the Brigade of Guards, they formed England's peculiar contribution to the art of land warfare.

Moore's goal was the 'thinking fighting man.' In the reconstituted 52nd—his own regiment—officers, themselves taught their drill in the ranks, were encouraged to get to know their men as individuals, to bring out the best of which each man was capable and teach him to think for himself. Wherever possible, he was to be shown the why and wherefore of things; to comprehend his duty instead of merely obeying it blindly out of fear or mechanical routine. Punishment, particularly of the 'curse, hang and flog' kind that robbed a man of dignity, was discouraged. Its place was taken by a discipline of example and encouragement. In an army notorious for inability to fend for itself in the field, every man of the Light Brigade—taking a leaf from the self-reliant French—was taught to cook and tailor and to take pride in living sparely against the day when he would have to depend solely on himself. Troops were trained for war under war conditions; when they marched, they bivouacked by the roadside instead of in town or village. The formal brass, feather and pipeclay review so dear to military pedants was abandoned for the field-day— an exercise in which war conditions were reproduced as closely as possible. Everything was made to serve the one great end of reality: the defeat of Napoleon's invincibles.

In all this Moore worked with nature instead of against it. In the quick march which he and his assistants devised for the light infantryman, the constrained and rigid move-

ments of the Prussian march were abandoned for a free
and natural rhythm whose object was the maximum of
speed with the minimum of fatigue. By being taught to
move quickly men became habituated to thinking quickly.
In the same way the art of fire was taught, not as an auto-
matic contribution to a blind mechanical volley, but as a
highly individualised application of the qualities of judgment, observation, vision and skill. Its object, Moore's
pupils were told, was 'to inflict death upon the enemy
rather than to confound, astonish and intimidate.' Armed
with a rifle capable of great accuracy up to 300 or even—
in the hands of a master—500 yards, the rifleman was
taught, first at the butts and then in the field, to judge and
use cover and varied ground, to fire always to kill and
never to waste a shot. He was trained not as a machine but
as a craftsman, the consciousness of whose skill—the best
guarantee for his survival on the battlefield—gave him
courage and self-confidence. So also the care of the rifle
was strictly inculcated, and distinguishing green and white
cockades awarded for marksmanship.

Above all, Moore's men were schooled in that art which,
though repeatedly forgotten under the shock of successive
inventions and weapons, is in all ages the ultimate arbiter
of war : the combination of fire and movement. The essence
of light infantry work was movement, whether in search of
information or in the protection of the heavy infantry of
the Line. And fire was taught as the concomitant of movement, so that at all times and in all places movement—with
its manifold dangers—should be covered by accurate, well-
timed and economical fire. A rifleman in battle was the
instrument of an orchestra in which every change of position, whether of individual or unit, was, wherever possible,
protected by co-ordinated fire, directed at the precise spot
from which any interference with that movement might
come. The Light Brigade's special system of drill was
directed to this end. Taught to the recruit by word of
mouth in close order on the parade ground, it was subsequently carried out in extended order by bugle, horn and
whistle. It aimed at combining the action of highly indi-

vidualised and rapidly-moving men and units, working together to destroy or outwit the enemy.

At the back of every rifleman's mind Moore instilled the principle that the enemy was always at hand ready to strike. Whether on reconnaissance or protective duty, he was taught to be wary and on guard : to explore country, gather information, watch and question travellers and inhabitants, investigate and map-out roads, paths, fords and bridges. It was the pride of a light infantryman never to be caught napping; of a light infantry regiment or company never to have an outpost or piquet surprised. When attacked, the latter were taught how to fall back without giving away the position of their main body; rules carefully devised, but always elastic and capable of infinite adjustment, were laid down for setting and relieving sentry lines and patrols by day and night, for defending approaches to villages, bridges and road junctions, for utilising hedges, woods and orchards and every incline of the ground for cover and fire. The British army of the future was to be encompassed at all times and places by an invisible screen of marksmen, watching the enemy from behind every bush and stone, each one an alert and intelligent individual acting in close but invisible concert with his comrades.

The leaven of Moore's training had only just begun to permeate the heavy, unthinking mass of the old Army when the opportunity came to test it and him. Even his Light Infantry regiments were still recruited from the national rag-tag-and-bobtail : penniless, drunken Irish peasants, village bad-hats, slum bullies and pimps, balloted Militia ploughboys with a penchant for drink and roving. But in 1808 the British soldier was summoned from the barrack-square to the battlefield by Napoleon's invasion of his satellite, Spain, and by the passionate reaction of the Spanish people to his treachery and their appeal to Britain for help. In July of that year a small British advance-guard under Sir Arthur Wellesley (the future Duke of Wellington) landed in Portugal and by its victory at Vimeiro succeeded in expelling the French from that country. Moore himself followed with reinforcements at the end of August, but, owing to the distrust felt of him by the politicians—who resented his outspokenness—only as a subordinate to two senior officers with a tithe of his ability and fighting experience. But their sudden recall, and that of Wellesley, in September to face a Court of Enquiry in London unexpectedly presented him with the greatest command held by any British general since Marlborough.

The decision to throw the whole weight of the nation's military effort into Spain was taken as a result of the surrender on July 23rd of a French army to the ragged patriots of Andalusia. When the astonishing news of the capitulation of Baylen reached him, the Secretary for War, Lord Castlereagh, urged the dispatch of a British Army to northern Spain to enable the men of Asturias and Aragon to strike at the enemy's communications. With this object he at once began collecting transports, and by September 3rd had completed preparations for sending 14,000 infantry, 4,000 cavalry and 800 artillerymen under Lieutenant-General Sir David Baird to Corunna. Three weeks later the Cabinet decided to add to them 20,000 of the 30,000 troops already landed in Portugal and to place the whole under the command of Sir John Moore.

The decision was based on a sound instinct : that a major test was imminent in Spain and that every available man would be needed. With hatred for his rule growing from Vistula to Ebro, Napoleon could not afford to admit defeat; when his troops abandoned Madrid, French funds fell from 94 to 70. He made no attempt to conceal the fact that he was preparing revenge. 'The hideous leopard,' he told his soldiers, 'contaminates by its presence the peninsula of Spain and Portugal. Let us carry our victorious eagles to the Pillars of Hercules. . . . No Frenchman can enjoy a moment's repose so long as the sea is not free.'

Yet Britain's military preparations were founded on an illusion. Ministers, and to a still greater extent the public to whom they were responsible, supposed that Spain was a modern, homogeneous State whose strength could be measured by its size and historic prowess. Palafox's defence of Saragossa stirred the popular imagination; the tale of the brave girl who, standing on her kinsfolks' heaped corpses and the ashes of her home, continued to train her gun on the invader, was in every mouth. The patriotism and the courage of the Spaniards became for the moment an article of British faith.

On the face of it, there seemed reason for confidence in Spain. Within a few weeks of Baylen the French had been expelled from every part of the peninsula save Navarre and Barcelona. Madrid had been reoccupied by Castaños on August 23rd, Saragossa relieved of all danger a week earlier; Joseph Bonaparte had abandoned Burgos and withdrawn as far as Vitoria without a fight. By the end of August a bare 60,000 French troops stood behind the Ebro in the extreme north-west corner of the peninsula they had hoped to conquer. Forty thousand of their comrades remained behind as prisoners or corpses.

British belief that the French had met their match in the Spaniards was more than shared by the latter. They did not merely suppose they could smash Napoleon: they knew it. 'They had no idea,' wrote *The Times* correspondent from Corunna, 'that it is possible for them to be beaten; their rage is unbounded when the name of Bonaparte is mentioned, but their hatred of the French is mixed with contempt.' All the fierce hereditary pride of their race had been re-kindled. A spontaneous popular outburst had thrown off both the French invader and the corrupt government that had obscured their national glories. Once more, as in the days of Charles V and Philip II, they were the greatest nation in the world. They took no thought for the morrow, but gave themselves up to unbridled rejoicing.

What this valiant and ancient people failed to see was that in overturning a corrupt Administration and scaring a few French generals they had not solved their real problem. They had merely exchanged, with Napoleon's help, a bad government for no government at all. Their grandees, poisoned by the same sterile pride and servile attendance on an idle Court that had ruined the aristocracy of France, were without backbone or political experience; for generations they had hardly been free to leave Madrid without the king's permission. Some of them, as a result of the former French alliance or because they feared anarchy, sympathised with the enemy or were suspected by the people of doing so. The lesser nobles, the provincial gentry and ecclesiastics, who, with the urban mobs, had taken the lead in raising the standard of independence, were mostly narrow provincials whose sympathies were bounded by their own mountain skyline. They were without the slightest capacity for administration or for co-operating with anyone whose views differed from their own. They shared to the full the national contempt for compromise and the strong national sense of personal pride. Within a few weeks of the French retreat several of the provincial Juntas were almost at open war and were threatening to employ their respective armies not against the enemy but each other. All competed for British arms and money, demanding fantastic quantities of both and doing their utmost to prevent their neighbours from getting any. Only with the utmost difficulty, and under pressure from England, could they be got to join in setting up a Supreme Junta. Nor, thereafter, did they pay it the slightest respect.

To local jealousies and vanity was added what a warm British admirer called the 'apathy and confidence of the Spanish character.' Every Spaniard seemed ready to postpone public business to an indefinite to-morrow. The need for application, perseverance and discipline was universally ignored. It was imagined that victories were made by instinctive courage, armies by popular enthusiasm, strategic combinations by eloquence. Ragged hordes of armed peasants and students trailed about the countryside, undrilled and unsupplied, discussing with all the fervour of their race the grand operations which were to overthrow the greatest soldier of all time. There was no supreme command, for no provincial Junta would allow the army to be commanded by any general but its own. Yet in imagination and boastful talk—to which the whole nation seemed prone—this leaderless force, exaggerated in numbers and untrained for war, was not merely to drive the veterans of

France from their strongholds in the north, but by a series of intricate converging operations over a three-hundred mile front, to encircle and annihilate them. Afterwards it was to advance to Paris and dictate peace.

With such confidence in their prowess the Spaniards were in no mood to take advice from British generals. They did not need amateurs to teach them how to make war. They took the money, arms and ammunition they proffered, but for the rest ignored the foreign heretics who until so recently had been their enemies. So long as the British remained at a distance, a warm and truly Spanish eloquence was extended to them; the moment they set their clumsy and unhallowed feet on Spanish soil or tried to interfere with the Spaniard's imperious preference for his own way, they became objects of loathing and suspicion. Any discipline, save of its own choosing, was anathema to this stark, passionate people. Thus the released Spanish prisoners from England, who had been feasted, clothed and armed by their former captors, mutinied on the way home and carried off the British ship in which they were sailing.

.   .   .

It was in such circumstances that at the end of the first week of October, 1808, Moore received his mission. Leaving 10,000 troops to defend Portugal, he was to proceed with the remaining 20,000 to northern Spain, where he would be joined by another 17,000 under Sir David Baird. He was to support the Spanish armies in their attempt to encircle the French and, in the event of a Supreme Commander being appointed by the Junta, to place himself— with reservations—under his orders. He was to convey his troops into Spain by land or sea as he thought best. A correct and friendly personal letter from Castlereagh assured him of every assistance.

The army heard of the appointment with satisfaction. A new spirit began to run through the dusty camp of Queluz; the men knew instinctively that the unaccountable inertia of the past six weeks was at an end. The new general appeared everywhere, inspecting regiments, reorganising magazines and stores, dismissing fraudulent contractors and talking to everyone he encountered. Men suddenly began to work with a will.

Yet some of those to whom the Commander-in-Chief spoke noticed an underlying gravity in his expression. Ministers might write of going into Spain like going into Hyde Park, but Moore as a practical soldier knew the difficulties. He could not effect his junction with Baird by sea because, without previously establishing magazines in the barren Galician hills, it would be impossible to march so large an army through the passes to Castile in time to succour the Spaniards. And though Ministers talked about the impending envelopment of the French—'a sort of gibberish,' Moore privately noted, 'which men in office use and fancy themselves military men without knowing how far it is susceptible of being carried into practice'—he was painfully aware that the problem was not, as people in England supposed, whether he could reach the Ebro in time to share the triumph of the Spanish armies but whether he could unite his own forces behind them before Napoleon launched his attack. His one chance of doing so in time— for he was convinced that Napoleon would strike before winter—was to march his men across the Portuguese highlands to Salamanca and join forces with Baird in the Castilian plain at Valladolid or Burgos.

For such a march—more than three hundred miles across mountains rising in places to 4,000 feet—Moore had neither maps nor magazines. His commissariat and Staff were both raw, and, owing to the Treasury's failure to supply bullion, it was impossible to obtain enough carts and draught animals. His men had therefore to carry the bulk of their equipment. And though he sent his engineers ahead to prospect, he was unable in the time at his disposal to discover whether any of the roads were fit for heavy artillery. The Portuguese seemed certain that none were, and, with the torrential autumn rains daily expected, Moore dared not risk it. He therefore dispatched all his guns save half a dozen light six-pounders by the Elvas and Badajoz highway to Madrid together with his transport park and an escort of 4,000 troops, including his entire cavalry force, under Lieutenant-General Sir John Hope. Only when they had gone too far for recall, did Moore discover that his allies had misinformed him.

On October 16th, while the foxhunters in England were riding out in their autumnal glory, the army turned its face towards Spain. 'A more glorious set of fellows,' wrote young George Napier, 'never was seen.' They wanted only experience in continental warfare. Their equipment was still incomplete, but Moore could wait no longer. 'The regiments are already marching,' he wrote to Pitt's niece, Lady Hester Stanhope, 'I pray for good weather. If it rains, the torrents will swell and be impassable, and I shall be accounted a bungler. I wish you were here with us, in your red habit *à l'Amazone*.'

For the next three weeks the troops pressed across the mountains into the north-east. The sand and olive trees of the Tagus plain, the crash of the muskets on the paving stones, the gloomy, stinking streets and high, shuttered houses, with barbers strumming on guitars in the doorways and loafing crowds in long brown cloaks and three-cornered hats, gave way to primitive hill villages where the corn was threshed by trampling bullocks and mules and the blow-flies swarmed over the middens in the central square. The roads became goat-tracks and ravines; every few minutes a cart would sink into a hole or overturn on a stone. Presently there were precipices and gullies over which the six-pounders had to be hauled on ropes by sweating, cursing infantrymen.

After the first week the rains came down : not ordinary rain such as Englishmen knew, but cascades of huge globular drops which soaked every one to the marrow and drew clouds of steam from the dripping columns. There was no shelter save for a rare mountain farm or peasant's hut, swarming with fleas and rank with the stench of the communal vessel round which the family and the livestock slept. Every mile the way grew more rocky and bleak.

Occasionally a ruined Moorish castle on a conical hill
guarding a defile would relieve the monotony. But still the
army pressed on, climbing ever higher into the cold, dripping clouds. As it approached the Spanish frontier, all sign
of human habitation vanished, save once in a glimpse
through clouds, a solitary convent nestling in a bunch of
trees on the bosom of the mountain, a vast abrupt vale, and
below, revealed in that apocalyptic second, the whole
system of the waters. Then the swirling mist closed down
again, and there was nothing to be seen but the bleak,
rocky, wretched road with a black hill on one side and a
precipice on the other, both lost in impenetrable, icy cloud.
It made a young officer with a touch of the poet feel as if
he were travelling on the bare outside of the world,
'bordered by the chaotic beginning of things.'

With the crossing of the frontier in the second week of
November spirits rose. First impressions of the new country
were greatly in its favour; the houses were cleaner and the
farms better stocked, the proud, courtly people more handsome and hospitable, the landscape more romantic. Ensign
Boothby, who had gone ahead of the right flank of the army
to Alcantara, where Trajan's viaduct over the Tagus reminded him of 'the bridge of Sin and Death striding over
chaos,' was greeted by the alcalde in his scarlet cloak and
treated to the fandango by girls whose graceful pride, as
they snapped their fingers and alternately raised and
lowered their heads, awed alike their rustic partners and
the watching redcoats. Later he was entertained in a
capital house with curtains and clean beds by 'a fine,
black, animated Spaniard' with a most beautiful wife, from
whose long, black mantilla, brilliant rolling eyes, Roman
nose, sweet mouth, jet black hair and graceful curls he
could not take his eyes. The quicker tempo of the land
affected the marching columns as they hurried on through
sparkling air and cork woods to Salamanca. They felt
ready for anything. 'We had fought and conquered and felt
elated,' wrote Rifleman Harris of the 95th; 'Spain was before us and every man in the Rifles seemed only too anxious
to get a rap at the French again. It was a glorious sight to

see our colours spread in those fields. The men seemed invincible and nothing, I thought, could beat them.'[1]

.   .   .   .

Meanwhile another British army had entered Spain. On the morning of October 13th, Mr. Crabb Robinson, *The Times* correspondent at Corunna, was startled by the report of cannon and, running to the ramparts, saw more than a hundred and fifty transports sailing in a double line before a gentle breeze; it made him proud to see them. It was Baird with the first 12,000 from England. Unfortunately there was a hitch, for no one had given authority for them to land, and the provincial Junta was either unable or unwilling to do so. In the end a special messenger had to be sent to Madrid to obtain the Supreme Junta's leave. Hookham Frere, however, who landed at Corunna a few days later as British Envoy, was given a tremendous reception. His carriage was dragged through the streets amid vivas, crackers and rockets, he was feasted at a banquet of countless dishes highly flavoured with garlic and treated to a theatrical performance at which Pluto appeared trampling Bonaparte under foot while the whole audience rose and sang 'God Save the King' and 'Rule Britannia'.

But not till October 25th was any reply received from Madrid. It then only gave authority for Baird to land if he insisted and strongly urged that he and his transports should remove themselves to some point on the coast less dangerously near the naval arsenal of Ferrol. Baird, a blunt Anglo-Indian soldier, however insisted, and next day his troops began to put ashore. But his difficulties had only just begun. The authorities objected to their disembarking in any but the smallest detachments and failed to make any arrangements for their feeding. It was not till November 4th that they were all ashore. Even then their progress was painfully slow. As in Portugal, the Treasury had omitted to provide bullion to hire forage wagons and draught cattle. There was not even money to pay the troops.

All this took place in an atmosphere of complete un-reality. Nobody in Corunna seemed to have the slightest idea what was happening elsewhere in Spain. The only information that could be obtained from the local leaders was that the French were flying; questioned as to where they were flying or from whom, they took refuge in vague generalities and evasions. Moore was faced by precisely the same difficulties : there was no Spanish Commander-in-Chief or General Staff, and the only authority to whom he could appeal was a Supreme Junta of thirty-four persons, all possessing equal powers and all apparently equally un-practical. So far as they gave their minds to military matters—most of their time was spent in discussing theo-retical constitutions and quarrelling with the provincial Juntas about their powers—they were obsessed by a fan-tastic plan for encircling the French with a converging movement of three almost completely unco-ordinated armies whose numbers in their own imagination they exaggerated as much as their fighting capacity. Any anxiety Moore might feel for the junction of his own forces, now moving across Spain in widely separated columns, he was assured, was entirely needless, since the enemy was securely hemmed in by immensely superior strength. The British Government seemed to share this illusion; misled by the uncritical optimism of its military agents with the Spanish armies, Castlereagh wrote on November 1st that the French were threatened from Saragossa to Bilbao by forces more than twice as large and that Napoleon's reinforcements could never reach them.

The Spanish leaders gave little thought to Napoleon. That he was likely to strike before their schemes matured never crossed their minds. Yet since the disaster at Baylen he had increased the year's levy of conscripts to a quarter of a million and transferred the pick of his veterans from Germany and Italy to Bayonne, using continuous relays of wagons to move them quickly. Within four weeks of leaving the Danube and Elbe they were concentrated on the Spanish frontier.

At the same time the Emperor took steps to safeguard

his rear. Putting his jack-boot down on underground patriotic activities in Prussia and browbeating the Austrian ambassador, he summoned his ally, the Czar Alexander, to Erfurt. Here at the end of September, amid servile princes and splendid pageantry, he secured a promise of Russian military aid against any uprising in the east. Then he hurried back home to Paris and told his Legislative Assembly that he was on his way to Spain to crown his brother in Madrid and plant his eagles on the towers of Lisbon. As his berlin drove southwards, the long columns of the Grand Army were already pouring along the trunk road to Vittoria. By November 1st, 1808, 120,000 troops were already on the Ebro.

Had the Spanish armies, though outnumbered, acted on the defensive, they might have been able to hold the French until the arrival of Moore's troops. But, having wasted three months in controversy, they chose the moment of the Grand Army's appearance for their long-advertised attack. On the last day of October Blake with the Army of Galicia, advancing without the slightest support from his colleagues, walked into Ney's lines at Durango. Here his troops, half naked and starving, were trounced and driven back to Bilbao. 'Intractable as swine, obstinate as mules and unmanageable as bullocks,' as a disgusted British officer wrote, they were 'cut up like rations or dispersed in all directions like a flock of sheep.'

A week later Napoleon reached Vittoria. He found himself in the centre of a horseshoe, with a compact force of the finest troops in Europe facing three widely separated bodies of peasant levies whose total numbers were inferior to his own. He struck immediately. In two successive days Blake was routed again at Espinosa, only escaping annihilation by a precipitate flight over the Cantabrian mountains, and the Army of Estremadura—theoretically in reserve—was utterly shattered at Gamonal village north of Burgos. On November 9th Burgos was a busy military base, supposedly far behind the lines and swarming with cheerful Spanish soldiers. A day later it was a deserted city full of untidy corpses and sacked houses while around it the

French cavalry hunted Count Belvedere's men over the
Castilian plain. Belvedere himself—a youth of twenty completely unaccustomed to command—fled with his Staff to
Aranda, 60 miles in the rear. The Spanish centre had
ceased to exist. On the 13th the French occupied Valladolid
—the intended rendezvous of the British army—while the
Supreme Junta was still debating the possibility of their
being able to advance at all.

.   .   .

Such was the state of affairs on November 13th when Sir
John Moore, having covered 250 miles of mountain track
in just over three weeks, was met at Ciudad Rodrigo by an
urgent summons from Belvedere. 'The Spaniards,' he
noted dryly, 'seem to think that everybody should fly but
themselves.' Two days later at Salamanca he heard the
news of Gamonal. He had arrived too late. Valladolid,
sixty miles to the north-east, was already in French hands;
without so much as a Spanish piquet between, his army
was threatened with destruction before it could assemble.
Baird, who had been expected at Astorga by November
14th, was still detained by the rains at Lugo nearly a
hundred miles to the north-west; his 5,000 horse under
Lord Paget had only landed at Corunna on the day Moore
reached Salamanca. Hope, with the artillery, was a hundred
miles away to the south on the far side of the Guadarramas.
A more depressing position for a commander it was
scarcely possible to conceive. Behind on Moore's only line
of retreat were the barren, rain-soaked mountains through
which he had come and a countryside in which he had no
hope of maintaining himself.

Yet the very folly of the Spanish generals that had betrayed him came to his aid. For Castaños and Palafox,
wholly regardless of the fate of their colleagues, proceeded
to advance on Napoleon's eastern flank with the insane
notion of cutting him off from France. The result was that
the French, not unnaturally supposing the British to be in
retreat to Portugal, switched their main forces eastwards
from Burgos towards the Ebro. Meanwhile Moore, being

Spain 1808-9

completely in the dark as to what either the French or the
Spaniards were doing—for no one troubled to send him
information—remained where he was, resting and regroup-
ing his army and trying to obtain intelligence. By November 18th he knew that Blake had been routed at Espinosa
on the 10th and that the chance of a junction with Baird
was even slighter than he had supposed. It did not add to
his comfort to receive on the same day a cheerful letter
from Castlereagh predicting an early advance by the
Spanish armies.

Moore's dilemma was pitiful. The assumptions on which
his instructions had been issued and which were still held
by the Cabinet no longer existed : they had vanished with
the Spanish armies of the North and Centre. The fog of
war had descended over the Castilian plain ahead, and he
had no cavalry with which to penetrate it. The Ebro was
nearly three hundred miles away and the whole French
army lay between him and it.

Yet so long as Castaños was fighting there, it would be
craven to abandon the Spaniards to their fate. Because his
first duty was to preserve his army—his country's only one
—Moore had sent Baird and Hope discretionary powers
to fall back on Corunna and Lisbon should they find their
way barred by overwhelming force. But until the attempt
to assemble his forces had been made, he felt he had no
option but to remain where he was. To Hester Stanhope,
perhaps his dearest friend on earth, he wrote that he was
in a scrape and that she must be prepared for bad news,
though his troops were in good spirits and eager to make a
fight for it. 'Farewell, my dear Lady Hester,' he added, 'if
I extricate myself and those with me from our present difficulties, I shall return to you with satisfaction; but if not it
will be better I shall never quit Spain.'

It was in this resolve that Moore on November 28th sat
down to reply to an urgent letter from Baird. Five days
earlier the latter at Astorga, a hundred and twenty miles to
the north, had heard of the disasters of Espinosa and
Gamonal and the French capture of Valladolid. Armed
with Moore's discretionary power to fall back on Corunna,

he had at once ordered a retreat. 'It certainly never could be the intention of the British Government,' he wrote, 'that we should engage in the defence of the country, unaided and unsupported by any Spanish force.' But Moore at once recalled him. 'I see my situation,' he informed him, 'in as unfavourable a light as you or any one can do. But it is our business to make every effort to unite here and to obey our orders and the wishes of our country. It would never do to retreat without making the attempt. If the enemy prevent us, there is no help for it, but if he does not, I am determined to unite the army. When that is done we shall act according to circumstances. There is still a chance that the presence of so large a British force may give spirits to the Spaniards.'

But late that night Moore learnt that the last Spanish army had ceased to exist. Riding five hundred miles in six days, a member of the British mission at Castaños's headquarters arrived from the capital to report that on November 23rd that general and Palafox had been routed at Tudela. The British were now the only undefeated force in northern Spain.

Around them was a population without the slightest outward trace of the fervid Iberian patriotism so extolled at home. The peasants continued their ceaseless labour in the fields. The townsmen, wrapped in their brown winter cloaks, lounged about in their hundreds in the sunshine, 'apathetic, indifferent, gloomy and sunk in utter idleness.' They seemed unmoved alike by Moore's appeals for help and the menace of the foraging cavalry which rode at will over the countryside. 'After leading us into a most dreadful mess through their deceitful and mendacious promises,' a Hanoverian officer wrote, 'they run away and say: "Now try to get out of it as best you can!" The people here have the cool effrontery to look upon the English troops as exotic animals who have come to engage in a private fight with the French, and now that they are here all that the fine Spanish gentlemen have to do is to look on with their hands in their pockets. They do not regard us in the least as allies who are prepared to shed their blood for Spain;

they simply look upon us as heretics. In our billets it is as much as we can do to get a glass of water.'

Under the circumstances there seemed nothing for it but to get out as quickly as possible. During the night Moore wrote again to Baird, ordering him to return to Corunna, re-embark in his transports and proceed to the Tagus. His own retreat through the Portuguese highlands to Lisbon would begin as soon as Hope's column, now at Villacastin seventy miles to the south-east, could reach him. He ordered it to proceed by forced marches to Alba de Tormes and thence to Ciudad Rodrigo on the Portuguese border where he proposed to join it. So long as Castaños's army remained in the field, he wrote, there had been hope, but now he could see none.

Till his guns and cavalry arrived Moore's position was one of acute danger. He had no idea how many troops Napoleon had with him on the Castilian plain : he knew that they could not be less than 80,000 to his own 17,000; he suspected that they were far more. To increase his troubles, protests began to arrive from Hookham Frere at Madrid urging him, in the name of the patriots, to stand firm, and repeating the old, familiar fables of impending Spanish victories. To support them came two Castilian generals—creatures of fantasy—who, declaring that 20,000 of their troops were barring the mountain road to Madrid, outlined fresh projects for the annihilation of Napoleon.

Yet at that moment the Emperor was in the suburbs of Madrid. As soon as he had learnt of the rout of the Spanish armies on the Ebro, he had marched on the capital. In his path was the snow ridge of the Guadarramas, where 12,000 Spaniards, hastily dispatched from Madrid, were holding the narrow and all but impregnable Somosierra defile. But once again the impact of cavalry proved fatal to undisciplined troops. Under cover of a mountain mist Napoleon launched the Polish lancers of the Imperial Guard against the guns at the head of the pass. The defenders fled in confusion, leaving the road to Madrid open. On December 1st Napoleon's advance guard appeared before the city.

Next evening Moore learnt what had occurred from his

aide-de-camp, Colonel Thomas Graham, who arrived from the capital just in time to give the Spanish generals the lie. As an exposé of their projects the news was conclusive. On the other hand, it temporarily relieved the British army of danger. Either because he was unaware of its position or because he viewed it with indifference, Napoleon had vanished over the mountains to the south. Two days later Hope, who had shown the greatest calm, initiative and judgment in a most trying situation, arrived with his precious guns and cavalry at Alba de Tormes, a day's march from Salamanca. For the first time since he left Lisbon Moore had a balanced fighting force under his immediate command.

On the morrow, December 5th, 1808, just as he was preparing to retreat at leisure on Portugal, further tidings arrived from the Spanish capital. The populace had risen once more, refused to admit Napoleon and appointed new leaders who were preparing to resist to the death. Madrid was to become a second Saragossa. The brave and generous British were urged to hasten to its aid.

In Moore's heart there flickered once more a faint spark of hope. He had little belief that Madrid could withstand the French assault; like Napoleon he knew the power of artillery. Nor was he in any doubt of the peril of remaining a day longer in northern Spain, now that his guns were safe. The odds against him—though he could not tell how great—were enormous. But he had been sent to save Spain, and, though her leaders had shown themselves worthless, her people, he was beginning to see, might be worth saving. A connoisseur in human virtue and courage, he saw—with a flash of poet's insight—that, under all its absurdities and fantasies, this strange, moody, mercurial race had bottom. The hardy, sober, industrious peasants who went about their daily affairs with such astonishing indifference when the French were at their doors, and who never gave them a thought till they were riding down the village street, were true men after all. Again and again during Moore's stay at Salamanca British officers were caught in villages overrun by the tide of French cavalry.

Yet though every Spaniard in the place knew of their presence, not one was ever betrayed.

Such a people, resolved to save itself, might still be saved. If British action could give them the will to fight on, Moore saw that it was his duty to give it. Deep down he knew that there was something more precious even than his country's only army : her honour. If he could use the fine instrument he had made—even if in doing so he should break or lose it—to create in Spain a permanent focus of resistance to Napoleon, he would have done what he had been sent to do. For the first time since he crossed the frontier his path became clear.

One thing the Spaniards needed above everything else : that of which in their brief hour of triumph they had been so prodigal—time. While Madrid held out, the southern provinces and Portugal were still free from the invader. Within a few weeks the winter would fall with its fierce winds from the mountains and the snowdrifts blocking the passes; if Napoleon's tempestuous advance could be held till then, the patriot leaders at Sevile, Valencia and Cadiz and the British and Portuguese at Lisbon might still be able to form new armies before the spring. To relieve Madrid, as the leaders of the populace demanded, was far beyond Moore's power : he could not, with half his little army and the bulk of his cavalry still in Galicia, cross the Guadarramas into the plains of New Castile. That would be to walk into the lion's den.

Yet a plan was taking shape in his mind. If he could join forces with Baird, he might strike eastwards with 35,000 men at Napoleon's communications with France. At the very moment that his contemptuous enemy thought he was retiring on Portugal, he would advance in the opposite direction. By doing so he would secure the support—for what it was worth—of the remnants of Blake's defeated army which La Romana had rallied on the Asturian border. Startling as such a move might seem, Moore saw what far-reaching effects it might have. Unable to feed his army on the wintry tableland of central Spain, the conqueror of Europe would be forced to recross the

Guadarramas in the December snows and deal with the threat to his life-line. Then the British army would become the quarry and have to run for its life over the mountains. But in the meantime Spain would have been given a respite —and a second chance.

Moore acted quickly, for speed was the essence of what he had to do. On the evening of December 5th he wrote two letters—one to Castlereagh, informing him of his intentions, and the other to Baird, recalling him to Astorga while warning him to be ready for an immediate retreat into Galicia. 'Madrid still holds out,' he told him, 'this is the first instance of enthusiasm shown. There is a chance that the example may be followed and the people be roused. . . . I mean to proceed bridle in hand, for, if the bubble bursts and Madrid falls, we shall have to run for it.'

Four days later, while Moore was waiting for Baird to retrace his steps, his aide-de-camp, Colonel Graham, returned to headquarters with the tidings that Madrid had capitulated. On the very day after the patriot leaders had dispatched their appeal to Moore they had entered into negotiations for surrender. Nor did they trouble to inform him that they had done so. On December 4th the Emperor had entered the capital. The way was open to Lisbon and Cadiz.

But Moore came of a stubborn race. He had made up his mind to harass Napoleon's communications, and, though Spain now seemed doomed, he meant, while his adversary's back was turned, to effect his junction with Baird and do what damage he could before he had to run for it. One of his officers, scouting to the north-west, had discovered that the French, in their southward surge, had evacuated Valladolid; they were obviously still unaware of his presence on the edge of the Castilian plain. He was free to advance to it and assemble his army where he had originally planned. His troops, who made a fine show parading in the noble square of Salamanca in the December sunshine, were now thoroughly rested after their march; strict discipline had been re-established and, careless of the future, they only asked to be led against the enemy. The weather had sud-

denly grown cold; at night the frost was so intense that a
Highlander of the 71st had his powdered pigtail frozen to
the ground as he slept. But the days were clear and exhi-
larating, and the ground had dried up.

On December 11th the advance began. But three days
later, when the army was half-way to Valladolid, a sheaf of
captured documents was brought into Moore's headquarters
at Alaejos. A French officer, carrying dispatches from
Napoleon's Chief-of-Staff to Marshal Soult near Burgos,
had been murdered in a roadside village for insulting the
postmaster. His papers came into the hands of the British
skirmishing cavalry. They showed that Napoleon had far
greater forces in Spain than had been supposed—well over
300,000 men—and that, all resistance in the centre of the
country having collapsed, he was advancing towards
Badajoz and Lisbon. But their most valuable disclosure was
that Soult, unaware that the British were in his path, was
moving westwards across the Carrion with 18,000 men,
while Junot was marching on Burgos in support.

It was the most useful information that Moore had
received from his allies since he entered the country, and it
reached him characteristically, not from their rulers but
through the rude and obscure. It revealed both his danger
and his opportunity. If Baird continued his march on
Carrion and Burgos unsupported by the rest of the army
fifty miles to the south, he would be overwhelmed. But if
the British united promptly and fell on Soult's lines on the
Carrion before Junot arrived, it would be Soult who would
be overwhelmed. With La Romana announcing his readiness to move from Leon against the marshal's right flank,
Moore had a chance of confronting an isolated group of
the French army with forces twice as large. If he could
only be quick enough he might, before retreating to the
sea, present his country with a resounding victory.

He therefore gave orders to change his march from
north-east to north so as to join Baird at the earliest
moment. On December 15th, with the latter's advance
guard at Benavente, he crossed the Douro in two columns
at Zamora and Toro. The snow from the mountains was

beginning to fall and the violence of the wind was such that the men could hardly stand. But nothing could halt Moore's pace; already his cavalry screen had made contact with Soult's patrols around Tordesillas and he knew that the alarm must soon be raised. Rifleman Harris of the 95th dropped under his load in the streets of Zamora like one dead; 'we staggered on,' he wrote, 'looking neither to the right nor to the left.' In his haste Moore was trying discipline high; the Spaniards still barred their houses and hid their food; the wintry plain was treeless and fuel unobtainable. But the troops were sustained by the thought of a fight; it was believed that Soult—the Duke of Damnation as they called him after his Dalmatian title—was flying before them and that they were near the end of the chase which they supposed had been going on ever since they left Lisbon. They were rough, unlettered men who knew nothing of strategy. But fighting the French was in their blood.

By December 20th the British forces had met, the infantry around Mayorga, the cavalry at Melgar Abaxo. The men surveyed each other curiously; those from Corunna, fresh from good quarters and rations, with bright jackets and shining accoutrements, those from Portugal gaunt, wayworn and rugged, with faces burnt dark by the sun. Next day they pushed on together towards Sahagun. Here at dawn on the 21st, after Lord Paget's cavalry had tried to surround a brigade of French horse, 500 men of the 15th Hussars charged and routed 700 French dragoons, capturing 13 officers, including two colonels, and 144 other ranks. Later, while the British marched into the town, Soult, now thoroughly alarmed, halted his advance and withdrew his outposts behind the Carrion.

· · ·

Though Moore could not know it, news of his move had reached Napoleon. Busied with edicts for reconstituting Spain, the Emperor had assumed that the British were in retreat before his vanguard down the Madrid-Lisbon road.

E

The capture of some stragglers from Hope's division at
Talavera had confirmed this impression. But on December
19th, just as he was about to set off from Madrid for
Badajoz, Napoleon learnt the truth. The swaggering
islanders, instead of retiring on their ships, had marched
out of Salamanca eastwards and were already half-way
across his lines of communication.

Napoleon retrieved his error with characteristic speed.
Halting his westward march, he ordered an immediate concentration on the Castilian plain north of the Guadarramas.
Leaving the Badajoz highway for Salamanca, his advance
guard was to sever Moore's communications with Portugal. Ney was recalled from Aragon to support Soult,
thus giving a respite to Saragossa, now facing a second
siege. Soult himself was to act on the defensive and decoy
the British on to Burgos. Meanwhile the flower of the
Grand Army was to cross the Guadarramas under
Napoleon's personal command and fall on Moore's flank
at Tordesillas and Valladolid. Everything was to give way
to the destruction of the arch-enemy.

But the price was the postponement for another year of
the conquest of the Peninsula. Napoleon already knew
that Austria was rearming, that his exactions and conscrip-
tions in Germany were rousing a Teuton hornets' nest and
that the example of Spain was awakening dangerous hopes
in every corner of Europe. With Russian revenues dwind-
ling under the pressure of the British blockade, he dared
not rely on the Czar's continued friendship. Once more
the islanders with their meddling and stupidity had spoilt
his best-laid designs. 'All the evils, all the plagues which
can afflict the human race,' he wrote to Josephine, 'come
from London!'

Only one thing could retrieve the situation : the complete destruction of the British army. And that, thanks to
Moore's temerity, was imminent. 'The day we succeed in
seeing these English,' Napoleon wrote as he hurried north
from Madrid, 'will be a day of jubilee. Ah! that these
20,000 were 100,000 so that more English mothers might
feel the horrors of war !' That night, while Moore's troops

were resting and repairing their boots, the Grand Army began to ascend the Guadarrama. It was bitterly cold, a blizzard was blowing and the track was thick with snow. Three times the officers of the advance-guard reported that the pass was impracticable in such weather. But nothing could shake Napoleon's purpose : linking arms with two of his generals, he marched with the leading files till the summit was reached. It almost seemed that night as though the Revolution incarnate was hunting the soul of England over the mountains.

By December 23rd, Napoleon was at Villacastin, only 60 miles south of Valladolid where—unaware of the last minute alteration in the British march—he supposed Moore to be. Actually the latter was at Sahagun—40 miles further north—issuing orders for an attack on Soult's lines across the Carrion. 'Sir John dines with General Paget,' wrote a subaltern, 'and battle is the word!' Advancing through the night, the troops were to fall on the French at dawn, following up with an assault on the enemy's main position at Saldana on Christmas Day. 'The movement I am making,' Moore reported to Frere, 'is of the most dangerous kind; I not only risk to be surrounded at any moment by superior forces, but to have my communications intercepted with the Galicias. I wish it to be apparent to the whole world that we have done everything in our power in support of the Spanish cause and that we do not abandon it until long after the Spaniards had abandoned it.'

Yet by a strange irony the unseeking soldier who was staking so much to keep his country's word was at that moment being reviled by ignorant amateurs as a timid procrastinator who had sullied England's honour by looking on while the Spaniards were overwhelmed. 'I can't bear to think of it,' wrote a grand lady; a retired ambassador at Brighton spoke with scorn of the British commander's readiness to get out of the way. Even Hookham Frere, flying with the Junta to Sevile, bombarded Moore with petulant notes charging him with an inactivity which had brought indelible disgrace to England and ruin to her ally. So outrageous did this brilliant man's letters become that

his friend Canning was forced to remind him that the
force he was seeking to commit to adventures in the Spanish
hinterland was his country's only army; another, he was
told, she had not to send.

On the evening of December 23rd, 1808, while Walter
Scott at Ashestiel was writing that little could be hoped of
a general who was always looking over his shoulder,
Moore's men set out on their momentous march. They
were in the highest spirits, telling each other that now they
would beat the French to death and have their ease. 'Every
heart,' wrote Captain Sterling, 'beat high, every breast was
buoyant for victory.' As each column moved off into the
snowlit night the regiments broke into cheers. Then they
marched in silence, though some, remembering that it was
the eve of Christmas, spoke of friends in England and of
the yuletide feast.

But a little after midnight the leading files of the Light
Brigade heard the sound of galloping on the road behind
and saw a dragoon spur furiously past towards General
Craufurd at the head of the column. Turning in his saddle,
the general, after a glance at the dispatch, gave the order,
'Halt!' A few minutes later the troops, grumbling furiously,
were retracing their steps. Everywhere, as the orders were
received, exultation gave way to gloom; even the best-
disciplined murmured. When the First Foot Guards, drawn
up outside Sahagun Convent, were told by Sir David Baird
to go back to their quarters and be ready to march in the
morning, 'nothing could be heard on every side but the
clang of firelocks thrown down in despair.'

For during the evening of the 24th Moore had learnt,
first from La Romana and then from his own cavalry
patrols, that Napoleon had recrossed the Guadarramas. At
Palencia, only twenty miles to the south of Carrion, billet-
ing officers had arrived with Imperial cavalry; the Emperor
himself was reported close behind. Any further advance by
the British would be suicidal. A day would be needed to

reach Soult, another to beat him and a third to return to Sahagun, and by that time Napoleon's forces would be all round them. There was only one thing to do : to get back to Astorga and the mountain road to Corunna before it was too late.

War is largely a matter of guesswork; a general can seldom see what is happening on the other side of the hill. He must form on imperfect evidence the picture on which his plan of campaign is based and constantly refashion it on better. Yet it is a frailty of the human mind to cling rigidly to conceptions once formed. The hall-mark of a great commander is that, while refusing to allow mere rumour to confuse his dispositions, he is quick on receiving fresh data to abandon a false conception.

On the evidence of Marshal Berthier's captured dispatch Moore had formed a picture of the military situation in northern Spain as it was in the third week of December. On that picture he had acted boldly and decisively. But, just as his stroke was in mid-air, he received new information showing that the picture on which he was acting was no longer true. He did not hesitate. He withdrew his army westwards as quickly as it had come.

By doing so he averted—just in time—what might have been the greatest military disaster in British history. Napoleon was seeking to avenge by a single decisive stroke the Nile, Copenhagen and Trafalgar, Egypt and Vimiero, his lost colonies and the blockade of the continent. He believed that England, war-weary and politically divided, would never recover from the catastrophe of her last military hope. Her striking force was within his grasp. While the Grand Army drove up like a thundercloud out of the south against Moore's exposed flank, Junot was about to reinforce Soult on his front and Lefebvre was hurrying up from the south-west to seize the Galician passes in his rear. Yet, by his sudden change of direction on December 13th and then by his equally prompt retreat on the 23rd, Moore still eluded that grasping hand. As the infuriated beast he had drawn charged down on him, he stepped quickly aside.

But, unlike a matador, a commander has more to control than his own body. He has to adjust his movements to his command. It is courting disaster to ask too much of it. And Moore's men had been sorely tried. During the past few days they had been driven forward at a pace only endurable under the conviction that victory was at hand. In bitter weather and an inhospitable countryside they had outrun their supplies. Half of them were young unfledged troops fresh from England; the other half had been marching, save for one halt, at extreme pressure since the middle of October. Now, without explanation, they were ordered to retreat at an even faster pace. Discipline threatened to crack under the strain.

Moore's problem was twofold. It was to cross the Esla and gain the mountain defile beyond Astorga before the fastest mover in the world could cut him off. It was also to hold his army together as a fighting, manageable unit. He could not defend any position for long or it would starve or be surrounded. He could not go too fast or his discouraged and uneducated men would lose cohesion. His assets were that his best troops were of his own training and that, by skilful and timely dispositions, he had left a margin of space and time between himself and the hunter. His handicaps were that his solitary line of supply was too congested and ill-found to maintain so large a force in mid-winter, and that, owing to the habit of his country, his army was drawn largely from the wastrel and criminal classes.

From Sahagun to Benavente and the Esla was nearly fifty miles : to Astorga and the Galician defile another thirty. Beyond that lay a hundred and fifty miles of mountain road to Corunna. There were few towns and villages on the way; the countryside afforded neither food nor fuel. The army was therefore forced to retire in corps by succession. Allowing La Romana with 7,000 ragged Spaniards to follow the safest route and that least likely to impede the British retreat, Moore sent off Hope and Fraser on the 24th and Baird on Christmas Day. He himself took the road nearest Napoleon's line of advance with

Edward Paget's Reserve division and the Light Infantry regiments he had trained. Lord Paget, Edward Paget's brother, covered the rear with the cavalry.

The advance had been made in frost and snow; the retreat began in a thaw. By day the roads were rivers of slush and mud; at night they became glaciers. All Christmas Day, while Napoleon rested his troops at Tordesillas, the English, soaked and frozen, pressed on. Tired, dispirited men looked in one another's faces and asked whether they were ever to halt again. 'By Jesus, Master Hill,' demanded an Irishman of the 95th, 'where the devil is this you're taking us to?' 'To England, M'Lauchlan,' came the disquieting reply, 'if we can get there.'

. . .

'Should the English pass to-day in their positions,' Napoleon observed at Tordesillas, 'they are lost.' 'Put it in the newspapers,' he ordered, 'and make it universally known that 36,000 English are surrounded, that I am at Benavente in their rear while Soult is in their front.' But, imagining them to be still at Sahagun, on the 27th he resumed his northward march towards that town instead of north-westwards to Benavente. So well did Paget's cavalry screen do its work that not till he reached Medina del Rioseco that night did the Emperor discover that Moore had been too quick. By then all but the British rearguard had crossed the Esla which, swollen by the thaw, had become a torrent.

But under the strain of the march, tempers and discipline collapsed. Dejection and shame now showed on every face. The men could not comprehend the leadership that refused to let them stand at bay. Forbidden to loose their anger against the French, they wreaked it on the Spaniards. There was a rumour that the retreat was due to La Romana's refusal to co-operate : the memory of barred doors and sullen scowls was in every heart. The villages on the road were mercilessly ransacked for firewood; 'everyone found at home,' wrote a private of the 71st, 'was looked upon as a traitor to his country.' All Moore's remon-

strances and rebukes could not stop the rot; his officers
were losing control. Wet and cold, with every door in the
town shut against them and the army commissaries hastily
burning the provisions and stores, the soldiers took the law
into their own hands. In the Duke of Ossuna's lovely
castle at Benavente—'surpassing anything I had ever
seen,' declared a Highlander, 'such as I have read the
description of in books of fairy tales'—they drove their
bayonets into the painted walls to hang up their knap-
sacks and washing, broke up priceless furniture for firewood and ripped up the tapestries for bed-clothes. 'What
the English soldiers cannot see any purpose in,' wrote the
German Schaumann, 'does not interest them.'[2]

Behind the dissolving army the Reserve Division and the
Light Brigade remained obedient to their orders. They
were facing the enemy and were therefore occupied and
cheerful. 'We are all well,' wrote General Paget, 'but a
good deal harassed.' The riflemen whom Moore had
trained at Shorncliffe lay in the path of the oncoming
French like cats watching for their prey, and, when their
chance came, they did not waste ammunition. On the
night of the 28th, after repeatedly driving off Napoleon's
Imperial Chasseurs, they filed silently across the bridge
over the Esla at Castro-Gonzala while the engineers prepared to fire the mine at which they had been working all
day. Yet though the men were so tired that they could
scarcely keep open their eyes, when the drums beat to arms
on an alarm every one was at his post in an instant.

The British cavalry, under Lord Paget's confident hand,
behaved, too, magnificently. On his arrival at Medina del
Rioseco Napoleon, realising that Moore had already
crossed his front, swung his columns to the north-west and
ordered his cavalry forward through Mayorga and
Valderas to drive the British rearguards into the Esla.
Hitherto these superb horsemen, drawn from the finest
fighting races in Europe, had been accustomed to carry
everything before them; in Spain the mere sight of their
brazen casques and streaming horse-hair had turned armies
into rabbles. But the British and Hanoverian cavalry were

quite unimpressed by them. Three brilliant regiments in particular—the 7th, 10th and 15th Hussars—proved, as at Beaumont fourteen years before, that, though inexperienced in the art of manœuvring with large armies, the British in personal encounter could match any cavalry in the world.

By the morning of the 29th the last patrols were across the Esla, and the Emperor, who had brought his headquarters forward to Valderas, ordered his horse to cross the river and discover whether the British were retiring on the wild Portuguese mountains to the west or on Astorga and Galicia. Accordingly 600 Chasseurs of the Imperial Guard under Colonel-General Lefebvre-Desnoëttes forded the swollen river a little above Benavente and appeared before the town just as the British rearguard was preparing to march out to the north-west. Suddenly the narrow streets, where the tired riflemen of the 95th were snatching a few hours' sleep, echoed with the clatter of hoofs, the rattle of sabres and shouts of 'Clear the way, Rifles! Up boys and clear the way!' The French general, driving in the piquets of the 18th Hussars outside the town, found that he had caught a tartar. Splendidly mounted, the British 10th Hussars and the 3rd Hussars of the German Legion, forming line as they rode, swept down on the surprised Chasseurs—big fellows with huge bearskin helmets and green uniforms—who, seeing what was coming, wheeled about and galloped for the ford. For a minute or two the race was equal; then a patch of swampy ground on the British left gave the fugitives a few breathless seconds to splash their way through the water. But nearly two hundred, including Lefebvre-Desnoëttes, were taken prisoner or left, sliced and mangled, on the bank or in the blood-stained stream. All the while the exultant riflemen in the town kept cheering like mad: it added much to their excitement when the rumour spread that Napoleon himself was watching from the heights beyond the Esla. Later, as they swung out of Benavente along the Astorga road, the captured French general rode in the greenjackets' midst—a big, sulky fellow in scarlet and gold with a bloody wound across his forehead.

Meanwhile the rest of the army was racing for Astorga as fast as its disorganised state would permit. Any thought of staying in the open plain till Napoleon's forces had had time to deploy was out of the question. Already wastage and sickness had reduced the British effectives to 25,000. There could be no safety for them until they reached the mountain defiles. Even then shortage of provisions and the danger of an outflanking movement through one or other of the converging valleys of that intricate region threatened to force them back to the sea. Moore saw clearly that it was Napoleon's game, not his, to fight a battle. The farther he could draw the Grand Army into the remote, inhospitable mountains of the north-west, the better for the Peninsula. 'The game of Spain and England,' he wrote to the Junta, 'must always be to procrastinate and save time.'

But for the moment the question was whether the British could escape Napoleon's converging jaws. Already the threat to their flanks was developing fast. On December 29th, the day Paget's rearguard evacuated Benavente, Soult's cavalry, fanning out to the north, overwhelmed La Romana's disintegrating army at Mansilla. By leaving the bridges over the Esla undestroyed the Spaniards opened the road through Leon and beyond. Meanwhile it was discovered from the captured Chasseurs that other forces were seeking to reach the great mountain defile at Villafranca. As soon, therefore, as he reached Astorga on the 30th, Moore sent officers ahead to watch any attempt either to cut the Corunna road from the direction of Leon or to use the track from Benavente to Orense to work round his southern flank. However bad such cross-country roads might be, he could not forget how often he had been misled about Iberian topography. Nor could he rely on the Spaniards defending their native passes; La Romana, ignoring every entreaty and his own promise, had failed to take his starving army over the Cantabrian range into the Asturias, and was now flying across the British line of retreat towards Orense. For these reasons Moore on New Year's Eve dispatched Major-General Craufurd's Light

Brigade towards Vigo to guard the valley of the Minho and his southern flank.

The threat of hunger kept pace with that of encirclement. Owing to the inadequacy of Baird's commissariat only two days' provisions were found at Astorga, while the flight of the Spanish bullock-drivers and their carts made it impossible to bring up supplies from the next magazine at Villafranca. The only course was to cover the fifty miles to that place before the army starved. Shortage of rations further undermined discipline; the natural tendency of the frightened inhabitants to hide what little food they possessed led to illicit house-to-house searches, and these in their turn to orgies in the cellars. The bad characters, who according to one witness numbered from fifty to a hundred in every battalion, came into their own. The national weakness for drink—always accentuated in an army recruited at the ale-house door—found a terrible vent, and hundreds of uncontrollable and armed men roved the streets in delirium. To add to the horror La Romana's troops poured into the town while the British were still evacuating it—a starving, shivering, stinking, typhus-ridden rabble who fell on the homes and chattels of their countrymen like a wolf-pack. Their example was eagerly followed by their allies.

The renewed retreat completed the army's demoralisation. In many units the sullen men became openly mutinous. The road into the mountains was knee-deep in snow and ice that became a river of slush by day and froze again at night. Boots, already in tatters, were wrenched off bleeding feet; horses could not stand and died in the snow or slid over frozen precipices. With every gust of wind clouds of snow blew in the men's faces. It was bitterly cold : there was no fuel, no shelter and nothing to drink but snow. 'We suffered,' wrote a soldier of the 71st, 'misery without a glimpse of comfort.' All the time La Romana's pitiful scarecrows kept getting in the way, swarming with famished howls through the battered doors of every wayside farm or hut.

At the top of the mountain a great pass ran through a

barren waste of snow. All the way through it, for eight or nine miles, the men trudged in angry silence broken only by the groans of the dying by the wayside or the occasional report of a pistol fired at the head of a fallen horse. Afterwards at the village of Bembibre hundreds of troops left the ranks and, burning and plundering, fought their way into the wine vaults. Here, as the old year went out, horrible scenes were enacted. 'Bembibre,' wrote an officer, 'exhibited all the appearance of a place lately stormed and pillaged. Every door and window was broken, every lock and fastening forced. Rivers of wine ran through the houses and into the streets, where soldiers, women, children, runaway Spaniards and muleteers lay in fantastic groups with wine oozing from their lips and nostrils.'

Here too on the first day of the New Year came the rearguard, sounding their bugles, hammering on the doors and rousing the insensible men in the cellars and streets with blows from their rifles. Behind them—though still at a respectful distance—came the French cavalry. As the rumours of their approach ran through the plundered town the streets filled with revellers whom all the efforts of their comrades had failed to rouse, reeling, staggering and crying out for mercy. They received none from the French dragoons who, eager to avenge Benavente, slashed at drunkards, cripples, women and infants in arms. Yet even in this pit of shame the stubborn English spirit flickered; during the night and following day with a wonderful persistence many stragglers regained the retreating columns —tattered soldiers with bloodshot eyes and festering wounds and women who had been raped in barns but had fled from their violators to rejoin the colours.[8]

It was this spirit almost as much as the valour of the Reserve and Light Brigade, that robbed Napoleon of his triumph. 'The English are running away as fast as they can,' he wrote from Benavente; 'they have abandoned the Spaniards in a shameful and cowardly manner. Have all this shown up in the newspapers. Have caricatures made and songs and popular ditties written. Have them translated into German and Italian and circulated in Italy and

Germany.' For, as his prey eluded him, the Emperor's indignation rose. He hated the British from the bottom of his soul. The man who had plundered half the cities of Europe felt genuine horror at the ill-disciplined rapscallions who had pillaged the wine shops of Benavente. He particularly disliked their barbaric destruction of bridges—one of the principal channels of civilisation.

On New Year's Day, 1809, while pressing forward from Benavente to Astorga to join Soult, Napoleon learnt that Moore had reached the mountains and that his last hope of forcing a battle on the open plain had passed. He at once resolved to leave Spain. As he approached Astorga a courier galloped up with dispatches from Paris. He dismounted, read them in the presence of his troops and paced angrily up and down. Later it became known that momentous tidings had arrived : that Austria was arming for war, that there had been a revolution in Turkey—incited by British agents—that traitors had been plotting in Paris. That night the Emperor handed over command of the army to Soult, and ordered the immediate return of the Imperial Guard to Valladolid. The English were beyond his reach. So for that winter were Portugal and southern Spain.

From this time, though 50,000 Frenchmen with more than fifty guns were still at their heels, the chief threat to the British came not from the enemy but from the weather and their own indiscipline. At Villafranca—a mountain town fifty miles from Astorga and a hundred from Corunna—where the main body of the retreating army arrived on New Year's Day, the troops refused to await the official distribution of rations and sacked the magazines while the commissaries stood by helpless. 'Every soldier took what he liked, everything was plundered, carried away and trampled under foot; the casks of wine were broken open so that half their contents were spilt over the floor, and the general fury and unruliness of these hordes of men was such that those officers who attempted to maintain order had to make haste to fight their way out of the crowds, if only to save their lives.' Fourteen days' store of biscuits, salt meat and rum vanished in a few hours, and with them all hope of a stand at Villafranca. Later houses were beaten up in search of drink and the disgraceful scenes of Bembibre re-enacted. Almost every sign of a disciplined fighting force disappeared. The artillerymen broke up their ammunition wagons for fuel and threw their contents into the river.

The rot continued until the 2nd when the Commander-in-Chief, who had been marching with the rearguard, arrived to restore order. All stragglers were at once arrested and locked up, and the emaciated, lacerated survivors of the French cavalry charge at Bembibre were paraded round the town as a warning. A man taken in the act of plundering a magazine was shot in the market place : another hanged for breaking into a house, while the troops were made to file past the dangling corpse. Later the army, with some semblance of discipline, marched out towards Lugo, and Moore rejoined the rearguard holding the bridge over the Cua at Cacabelos five miles to the east.

Here also, since the drunken orgy at Bembibre, there had been some loss of discipline. Sir John, whose faith in his army had been almost broken, ordered the division to parade in close column and addressed it in forcible terms. Sooner than survive such conduct, he announced, he trusted that the first cannon-ball fired by the enemy would remove him from the scene of his disgrace. 'And you, 28th'—turning on a famous regiment that had fought by his side in Egypt—'are not what you used to be. If you were, no earthly temptation could tempt one of you away from your colours for an instant.' Next morning, some plundering having occurred in the village during the night, Major-General Paget had the culprits paraded in a hollow square and flogged. While the last offenders, who had been sentenced to be hanged, were waiting their turn under the triangles, the French were reported approaching, whereupon the thirty-three-year-old general—most impressive of disciplinarians—turned on his division with, 'My God ! is it not lamentable that, instead of preparing the troops confided to my command to receive the enemies of their country, I am preparing to hang two robbers?' He then paused. 'If I spare the lives of these two men, will you promise to reform?' There was a great shout and the prisoners were taken down.

Immediately afterwards, as if the affair had been staged, the enemy appeared on the skyline in action with the piquets. Battle was immediately joined. It was the tonic the men required. In the fighting the 52nd, the Light Company of the 28th—the 'Old Slashers'—and a battalion of the 95th that had not accompanied the other half of the regiment to Vigo covered themselves with glory. The French cavalry were repelled and their leader, General Colbert, killed. 'We popped them off whenever they showed their ugly faces,' said a rifleman, 'like mice in the sun!'

After that there was no further difficulty with the rear-guard. That night, after Villafranca had been evacuated, the men marched eighteen miles to Herrerias without losing a straggler. The retreat now bore two faces, one of shame and suffering, the other of glory: the demoralised misery of the main body trudging over the frozen hills, and the splendour of the fighting division which covered its retreat. During the next fifty miles to Lugo the agony of the army surpassed anything yet encountered. Drenched with rain, famished with cold and hunger, ignorant when their torture was to cease, thousands of redcoats toiled up the agonising slope of Monte del Cabiero, leaving behind a trail of dying men, women, horses and mules. Above the howling of the wind nothing could be heard but groans and curses. In the terrible defile beyond Villafranca, where the road ran between enormous precipices round the bends of the raging Valcarso, the men, worn out by their excesses, dropped in shoals. The worst was endured on the high ground near Los Royales and Constantino. On the desolate, wintry height many, through the failure of the commis-sariat, died of starvation clasped in one another's arms in the snow. 'The misery of the whole thing was appalling,' wrote Schaumann, 'huge mountains, intense cold, no houses, no shelter or cover of any kind, no inhabitants, no

bread. The howling wind, as it whistled past the ledges of
rock and through the bare trees, sounded to the ear like
the groaning of the damned.' At one point on that march
of death a dying woman gave birth in an overturned
bullock cart; an officer of Moore's Staff, finding the living
infant whimpering at her frozen breasts, wrapped it in his
cloak and carried it away with him. Then 'the dark, almost
polar night fell' and concealed such sights from men's eyes.

Occasionally, where the mountains permitted, French
cavalry patrols swept round the flanks of the rearguard to
fall on the stragglers. Yet though they gathered in nearly
a thousand prisoners by this means, they always encountered more than they bargained for. The sound of their
trumpets borne on the wind had an electrifying effect.
However desperate their plight, the pallid British scarecrows would instinctively face about, level their muskets
and fire. 'I heard them more than once say,' wrote a
private of the 71st, 'as they turned from the points of our
bayonets, they would rather face a hundred fresh Germans
than ten dying Englishmen.' Nothing in all their sufferings
so enraged the latter as the failure of the enemy to close.
'Why don't they come on like men,' cried one, 'whilst
we've strength in us left to fight them?'

Scenes not dissimilar were enacted in the parallel march
on the road to Vigo. Here Brigadier-General Craufurd—
the little, dark, wiry man whom the men of the Light
Brigade called Black Bob—kept his troops in heart and
good order by sheer strength of personality. Wherever
suffering or danger was greatest, he was certain to appear,
growling like a worried bulldog and bearing a canteen of
rum and a small cup which he offered to his men with
oaths and homely counsel. 'Many a man in that retreat,'
wrote one of them, 'caught courage from his stern eye and
gallant bearing. . . . He did not like retreating, that man.
War was his very element, and toil and danger seemed to
call forth only an unceasing determination to surmount
them.' Once he caught an officer crossing a stream on a
soldier's back : 'Put him down, sir, put him down,' he
shouted, plunging into the icy water, 'go back, sir, and go

through the water like the others!' On another occasion he halted the brigade and sentenced two men to be flogged by drumhead court-martial, standing beside them while the sentence was carried out. 'If he flogged two,' wrote Rifleman Harris, 'he saved hundreds.' His troops looked upon him as the finest soldier in the world and would have followed him to hell. They walked at his side like familiars and, whenever he halted to deliver one of his stern reprimands, half a dozen of them—unshaven, shoeless and savage—would stand 'leaning upon their weapons and scowling up in his face as he scolded; and, when he dashed the spurs into his reeking horse, they would throw up their rifles and hobble after him again.'

Such troops and their fellow light-infantrymen of Edward Paget's rearguard developed as the retreat went on an immense pride in their powers of endurance. At night they lay down, as 19-year-old Lieutenant Blakeney wrote, in martial wedlock, each folding to his breast his better half—his musket. For the stragglers and weaklings littering the way they felt nothing but contempt; clodhoppers they called them. At every village along the line of retreat the angry shout would go up: 'Burst open the door!' and the laggards would be frog-marched into the street and set marching with kicks and blows. 'Now show yer nerve,' cried the sergeant of the 43rd, throttling his own racking cough; 'if you die to-day, you won't have to die to-morrow. Fall in!'

.   .   .

At Lugo on January 6th Moore halted his army and prepared to give battle. Despite the wet and dreadful cold the effect on discipline was instantaneous. The men asked only one thing: to be allowed to visit their sufferings and injured self-respect on the enemy. For two days they bivouacked on an icy ridge without shelter and with scarcely any food, hoping against hope that the French would attack. On the third day, as the enemy made no sign and the last provisions were exhausted, the retreat was resumed in a terrible night of sleet and hail. Two more days of suffering and demoralisation followed, during which the French captured another five hundred footsore, starving laggards, though only after the latter, forming square under the orders of a sergeant, had put up a desperate fight. By the second night the march had become not a succession of battalions but a vast, disorganised multitude without respect of regiment, brigade or division; the colours of that famous corps, the Royals, were attended by nine officers, three sergeants and only three privates. During this time the rearguard repeatedly saved the army.

In the course of January 10th the hills were left behind and the main body reached Betanzos on the coastal plain. Here the sun was shining and the orange and lemon trees were in flower; there was ample provision of food, and the famished troops were able to fill their stomachs. Next day, with indescribable feelings, they caught their first glimpse of the sea and the distant masts of ships. A thorough re-organisation having taken place under the supervision of the Commander-in-Chief, the army entered Corunna that night in tolerable formation, the ragged, shoeless scarecrows stumping on frostbitten, bleeding feet through the streets with every commanding officer leading his regiment and every captain and subaltern flanking his section. The highlight was the performance of two battalions of the First Foot Guards, each 800 strong, who marched in perfect formation in column of sections, with drums beating and the drum-major twirling his staff.

Before the retreat Moore had urged the Government to send transports to Corunna or Vigo—a summons which had caused great indignation among the more sanguine Ministers. But not till the night of January 3rd–4th, during the midnight halt at Herrerias after the action on the Cua, had he decided, on receiving his engineers' reports, to embark the main army at Corunna. When, therefore, it arrived, though the bay was filled with hospital and store ships, the transports were still wind-bound at Vigo. There was nothing for it but to wait for them and trust to their coming before Soult, who had lost a day or two on the march, could bring up his reserves and heavy guns.

Nor had the general been well served by his engineers. Corunna was protected on the south by a range of heights. But, like those at Toulon fifteen years before, they were too extensive for the army to hold. Sickness, the detachment of Craufurd's contingent to Vigo and heavy losses on the retreat—at least 5,000 had fallen or had been captured —had reduced Moore's infantry to a bare 15,000. The only position on which so small a force could fight a delaying action was an inner ring of low hills completely dominated by the outer heights. Moreover embarkation presented grave risks, since it was almost impossible to get out of the harbour in certain winds. 'Figure to yourself,' wrote a naval officer, 'two or three hundred sail of bad-sailing merchantmen, crammed chock full, and a French army at hand who, possessing themselves of the place, would be enabled from both sides of the entrance to throw shot and shells at leisure at the unhappy transports attempting to work out. Such a situation makes me shudder!' To make matters worse, until the transports should arrive, there was a serious shortage of food; on the day the British marched into the town every provision shop closed its doors.

Therefore, though the soldiers rejoiced at the end of their sufferings and a happy commissary sat over Don Mascosa's mulled wine, smoking cigars and admiring the beauties of the harbour, those charged with the army's safety continued deeply anxious. Some even urged the Commander-in-Chief to ask Soult for a negotiated evacuation. But Moore rejected this proposal and proceeded with his usual energy to make the best of the situation. He at once embarked as many of his sick and wounded as possible in the store and hospital ships and began to fortify the landward approaches to the town. In this he was aided by the townsfolk, who, regardless of their own bleak future, threw themselves, men, women and children, with wholehearted abandon into digging trenches, strengthening the neglected ramparts and carrying ammunition to the forts and batteries. It was as though, touched by the sufferings of their allies, they had resolved by a single impulse to make amends for all the improvidence and procrastination of the

past six months. Among the consequences of the latter was
a huge magazine of four thousand barrels of powder, sent
out in haste from England at the beginning of the war and
since left undistributed and unused. This was fired on the
13th, causing an explosion which broke every window in
the town, swept the harbour with a tidal wave and killed a
sergeant and two men on piquet more than a mile away.

Moore did not destroy everything that he found at
Corunna. From the stores he took arms and ammunition,
giving to every man a new firelock and a pouch filled with
fresh powder—an instance of the effects of sea power, for
the French, with the long mountain road behind them and
their powder and arms damaged by exposure, could hope
for no such advantage. And Moore needed all the help he
could get. The rearguard after its superb performance
during the retreat—in which, though continuously engaged,
it had lost fewer men than any division in the army—was
holding the crossing over the Mero at El Burgo, four miles
east of the town. But, with the enemy massing beyond the
river, the position ceased to be tenable after the 13th when
a partially masked battery was disclosed commanding the
broken bridge. General Paget's small force had no alter-
native but to withdraw in haste, leaving the French free to
cross. A battle under the walls of Corunna could no longer
be avoided.

Fortunately on the evening of the 14th the missing transports arrived, 110 sail strong, bringing the total at anchor
in the harbour to 250. With them came a squadron of
battleships—*Ville de Paris, Victory, Barfleur, Zealous,
Implacable, Elizabeth, Norge, Plantagenet, Resolution,
Audacious, Endymion, Mediator*—a glorious spectacle,
thought an onlooker, had it been possible to forget the
service for which they had come. Yet it was one which
brought relief to thousands of British hearts. That night
Moore, not daring to waste an hour lest a sudden change
in the wind should enable the French artillery to destroy
the fleet at anchor, embarked the remainder of his sick, all
but eight of his guns and, since the rocky terrain did not
admit of their use in battle, the whole of his cavalry. Only

a thousand horses could be taken. The remainder, many having foundered during the retreat—not for want of shoes but for nails and hammers—were shot on the beach.

During the morning of the 15th Soult, forcing back Paget's outposts, occupied the heights round the town, overlooking and partially enclosing the inferior British positions on the slopes of Monte Mero. Sharpshooting and cannonading continued all day, about a hundred men falling on either side. Sir John Moore spent the afternoon inspecting his lines, talking as usual to every officer and giving cautions, orders and exhortations. 'He looked wistfully at the enemy,' wrote young Boothby who rode with his Staff, 'apparently wishing with painful eagerness for a battle.' Those, Boothby added, who supposed that such wishes were excited by any thought of his own fame did not know Sir John Moore; only that morning in a letter to the admiral he had expressed his anxiety for an engagement as the only means of securing an unmolested embarkation.

Yet possibly another—and not ignoble—thought was in Moore's mind. In his last dispatch, sent off two days earlier, he had told Castlereagh that he could never have believed that a British army could become demoralised in so short a time; its conduct in retreat had been infamous beyond belief. Yet he could not refrain from also stressing his unbroken confidence in the valour of his troops; whenever there had been any prospect of fighting, the men had shown their determination to do their duty. In a retreat of nearly three hundred miles, carried out under appalling conditions in the face of a superior foe and without the slightest help from the Spaniards, they had not—for all their insubordination—lost a gun or a colour.

But next day—January 16th, 1809—though their drums beat early to arms and a battery of eleven twelve-pounders had appeared during the night on a rocky eminence overhanging the British lines, the French made no move. During the morning, while the last stores and baggage were embarked and Mr. Robinson of *The Times* paid farewell calls in the town, the scarlet lines waited unmolested under a cloudless sky among the Monte Mero rocks and heather.

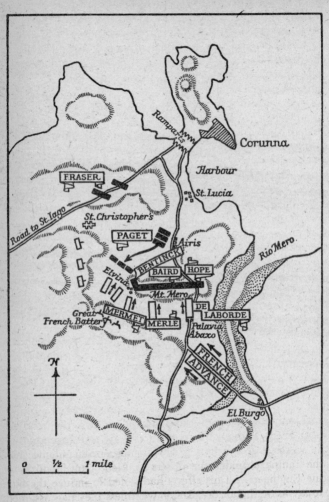

Corunna

At midday, when it seemed clear that the enemy were not going to attack, Moore gave orders for the Reserve to embark during the afternoon and for the rest of the army to follow as soon as it was dark. Among the white houses of Corunna two miles away Crabb Robinson, going to dine at the hotel, found the table d'hôte packed with departing English officers.

But between one and two o'clock, just after Moore had observed to his secretary, 'Now if there is no bungling, I hope we shall get away in a few hours,' the French began to move. Soult, supposing that his enemies were breaking formation, had decided to destroy them as they went down to their ships. He had a score of heavy calibre guns to their eight light six-pounders, a superiority in manpower— 16,000 or more to their 15,000—and far greater forces coming up over the mountains in his rear. The ground and all the circumstances were in his favour. He waited no longer but launched his troops at a run down the mountain side in three columns, with a cloud of voltigeurs swarming ahead into the valley below the British lines. At the same time the great battery of heavy guns on the rocks opposite the British right opened with terrible effect.

Down by the harbour, as the firing broke out, everything changed. Crabb Robinson looked up from his dinner to find that the redcoated officers had all left. Crowds of people gathered in the streets and on the roofs to hear the musketry and watch the smoke rising like mist from the nearby hills. The Reserve, marching down to the quayside with thoughts set on England, halted to a man as if by word of command at that compelling sound; a few minutes later an aide-de-camp came spurring down the road to recall them. Perhaps the most astonishing transformation of all was that of a fatigue party digging entrenchments near the ramparts under the orders of Lieutenant Boothby of the Engineers. All his efforts had failed to induce the men to lay aside the air of extreme weariness they had assumed. Each shovel of earth approached the top of the bank as slowly as the finger of a clock. Boothby was therefore considerably astonished at their behaviour when an order came

for them to join their regiments marching to the field.
'They threw down their tools, jumped to their arms, halloed and frisked as boys do when loosed from school, these
poor, tattered, half-dead looking devils.'

Meanwhile the French had taken all their first objec-
tives. Pouring down the hillside in a torrent, 600 voltigeurs
under old General Jardon—a true, foul-mouthed, gallant
son of the Revolution, who never changed his linen and
always marched on foot with the leading files, carrying a
musket—drove the defending piquets out of Elvina village.
He was closely followed by General Mermet with the main
column. Another phalanx on its right made for the British
centre. Behind, the guns of the great battery pounded
cannon-balls over their heads into the British lines. Here,
on the extreme right of the ridge above Elvina, twenty-six-
year-old Charles Napier, commanding the 50th Foot,
walked up and down the ranks making his men shoulder
and order arms to distract their minds from the round shot,
while his piquets fifty yards below disputed with the French
skirmishers.

Suddenly above the thunder of musketry and the cries
of 'En avant, tue, tue, en avant, tue!' of the French
column, he heard the gallop of horses and, turning round
saw Sir John Moore. 'He came at speed,' he wrote, 'and
pulled up so sharp and close he seemed to have alighted
from the air; man and horse looking at the approaching
foe with an intenseness that seemed to concentrate all feeling in their eyes. The sudden stop of the animal, a cream-
coloured one with black tail and mane, had cast the latter
streaming forward; its ears were pushed out like horns,
while its eyes flashed fire, and it snorted loudly with
expanded nostrils, expressing terror, astonishment and
muscular exertion. My first thought was, it will be away
like the wind! but then I looked at the rider, and the horse
was forgotten. Thrown on its haunches the animal came,
sliding and dashing the dirt up with its fore feet, thus bend-
ing the general forward almost to its neck. But his head
was thrown back and his look more keenly piercing than I
ever saw it. He glanced to the right and left, and then

fixed his eyes intently on the enemy's advancing column, at the same time grasping the reins with both his hands and pressing the horse firmly with his knees : his body thus seemed to deal with the animal while his mind was intent on the enemy, and his aspect was one of searching intenseness beyond the power of words to describe. For a while he looked, and then galloped to the left without uttering a word.'

Here the other two columns were attacking the British line which ran for about a mile along the scrubby ridge to the marshes of the Mero on its left. On the fringe of the latter the easternmost column had driven Lieutenant-General Hope's outposts out of Palavia Abaxo village and was coming on towards the slope at the double. But it soon became clear that the real danger was to Baird's division on the other flank opposite the great battery, and particularly to its extreme right where Lord William Bentinck's brigade—consisting of the 4th, the 50th and the 42nd—was holding a small knoll above Elvina. A further French column, supported at a distance by cavalry, was now surging round the western edge of the ridge into the valley which ran down behind the British position towards the harbour two miles away. To protect the latter the 52nd and the Rifles had been hastily extended, screening the rest of Paget's Reserve which had taken up its position in the suburb of Airis behind the British lines. Though the French were swirling all round the knoll on which he was posted, Lord William—an habitually placid man—was ambling about on an old mule, which seemed as indifferent to the fire as he, and talking to every one with the utmost good humour. 'I only remember saying to myself,' Charles Napier wrote, 'this chap takes it coolly or the devil's in it.'

Presently Moore returned and joined the group on the knoll. A round-shot struck the ground close to his horse's feet, causing it to spin round, but he never took his gaze from the enemy. A second shot tore the leg off a 42nd Highlander who started screaming and rolling about, much to the agitation of his comrades. 'This is nothing, my lads,' Moore called out, 'keep your ranks, take that man away;

my good fellow, don't make such a noise, we must bear these things better.' His sharp tone had the calming effect intended, and the ranks closed again.

The battle was now reaching the climax he had foreseen. While Baird's and Hope's battered divisions continued with their sustained musketry to hold the ridge against frontal attack, the French—deceived by appearances—were pouring into the valley towards Airis and the approaches to Corunna, imagining that they had encircled the British right. They had completely failed to realise that Moore had two unused divisions behind his lines. He now gave the order for the rest of the Reserve to reinforce the 95th and 52nd and expel the intruders and for Major-General Fraser's division, lying back near the port on the Corunna-St. Iago road, to move up in support. At the same time he launched the 4th Foot from the right of the ridge against the flank of the incautious French and sent the 50th and 42nd forward against Elvina.

In the smoke-filled valley on his right everything went as Moore had intended. As Soult's troops surged forward they encountered Paget's advancing line and discovered—for the first time—the real right of the British army. Enraged by the memory of all they had suffered on the retreat and supported by the enfilading fire and bayonets of the 4th, the veterans of the Reserve quickly turned the enemy's advance into a rout and, carrying all before them, surged up the valley towards the great battery itself. Meanwhile, led by Napier and his young fellow major, Charles Stanhope—Pitt's nephew—the 50th cleared Elvina and dashed on in a rough, scrambling fight into the stony lanes and fields beyond. Owing to a misunderstanding, however, the Black Watch fell back to replenish their powder; on seeing this the general rode up to them, exclaiming, 'My brave 42nd, if you've fired your ammunition, you've still your bayonets. Remember Egypt! Think on Scotland! Come on, my gallant countrymen!' Then, sending back young George Napier, his aide-de-camp, to bring up the Guards in support, he remained erect and motionless on his horse, watching the development of the attack on the French battery.

At any moment now the guns would be his; the 14th Foot on his left had retaken Palavia Abaxo; the discouraged enemy, their ammunition failing, were everywhere giving ground. Behind them lay the swollen Mero and the solitary bridge at El Burgo. The experienced eye of the great Scottish soldier told him that victory was his; the sufferings he and his men had endured for so long were about to be avenged.

At that moment a cannon-ball from the threatened battery struck him from his horse, carrying away his left shoulder and part of his collar-bone, and leaving his lungs exposed and his arm hanging by a torn string of flesh. For a moment he lay motionless, then raised himself to a sitting position and, with eyes kindling with their habitual brilliance, resumed his gaze on the smoke and turmoil ahead. So unmoved was his face that those about him could scarcely realise the deadly nature of his wound.

A little later Commissary Schaumann saw him being borne by six Highlanders through the streets of Corunna on a blood-stained blanket, with a little group of aides-de-camp and doctors walking beside. He had refused to be parted from his sword which he carried out of the field with him like a Spartan his shield. Though breathing only with intense pain, he repeatedly made his bearers pause so that he might look back on the battle. 'You know,' he murmured to his friend, Colonel Anderson, 'I have always wished to die this way.'

After Moore's departure—for Baird had also had his arm shattered by the great battery's raking fire—the command devolved on a fellow Scot, Sir John Hope. The latter, isolated on the left from the decisive events which had been taking place elsewhere, was unable to follow up the swift succession of blows planned by his fallen chief. The gallantest of men, pottering instinctively—as one of his officers testified—to wherever the fire was hottest, he was a little overawed by the weight of the responsibility that had suddenly fallen on him; England's only army was in his keeping and her fleet was waiting in a perilous anchorage. It was growing dark and, seeing that the French attack was broken, he called off the pursuit and ordered Moore's instructions of the morning to be put into immediate operation. It was certain now that the embarkation would be unmolested.

In darkness and weariness the men marched to the quay-side while the rearguard piquets lit bivouac fires on the abandoned ridge. Hollow-eyed and covered with blood and filth, they looked so terrible that the townsfolk crossed themselves as they passed. But the withdrawal was carried out in perfect order, so well had Moore's measures and a brush with the enemy restored the discipline of his tattered troops. Presently, on the dark, tossing water-front they were grasped by the mighty fists of the sailors and pulled into the boats. As they were rowed across the harbour to the waiting ships, their general lay breathing his last on the soil of the land he had come to save. 'I hope the people of England will be satisfied,' he whispered, 'I hope my country will do me justice.' He repeatedly enquired after his officers, urging that this one should be recommended for promotion and begging to be remembered to another. 'Is Paget in the room?' he asked, 'remember me to him, he is a fine fellow.' Then, as his wound congealed and grew cold and the agony increased, he became silent lest he should show weakness.

By the morning of the 17th the whole army was on board except for 1,500 troops whom Hope, resolved to depart in dignity, had left under Hill and Beresford to cover the embarkation of the wounded. The Spaniards, stirred by the battle to a sudden ecstasy of generous enthusiasm, had volunteered to defend the ramparts while the fleet got to sea. The whole town, men, women and children had turned out; 'everybody commanded, everybody fired, everybody halloed, everybody ordered silence, everybody forbade the fire, everybody thought musketry best and everybody cannon.' 'Thus, after all,' wrote Schaumann, 'we became reconciled to the Spanish character.' About the same time Napoleon, having threatened to hang the municipality for the murder of a French soldier, was preparing to leave Valladolid for Paris. His eagles had not been planted on the towers of Lisbon after all. Nor had he destroyed the British army. As it began to grow light and the wind in the bay of Corunna freshened, a party of the 9th Foot with a chaplain and a few mournful officers could be seen making their way along the ramparts on the landward bastion of the citadel. They carried the body of their dead commander, wrapped in his military cloak. Presently they committed it to the ground, and 'left him alone with his glory.'

CHAPTER SIX

WATERLOO, 1815
The Last Battle

During the afternoon of Sunday, June 18th 1815, the city
of Brussels was in a state of panic. Since three o'clock a
stream of fugitives had been pouring in from the plain
beyond the forest of Soignes where, twelve miles to the
south, Wellington, with 25,000 British and 42,000 Germans
and Netherlanders—most of them inexperienced or unreliable—and 156 guns, was barring the way of a victorious
French army of 74,000 veterans and 246 guns commanded by Napoleon himself. Most of the British visitors
who had invaded the city in the wake of their army had
already fled to the north and were crowding the roads and
waterways to Antwerp, where, on Wellington's orders, a
state of siege had been proclaimed and crowds waited all
day in the rain for news. But hundreds more, unable to
obtain transport in the panic—for everything on wheels
had been requisitioned—remained in the city without hope
of escape. Every few minutes fugitives from the battlefield
kept galloping into the town, shouting that all was lost and
that the French were at their heels. Once a whole regiment of Hanoverian cavalry poured in through the Namur
gate with swords drawn and foam-flecked horses and rode
through the town towards the north, upsetting everything
in the streets on their way. There were other fugitives with
bloody and bandaged heads, cartloads of wounded, and
occasionally, towards evening, an officer of high rank,
British or Belgian, extended upon a bier borne by soldiers.
As the dreadful afternoon advanced and the distant cannonade grew in intensity, the rumour spread—possibly
circulated by French sympathisers, of whom there were
said to be many—that Napoleon had promised his soldiery
the sack of the city. Every woman knew what that meant.

'I never saw such consternation,' wrote Fanny Burney. 'We could only gaze and tremble, listen and shudder.'

Yet three days earlier Brussels had seemed as securely held by British wealth and the martial power of united Europe as London. For weeks it had been a scene of gaiety and military pageantry, with the brilliant aristocracy of Britain flooding the city in the wake of her army and spending money with a profusion never matched by its successive Spanish, Austrian, French and now Dutch rulers. The nearest French vedettes had been forty miles away beyond the Sambre, and between them and the Belgian capital two great armies had guarded every road on a hundred-mile front, growing daily in strength and commanded by the two most famous soldiers (the 46-year-old Field Marshal the Duke of Wellington and the 70-year-old Prussian, Marshal Blücher) of the European alliance which had defeated and dethroned Napoleon. The Prussian host of around 113,000 men—almost as numerous as the largest striking force Napoleon could be expected by then to raise from an exhausted and divided France—had entered Belgium under Blücher to hold the frontier from the Ardennes to Charleroi, while a smaller joint British, Netherlands, Hanoverian and Brunswick army guarded it from Mons to the North Sea. Soon the young, under-strength battalions sent out in haste from England were expected to be joined by the veteran regiments which had driven the French from Spain and which were now returning from America. Elsewhere more than half a million men, mobilised by the Sovereigns of Europe, were on the march, their vanguards already closing in on the French frontiers. The danger to Brussels and the Low Countries, so great three months before, seemed to have passed. Though no official state of war existed—Napoleon being merely treated as an outlaw under the new international system of collective security—it had been known that an invasion of France was to begin in July. It had even seemed likely that the French, republicans or royalists, would themselves throw out the returned usurper and so avoid the necessity of invasion.

On the night of Thursday, June 15th, there had been a ball in the city. It had been given by the wife of a British milord of fabulous wealth—the Duchess of Richmond—and the principal officers of the British and Allied army had attended it, including the Duke of Wellington, most of his generals and the leader of the Netherlands forces, the Prince of Orange. But during its course, and even before it had begun, it had become known that something was amiss. Several times Wellington had been interrupted by messages and was seen to write orders, and at an early hour many of his officers took their leave. During the small hours of the 16th the squares and streets of Brussels had filled with troops as the trumpets sounded and drums beat to arms. Presently the troops—green-jacketed Riflemen, scarlet-clad infantry of the Line and Highlanders, blue-coated Belgians, and Brunswickers in black—had moved off, laughing and joking in the early morning sunshine, and asking one another what all the fuss was about. The stolid Flemish country folk, rolling into the city in their carts, had watched them with curious eyes as they marched out down the Charleroi road. Everyone in command had seemed very composed and quiet; old Sir Thomas Picton, commander of the British 5th Division, with top-hat and reconnoitring-glass slung over his shoulder, cheerfully accosted his friends as he rode through the streets.

Elsewhere—at Enghien, Ath, Grammont, Nivelles, Oudenarde, and even as far away as Ghent—other troops, British, German and Netherlander, roused from their cantonments, had assembled to the sound of trumpets and bugles and, marching off along the hot, dusty high-roads southwards and eastwards, had begun to converge on the assembly point. It had been a day of intense heat. As they emerged from the beech forests on to the great corn plain which fringed the Sambre to the north, the tramping infantrymen and jingling cavalry and gunners heard a dull, sullen sound like distant thunder and saw on the horizon columns of smoke arising.[1]

For at dawn on June 15th, after one of his incredibly swift and secret concentrations, Napoleon had sprung like a tiger across the Sambre and driven in the outposts of Blücher's army not far from the point where its right touched the left of Wellington's equally scattered force. With 124,000 men he had placed himself, as he hoped, between them. His object was to defeat the Prussians before they had time to concentrate, forcing them back eastwards on their Rhine communications and then, brushing aside Wellington or driving him back towards the sea, to enter Brussels as a conqueror. Thereafter, he believed, the Belgian common people would rise against the Dutch, the war-weary French take heart and unite behind him, the Tory Government in London fall, and his Austrian father-in-law, deprived of British subsidies, sue for peace.

It was not true, as is sometimes said, that Wellington had been caught off his guard. Neither he nor Blücher could have known at what point on the French-Belgian frontier Napoleon would choose to strike. Of the three main roads to Brussels one, through Charleroi, crossed the Prussian sector, the other two, through Mons and Tournai, the Anglo-Dutch. But though that through Mons was the shortest and, therefore, constituted the greatest threat to the Belgian capital—Napoleon's political objective—until that past-master of strategic surprise and sudden, concealed movement showed his hand, it was guess-work which he would take. Wellington had therefore had to be equally ready both to resist an advance along either of the roads crossing his own sector and to hasten eastwards to join the Prussians if they were attacked first. True, therefore, to his unchanging principle of so disposing his forces as to be able to respond to any move of an enemy, instead of keeping them strung out and exposed he placed them in commanding positions well back from the frontier whence they could march to one another's or their allies' aid in the shortest possible time. Two thirds of them could be assembled at any point within twenty-two hours and the whole in not more than forty-eight.[2]

As, however, the French had struck at the Prussian

F

outpost line and not his own, Wellington was dependent on
his ally for information of their initial direction and
strength. And, owing to defective Prussian staff work, no
authentic news of what was happening reached the British
Commander-in-Chief till the middle of the afternoon and
then many hours too late and out of date. Even then it was
not clear whether the reported attack was a feint to draw
off forces from some real danger-point elsewhere. It was
not till after dark that, just before he left for the Duchess
of Richmond's ball, Wellington learnt that it was something more than an affair of outposts and that Napoleon
had thrown his whole weight against the Prussians. Only
then had he felt justified in ordering an immediate concentration of his entire army at Nivelles, a few miles west of
the Charleroi-Brussels road.

When at midnight he arrived at the ball—which, like
Drake before the Armada, he insisted on attending lest a
panic flight of civilians from the Belgian capital should precipitate a pro-French rising—his troops were already
marching. An hour later, just as supper was being served,
an A D C arrived with news that a brigade of Nassauers
under Prince Bernhard of Saxe-Weimar had made contact
with French patrols at Quatre Bras where the road from
Nivelles to Namur crossed the Charleroi-Brussels highway.
Before retiring at 2 a.m. to snatch three hours' sleep before
setting out to the south, Wellington, therefore, issued
further orders to make Quatre Bras—essential for keeping
open communications with the threatened Prussians—the
assembly-point for his entire army.[3]

.   .   .

All afternoon on Friday 16th—the day after the French
had crossed the Sambre—the people of Brussels had heard,
through the hot airless haze, the sound of cannonading
from Quatre Bras, where twenty miles to the south of the
Belgian capital Marshal Ney, commanding the left wing
of Napoleon's advancing army, was trying to brush aside
a still weak but growing British and Netherlands force

from the cross-roads which preserved communication between the two allied armies and alone prevented him from falling on the flank of the Prussians whom Napoleon was assailing frontally at Ligny a few miles to the east. When at 10 a.m. that morning, after passing on the road his Reserve Corps, which he had sent off at dawn from Brussels with Picton's British division in the lead, Wellington had arrived at Quatre Bras, he had found all quiet and a Dutch-Belgian division of 8,000 men under the young Prince of Orange strongly placed at the crossroads. Having already made dispositions for an early concentration of his army at this vital point, he had ridden over to Sombreffe on the nearby Plain of Fleurus to take counsel with Blücher who was awaiting Napoleon's attack in a position which did anything but inspire him with confidence. 'If they fight here,' he had remarked to Colonel Hardinge, his liaison officer at Prussian headquarters, 'they will be damnably mauled.'

When, shortly before 3 p.m., the Duke had returned to Quatre Bras he had found that the French were about to attack the Dutch-Belgian lines there. The latter were strongly posted, but as soon as the enemy's offensive developed, they gave way. There was a moment when, but for Wellington's timely arrival, there would have been a disaster, as the young Prince of Orange had completely lost his grip on the situation and assumed that a wood full of advancing French troops was held by his men. 'It is all over,' he had assured the Duke, 'they are driven back!' 'Over, but what are those in that wood?' 'They are Belgians.' 'No, by God, but they are French and the wood is full of them!'[5] Fortunately the head of Picton's British division was then just arriving on the field, headed by the veteran 1st battalion of the Rifles, probably the most resourceful and versatile fighting unit in any of the three armies. For the next hour or two, under the Duke's tactical command, a British infantry force of divisional strength, without cavalry and at first only partially deployed, had held off three veteran French divisions under one of Napoleon's greatest marshals, supported by 4,000 horse. Reckoning, as at Assaye, that in an apparently hopeless situation boldness is the best policy, and relying on the fact that reinforcements were on the way, the British commander, directing every action down to battalion and even, at times, company level, hit back wherever possible and gradually gained the breathing-space he needed to hold the vital crossroads. At one moment, while trying to rally a force of Dutch-Belgian and Brunswick light horse, he was all but surrounded by French lancers and only reached safety by putting his horse at a ditch lined by the 92nd Highlanders and jump-ing clear over their heads and bayonets. By a miracle of tough, confused fighting in which Picton's veteran Scottish and English regiments, though suffering heavy losses, covered themselves with glory and the Duke of Brunswick fell at the head of his troops, Wellington for six hours clung to a weak but essential strategic position and then, as little by little his numbers rose from 7,000 to 36,000, took the offensive and drove back Ney's 20,000. By doing so, he saved the Prussian army from an assault on their western flank which would have involved them in utter disaster.[6] As it was, by nightfall—though as yet unbeknown to him—63,000 French veterans under the Emperor, attacking with magnificent *élan*, had beaten 80,000 Prussians at Ligny and inflicted on them between 15,000 and 20,000 casualties. Their gallant septuagenarian commander, Blücher, only narrowly escaped capture after being ridden over by French cavalry.

Yet Napoleon's victory had not been as complete as he had hoped. Owing to Wellington's success in withstanding and defeating Ney, and the failure of a French corps which, through the Marshal's and Napoleon's contradictory orders, had marched and countermarched all day between the two battlefields without taking part in either, the Prussians had escaped annihilation and had been able to withdraw northwards in tolerable order into the night. Next day, when, after detaching 33,000 troops under Marshal Grouchy to follow them, the victorious Emperor threw the rest of his army against Wellington, the latter, retaining contact with his defeated ally, fell back in good order up the Charleroi-Brussels highway. And though Napoleon had meant to drive the Prussians eastwards on their communications, Blücher, in loyalty to Wellington, and contrary to the advice of his Chief of Staff, Gneisenau, had retreated northwards towards Wavre on a road parallel to the British and only a dozen miles to the east. The Allied armies thus remained in touch, and, though the Emperor had reduced their numerical superiority and shaken their morale, he had not, as he supposed, divided them. And, though the people of Brussels had expected all day to see the victorious French emerge from the Forest of Soignes, the British withdrawal on the afternoon of the 17th, brilliantly directed by Wellington, had not been in the least precipitate. Covered by Lord Uxbridge's cavalry and horse artillery, by nightfall he had concentrated his entire army on the ridge of Mont St. Jean twelve miles south of the city. During the late afternoon the retreat of the cavalry rearguard and Napoleon's pursuit were delayed by torrential thunderstorms which converted the Charleroi *chaussée* and the fields on either side into quagmires. It had seemed, recalled one officer, as if water was being tumbled out of heaven in tubs.[7]

The two armies had spent a most uncomfortable night. The rain fell almost continually, with flashes of lightning and violent gusts of wind. The ground on which the men lay, drenched to the skin and shaking with cold, was sodden with wet crops. A few old campaigners made themselves tolerably comfortable by smearing their blankets with clay and making pillows of straw. Few of the newcomers to war, who in the Allied army by far outnumbered the old hands, got any sleep at all.

. . .

The ridge, or rather rolling plateau, on which the British army had halted was one which the Duke had long marked as a favourable position for the defence of the Belgian capital. It crossed the highroad from Brussels to Charleroi

a mile and a half south of the village of Waterloo and the
Forest of Soignes. It was named after the farm of Mont St.
Jean which nestled by the roadside in one of its northern
folds. In the course of riding and hunting expeditions, Wellington had carefully studied its gentle undulations and
contours.[8] It was here that twenty-one years before, when
he was a young lieutenant-colonel, his chief, the Duke of
York, had urged the Austrian Generalissimo, Coburg, to
give battle to Jourdan's levies after Fleurus. But Coburg
had chosen to fall back eastwards on his communications,
leaving Brussels to its fate and the British to shift for themselves. It was because, after a generation of disaster and
servitude, a Prussian Field-Marshal had learnt the necessity
of unselfish co-operation between allies, that Wellington
was able to take his stand here. For, though his only reliable
troops were outnumbered by two to one and though the
French had nearly double his weight of artillery, he knew
that he had only to hold his ground with one wing of an
international army until the other under Blücher, who had
given him his assurance that he would so do, could reach
the battlefield. For while neither the British nor the Prussians, acting alone, were strong enough to defeat Napoleon's
army, together they were too strong for him. To keep them
together was, therefore, the basis of Wellington's strategy,
and to do so he was ready to sacrifice temporarily, if
necessary, both the Belgian capital and his communications
with England. For if he and Blücher could unite, on the
morrow their joint forces could take the offensive and
sweep Napoleon back to France.[9]

Unlike Blücher at Ligny, who, in the normal continental
manner, had drawn up his army in view of Napoleon,
Wellington—the greatest master of defensive tactics in
Europe—had chosen a position where his infantry could
inflict the utmost damage on the attackers while suffering
the least themselves. Its reverse or northern slopes, in whose
undulations he concealed his forces, gave him precisely the
cover and field of fire needed for an active defence. Behind
it lay the forest which, stretching for miles on either side
of the Brussels highway, constituted, with its open pines

and beeches and freedom from undergrowth, an excellent temporary refuge into which to withdraw inexperienced troops if they proved unable to withstand Napoleon's attack. Once inside it, he remarked, he would have defied the Devil himself to drive him out.[10] But as, like his ally, he was thinking in ultimate terms, not of defence but of offensive action, he gave battle on the open plain where the full strength of the Prussian and British armies could later be brought to bear on the enmy.

Until then, however, Wellington knew that his rôle must be strictly defensive. At least half the foreign troops under his command could not be trusted to manœuvre. Kincaid of the 95th drew the picture of a detachment of them at Quatre Bras, behaving for all the world like the comedian Mathews's ludicrous sketch of the American Militia; whenever, after a careful explanation of their rôle, they were given the word to march, they had started blazing away at the British skirmishers ahead of them. 'We were at last,' Kincaid wrote, 'obliged to be satisfied with whatever advantages their appearance would give, as even that was of some consequence where troops were so scarce.' Later in the day, he admitted, when they got used to the sensation of being fired at, they behaved quite well. Having fought for Napoleon when Belgium, Holland and Western Germany formed part of his empire, however, they had little stomach for fighting against him. Many more were boys and raw Landwehr, though, in the case of the Brunswickers, with good officers and NCOs. Few were adequately equipped or trained.[11] Of the 42,000 foreign troops in Wellington's army only the 5,500 men of the veteran King's German Legion—an integral part of the British Army—could be described as first-line troops.

Wellington was, therefore, forced to do as he had done in early Peninsular days; to stiffen his foreign formations with redcoats. In the teeth of opposition, particularly from the King of the Netherlands, he had tried to make his force as international in organisation as possible; to this end he had not only worn the national cockades of all the Allies in his hat but had forbidden the playing of 'Rule

Britannia' at regimental concerts. As at Talavera, the most immobile troops of all he stationed among buildings and behind walls. Fortunately one of the features of his position was the presence of villages and farms on either flank of his two-and-a-half-mile front—Smohain, Papelotte, La Haye and Frischermont to the east, and Merbe Braine and Braine l'Alleud to the west. In these he placed some rather uncertain Nassauers—who, however, defended them bravely—Chassé's Belgian division and the youthful Brunswickers who had suffered so severely at Quatre Bras. They thus served—an old device of Wellington's—both as flank guards and reserves.

The backbone of his polygot, and what for this reason he afterwards described as his 'infamous army,'[12] were its 21,000 British regulars—of whom more than 2,000 had arrived from Ostend only that morning—and their comrades of the King's German Legion. Yet of this vital 26,500 —a smaller British force than any he had commanded since his first Portuguese campaign—only about half had ever been under fire. Several of its units were weak second-line battalions, scarcely out of the goose-step. Even most of the eighteen infantry battalions which had fought in Spain had been brought up to strength by recruiting from the plough before they left England. Probably not more than 12,000 of his men had served in the incomparable army which had marched from the Douro to Toulouse, and with which he had said he could have done anything.

Compared with his Peninsular army, Wellington's force was relatively stronger in cavalry than infantry. Its 7,000 British and King's German Legion horse, though far outnumbered by Napoleon's cuirassiers and lancers, made an imposing spectacle, superbly uniformed and caparisoned— the Prince Regent saw to that—and mounted on the finest horses in the world. They could ride across country like a field of high-mettled foxhunters, for they came from a land where horsemanship was a passion. At a review they left Blücher speechless with admiration. 'It did one's heart good,' wrote a Rifleman, watching them on the retreat from Quatre Bras, 'to see how cordially the Life Guards went at their work; they had no idea of anything but straightforward fighting and sent their opponents flying in all directions.' Their chief, the Earl of Uxbridge, was the Lord Paget who had commanded Moore's cavalry so brilliantly during the Corunna campaign, but whose service in the Peninsula had been cut short by an elopement with the wife of Wellington's brother, Henry. Apart from his amatory exploits,[13] he was an excellent officer, quiet and incisive, though, like his command, rather too dashing.

What the British cavalry lacked, except for the King's German Legion and a few fine Peninsular regiments like the 23rd Light Dragoons, was experience of war and, in their high-spirited younger officers, discipline. Too many of the latter held their commissions, not because they wanted to be professional soldiers, but because a few years in a crack cavalry mess was a mark of social distinction. Their courage and dash were indisputable; their self-control and staying-power less certain.[14] The troopers, magnificent fighting material, were what the officers—so much less experienced and realist than their humbler infantry colleagues—made or failed to make of them. The same witness of the Lifeguards' charge during the retreat noticed with amusement that, whenever one of them got a roll in the mud, he went off to the rear as no longer fit to appear on parade.[15]

In artillery, though he acknowledged it only sparingly, Wellington was brilliantly served. Its mounted branch was magnificently horsed,[16] and, Horse and Field Artillery alike, officers and men were animated by the highest professional spirit. Only 96 of the 156 guns opposed to Napoleon's 246 pieces were British or King's German Legion, but they were probably better handled than any even on a battlefield where one of the commanders was the master gunner of all time. They were lighter metalled than the French guns, many of which were the dreaded twelve-pounders. Yet, thanks to the foresight of Sir Augustus Frazer, their commander, three of the seven mounted batteries had recently substituted nine-pounders for the normal six-pounders. There were also some howitzers.

The weakest branch of the army was its staff. 'I command,' Wellington had written to a friend a few weeks before Napoleon crossed the frontier, 'a very small British army with a very large British staff,' and to another, 'I have more generals and officers of all nations than I know how to employ.' 'To tell you the truth,' he told the Secretary of State, 'I am not very well pleased with the manner in which the Horse Guards have conducted themselves towards me. It will be admitted that the army is not a very good one and, being composed as it is, I might have expected that the generals and staff formed by me in the last war would have been allowed to come to me again. But, instead of that, I am overloaded with people I have never seen before, and it appears to be purposely intended to keep those out of my way whom I wished to have.' 'However,' he added, with his customary philosophy of obedience, 'I'll do the best I can with the instruments which have been sent to assist me.'[17]

Of these by far the best were his British and King's German Legion infantry; on them in the last resort everything depended. There were too few of them, and far too few with battle experience; as he carefully sent them off on the retreat from Quatre Bras before the rest of his troops, he remarked, 'Well, there is the last of the infantry gone, and I don't care now.' A few weeks earlier, Thomas Creevey, encountering the Duke in a Brussels park, had asked him his view of the military prospects. He had stopped and said in the most natural manner, 'By God, I think Blücher and I can do the thing.' 'Do you calculate,' Creevey asked, 'upon any desertion in Bonaparte's army?' 'Not upon a man,' he replied, 'from the colonel to the private in a regiment—both inclusive. We may pick up a marshal or two, perhaps, but not worth a damn.' Then, seeing a private of one of the Line regiments who was gaping at the statues in the park, he added, 'There, it all depends upon that article whether we do the business or not; give me enough of it, and I am sure.'

He therefore placed his thirty-five under-strength British and King's German Legion infantry battalions where he thought the danger was greatest, but left no part of the battlefield without them. He had received in the small hours of the morning Blücher's assurance that he would join him in the course of the day with not less than two corps—a force as large as his own. His anxiety was, therefore, for his right rather than his left. Believing it to be to Napoleon's interest to shift the battle away from the Prussians' impending flank-march and so separate the two allied armies, he expected him to incline to the west, possibly even striking as far as the Mons-Brussels road to seize the Belgian capital in his rear. For this reason he had posted at Hal and Tubize, some ten or twelve miles to the west, 15,000 Dutch and Hanoverian and 3,000 British and King's German Legion troops to guard the Mons-Brussels road, protect the capital, and keep open his communications with Ostend, where more veterans from America were expected. In the event of the battle shifting to the west this force might have an important effect, either against a French offensive move or in pursuit of a French retreat towards Maubeuge or Lille.[18] For, since Wellington was unaware that his world-famous adversary, having beaten the Prussians, had not taken the trouble to verify their subsequent movements but had assumed—merely because he wanted to—that they had retreated eastwards towards Liège instead of, as Wellington knew, northwards on Wavre, it would have been flying in the face of all military common sense and prudence not to have guarded against the probability of Napoleon manœuvring to the west to separate him from his ally instead of committing his army to a frontal attack against a well-defended position where, by the afternoon, he would have to fight both allied armies instead of only one. For this reason also, Wellington placed his main reserve behind and beyond his right or western flank under his most experienced and reliable corps commander, General-'Daddy'-Hill.

There was another reason why Wellington felt anxious about his right. The unobtrusive but fine defensive position he had chosen had one flaw—a narrow, winding, shallow depression which, passing under the walls of a country house called Hougoumont in the plain below the ridge, afforded an approach by which a column could climb round the west shoulder of the plateau out of direct gun-fire and debouch on to the reverse slope where his army was drawn up. For this reason he placed near the danger spot on the right of his front line the First or Guards Division, and behind it, in reserve and *en potence,* Clinton's fine 2nd Division which, with its two brigades of veteran British and King's German Legion infantry, was the nearest he possessed to his old Peninsular Light Division—a force which could manœuvre quickly. Beyond it he stationed at Merbe Braine and Braine l'Alleud his less mobile reserve of Brunswickers and Chassé's Belgians. In addition, since the winding hollow which his experienced eye had perceived could be commanded by musketry fire from Hougoumont, he adopted the, for him, unusual but, under the circum-stances, necessary expedient of fortifying and garrisoning an outpost nearly a quarter of a mile in advance of his main position on the ridge. With its château, barns, orchards, gardens, park and woods, the estate of Hougou-mont formed a 500 yards square whose wooded southern border extended almost to the ridge occupied by the French. Without its possession Napoleon could neither move a column up the concealed hollow nor, unless he divided his army in the presence of his enemy's best troops, envelop the Allied right. Wellington, therefore, placed seven hundred Hanoverians and Nassauers in the Hougou-mont woods, and four light companies of the Guards, detached from the Guards Division on the ridge behind, to hold the house, gardens and orchard and command the sunken way. To the west, defending the avenue to the house from the Nivelles road, he stationed Mitchell's British brigade with some light cavalry in rear. Thus garri-soned, the Hougoumont estate outflanked from the west the plain between the rival armies; if it could be held till the Prussians arrived, Napoleon's position would ultimately become untenable. In the meantime it would gravely delay and impede his attack.

Having secured his right, Wellington strengthened the

remaining two miles of his front in his usual way by placing his formations, except for the guns and skirmishers, on the reverse slopes of the ridge. They were thus out of sight, though not out of range, of the enemy's cannon. They were deployed in broken and staggered lines so as to present single rather than double targets for the enemy's round-shot. The artillery, save for the reserve batteries, Wellington placed along the summit of the ridge, with orders to keep its fire for the enemy's columns and not to waste ammunition in duels with his guns. The skirmishers and riflemen were stationed on the forward or southern slope, concealed, as were all his troops, in the corn which, almost shoulder-high, covered the entire battlefield. By this arrangement the French masses would have to advance through three successive zones of fire—the rifle fire of picked marksmen, the round-shot and grape of the guns, and, as they came over the crest, the musketry volleys of deployed and, till then, invisible infantry.

Apart from Hougoumont on the west, Smohain, Papelotte and La Haye on the east, and the little farm of Mont St. Jean just behind the centre of the British lines, there were no buildings on the open ground Wellington had chosen for battle except the farm of La Haye Sainte. This lay a hundred yards or so down the slope on the southern side of the ridge, abutting on to the straight-paved *chaussée* from Charleroi to Brussels which, ascending the hill here through a cutting, intersected it and the British line at right angles. Here Wellington placed a battalion of the King's German Legion under Major Baring with close by, in an adjoining gravel-pit, part of the 1st battalion of the 95th Rifles, the remainder of which lined a sunken road and hedge on the ridge above. This sunken road crossed the Charleroi-Brussels road at right angles and, following the crest from east to west, joined, north of Hougoumont, another highway that fanned out of the Brussels road at Mont St. Jean and ran through a cutting south-westwards towards Nivelles. This road, like the orchards and woods of Hougoumont, had the effect of constricting the frontage on which the French could assail

Wellington's right. It helped, too, to form those lateral communications by means of which, in all his chosen defensive positions, he could reinforce any point on the battlefield as circumstances dictated.

For the essence of Wellington's defensive tactics was freedom to manœuvre and the ability to react in strength to whatever the enemy might do. Before retiring for three brief hours of sleep in the village inn of Waterloo which was his headquarters, he was asked by Lord Uxbridge, whom, to his annoyance, the Horse Guards had sent him as commander of his cavalry and who, by seniority in the Army List, was his nominal second-in-command—an office he resented and ignored—what his plans for the morrow were. 'Who,' the Commander-in-Chief replied, 'will attack tomorrow, I or Bonaparte?' 'Bonaparte.' 'Well, Bonaparte has not given me any idea of his projects; and, as my plans will depend upon his, how can you expect me to tell you what mine are?' Then, as though to make amends for his terseness—for Uxbridge had only wanted to know what instructions to carry out in the event of his death—he laid his hand on his cavalry commander's shoulder, and said : 'There is one thing certain, Uxbridge, that is, that whatever happens, you and I will do our duty.'[19]

For the second night running Wellington rose at 3 a.m., for he had another twenty hours' day—the third in succession—before him. It may have been that he was woken by a letter from Blücher which is known to have reached him early on the 18th, informing him that two Prussian corps were setting out at dawn to march to his assistance.[20] There was no question now but that he and his men must fight where they stood, and, if necessary, to the death, for to retreat would be to expose these loyal allies to the full force of Napoleon's counter-attack. His only doubt was lest Napoleon, instead of attacking frontally, should strike westwards through Tubize and Hal and so force him temporarily to uncover the Belgian capital. For this reason Wellington wrote in the small hours of the morning several letters warning the British Ambassador at Brussels and

others of this contingency. 'Pray keep the English quiet if
you can,' he told the former. 'Let them all prepare to
move, but neither be in a hurry or a fright, as all will yet
turn out well.' One letter was a personal one to Lady
Frances Webster, then *enceinte*—the neglected wife of one
of Uxbridge's aides-de-camp and a great favourite of his.

> Waterloo. *Sunday morning,*
> *3 o'clock.* June 18th 1815
>
> 'My dear Lady Frances,
>   'As I am sending a messenger to Bruxelles, I write to
> you one line to tell you that I think you ought to take
> your preparations to remove from Bruxelles to Antwerp
> in case such a measure should be necessary. We fought a
> desperate battle on Friday, in which I was successful,
> though I had but very few troops. The Prussians were
> very roughly handled, and retired in the night, which
> obliged me to do the same to this place yesterday. The
> course of the operations may oblige me to uncover
> Bruxelles for a moment, and may expose that town to
> the enemy; for which reason I recommend that you and
> your family should be prepared to move to Antwerp at a
> moment's notice.'[21]

Whatever doubts Wellington may have had as to the issue
—knowing that only half his army could be trusted to stand
if attacked, he must have had many—he did not show them
to his troops. When, in a deep gloom—feeling that his
former chief was certain after the Prussian débâcle to be
defeated by a veteran army numbering twice as many
battle-worthy troops as his own and commanded by the
great Napoleon himself whom Wellington had always said
was worth 40,000 men on the battlefield—General Alava
rode out early from Brussels to join him, he was greeted
to his amazement by a smiling Commander-in-Chief who,
instead of dwelling on his difficulties, plied him with questions about Lady Charlotte Greville's latest party. From
that moment, Alava recalled, he felt assured.

Alava was not the only man on the battlefield who took

courage and confidence that morning from Wellington's
bearing. Dawn on the 18th was cold and cheerless; everyone was soaked and covered in mud from head to foot.
Presently the thunder-clouds began to lift, and the men
managed to get their camp-fires lit and to cook breakfast.
Afterwards, on their officers' orders, they dried their ammunition and cleaned their arms. Later as the sun came partly
out, Wellington rode round the lines with his glittering
staff of aides and foreign attachés, looking, wrote a young
Guards' officer, as gay and unconcerned as if they were
riding to a meet in England. He was wearing a low cocked
hat, bearing the four cockades of Britain, Spain, Portugal
and the Netherlands, a white cravat and blue civilian coat,
white buckskin breeches and a pair of Mr. Hoby's—the
famous St. James's Street bootmaker's—shining top-boots,
together with a blue cape which he was to put on and off
repeatedly on that long day of showers, fog and mist.[22] To
everyone, as he rode along the ridge, visiting every unit and
outpost, he gave the impression that he knew what he was
about and was confident of teaching the French another
of his familiar lessons, Napoleon, his *Grande Armée* and
Imperial Guard notwithstanding. 'The very sight of him
put heart into us all,' wrote a young officer who saw him
pass. Beside the *chaussée* above La Haye Sainte, Captain
Kincaid of the Rifles had brewed a huge camp-kettle full
of sweet tea, out of which the smiling Duke and his staff
partook. 'It was delightful,' wrote Harry Smith of the same
regiment, who was acting as Brigade-Major to General
Lambert whose brigade was stationed in reserve at Mont
St. Jean, 'to see His Grace that morning on his noble horse,
Copenhagen, in high spirits and very animated, but so cool
and so clear in the issue of his orders that it was impossible
not fully to comprehend what he said; delightful also to
observe what his wonderful eye anticipated while some of
his staff were of the opinion the attack was not in progress.' For when one of his entourage remarked that he did
not believe the French would attack that day, Wellington,
who had been closely watching the opposing ridge through
his telescope, replied, 'Nonsense! The columns are already

forming and I think I have discerned where the weight of the attack will be made. I shall be attacked before an hour.' And he gave orders to Harry Smith to instruct General Lambert to be ready to reinforce General Picton's division half a mile ahead, where he could see the French main attack was likely to fall. Soon afterwards he turned to the Duke of Richmond who, with a sixteen-year-old son, had ridden out from Brussels that morning, saying, 'As the father of ten children, you have no right to be here. You must go. You may go now, but a quarter of an hour or twenty minutes hence, you could not go—it would no longer be right.' For, with his experience of battles, he could foretell the storm that was coming. 'It was only just beginning,' he recalled afterwards, 'but it was already quite clear that we should have a terrible day.'[28]

For in the course of the morning it had become plain that the enemy advanced-guard, which had bivouacked during the night on the parallel ridge three-quarters of a mile to the south, was now being joined by the entire French army. Presently watchers could see long lines of massed troops, with their glittering helmets, cuirasses and arms, forming a magnificent spectacle on the ridge of La Belle Alliance—named after the solitary, red-tiled public house of that name. The spectacle was no doubt meant to intimidate Wellington's raw young soldiers and encourage his French-speaking Belgians to desert. At one moment there was a burst of cheering as a grey figure on a white horse, accompanied by a cavalcade, rode down the lines. For the French were not only intending to attack, but in their resolve to conquer, were partaking of a sacrament. Napoleon might not have France, or even all his anxious generals, behind him, but there was no question of the devotion of his fighting men. Between him and his old *moustaches* was a bond to be found in no other army on earth. For all his grandiloquent pretensions, he and they were familiars. Cam Hobhouse, watching him review the Imperial Guard just before the campaign began, had been amazed at the way he mingled with his troops, leaving the saluting base and marching in time beside each column;

once he had gone up to a grenadier and affectionately pulled his nose. He might be prodigal of his men's lives, but, unlike Wellington, who was not, he valued his command of their hearts. It was the foundation of his fortunes. At that moment, as he rode along the lines amid shouts of '*Vive l'Empereur*!', Leipzig, the retreat from Moscow and the Abdication were as though they had never been.

Neither Napoleon nor his men doubted their ability to destroy Wellington's army and reach Brussels by nightfall. Their triumph over the Prussians two days before—achieved against superior numbers—had whetted their appetite for glory. They saw themselves, for all their difficulties, on the verge of a new Marengo. Nor was the urgent victory Napoleon needed the key only to political salvation. It would be a revenge for all the humiliations the English had heaped on him. Wellington was the one commander with a European reputation whom he had never beaten, and the British the one army. 'Because you have been defeated by Wellington,' he told his Chief of Staff, Soult, who dwelt on the British capacity for recoil, 'you think him a great general! I tell you that Wellington is a bad general, that the English are bad troops and that this will be a picnic!' His only fear was that they would vanish before he could attack them, as they had done on the previous day at Quatre Bras and seven years earlier under Moore on the Carrion. As, however, they now appeared to be calmly waiting for him, their doom was certain. 'We will sleep tonight,' he told his officers, 'in Brussels.'

Owing to the usual dispersal in search of food and plunder the last of the French only reached their battle stations at midday, three hours after the time originally ordered. Napoleon, however, was not hurrying, since to make full use of his superior artillery and cavalry, he wanted the soaked ground to dry. Despite warnings from those who had fought in Spain, he was quite sure that, once he struck in overpowering force, there would be little need to waste time in manœuvring. Most of Wellington's foreign auxiliaries, he reckoned, would bolt at the start, and the stiff redcoats would then break under the triple

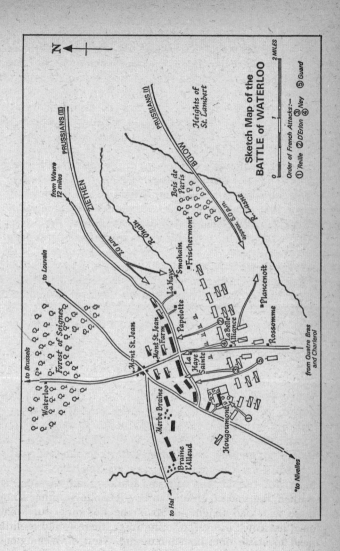

Sketch Map of the
BATTLE of WATERLOO

0   1   2 MILES

Order of French Attacks:—
① Reille ② D'Erlon ③ Ney
④   ⑤ Guard

N

Heights of
St. Lambert

PRUSSIANS II

BÜLOW

PRUSSIANS III

ZIETHEN

from Wavre
12 miles

R. Dyle

Bois de
Paris

R. Lasne

approx 5.0 p.m.

Frischermont

Plancenoit

Smohain

La Haye

Papelotte

La Belle
Alliance

Rossomme

from Quatre Bras
and Charleroi

to Louvain

Mont St. Jean

Mont St. Jean
Farm

La
Haye
Sainte

to Brussels

Forest of Soignes

Waterloo

Herbe Braine

Hougoumont

to Hal

Braine
l'Alleud

to Nivelles

shock of his massed bombardment, veteran columns, and discharge of grape at close range. 'I shall hammer them with my artillery,' he announced, 'charge them with my cavalry to make them show themselves, and, when I am quite sure where the actual English are, I shall go straight at them with my Old Guard.'[24]

As for the Prussians, he was so convinced that they had retreated eastwards, as he wished, that he never considered the possibility of their appearance on the battlefield at all. After the hiding he had given them at Ligny they were manifestly incapable of further fight for the present. Having detached Grouchy to shepherd them out of Flanders, he felt he could discount them. They could be trusted, as in the past, to act selfishly and leave their allies to their fate. It had never been his habit to keep faith with anyone unless it suited him. That a Prussian commander should endanger his army and strain his communications to keep faith with Wellington never occurred to him.

The Emperor therefore decided to open his main attack at one o'clock. In the meantime, while he massed eighty field-pieces on a spur of high ground in the middle of the valley opposite and about 600 yards short of the British centre, he ordered the troops on his two flanks to engage the extremities of the defenders' line at Papelotte and Hougoumont in order to distract attention from his impending blow, and probably—though of this there can be no certainty—to clear a way for the use, at the decisive moment, of the sunken hollow leading to the heart of Wellington's right. In that case, however, he was unfortunate in his adversary.

The first shots of the battle were fired shortly before noon in front of Hougoumont where Prince Jerome's division had been massing for some time. Actually Wellington himself had already been under fire there, but not from the enemy. For when earlier he had ridden down to check its defences, a battalion of Nassauers, lining an outlying hedge, believing the French to be about to attack, had suddenly panicked, and when, after rallying them and calming their fears, he was riding away, some of them, whether deliberately or unintentionally, had opened fire on him.[25]

At midday, after a short preliminary bombardment, four battalions of Prince Jerome's division advanced against the wood to the south of the château. During the next hour they succeeded in driving out its German defenders. But they then went on to attack the gardens and mansion and, in doing so, came up against a far more formidable adversary, the four light companies of the British Guards under Lord Saltoun. The attackers, closely watched by Wellington, who had stationed himself on the ridge immediately above, suffered exceedingly heavy casualties—1,500 in the first forty minutes—both from the aim of the British guardsmen, firing through embrasures in the walls, and from the accurate fire of Bull's howitzer battery stationed on the ridge. When the Guards counter-attacked and drove them back, Jerome threw another brigade into the assault and tried to gain a lodgment in the courtyard of the château. So furious was his attack that at one moment a detachment of his men broke open the great gate with an axe and swarmed in, only to be surrounded and destroyed inside, while four officers and a sergeant of the Coldstream closed the door behind them by main force. Once again the British counter-attacked with four companies of the Coldstream whom Wellington sent down from the ridge. 'There, my lads, in with you,' he said as they moved off, 'let me see no more of you.'

Jerome's answer, and that of the commander of the French left, General Reille, was to undertake—a quarter of an hour before Napoleon's main attack on the centre was due to begin—a third attack on Hougoumont with still larger forces. For every regiment they committed, the frugal Wellington staked no more than a company or whatever smaller force was necessary to hold the position. All the while his guns continued to shell the wood with such effect that, as one unending column of fresh attackers poured into it, another—of wounded—as continuously poured out.[26]

So far Napoleon had been only partially successful. His

diversion to the east had made little effect on the Netherlanders in Papelotte and La Haye, while the more important one to the west, though occupying Wellington's
attention, had failed either to by-pass or capture Hougoumont. It was now one o'clock, the hour at which the
bombardment of the Allied centre was due to begin. But
before its smoke enveloped the battlefield, Napoleon, watching the preparations from a knoll beside the Brussels road,
observed through his telescope a suspicious movement on
the high ground towards Wavre, five or six miles to the
east. Wellington, who knew what it was, had earlier seen it.
It might—at first it seemed to Napoleon that it must—be
Grouchy, from whom he had just heard that the Prussians
were retiring, not on Liège as both had thought, but on
Brussels. Yet this was now scarcely likely, as Grouchy, in
his dispatch, dated at six that morning, had announced his
intention of following them northwards on Wavre. And, as
Grouchy, like Napoleon, had been wrong once about the
Prussians' movements, there was another and less pleasant
possibility.

At that moment this terrifying suspicion was confirmed.
For a Prussian hussar—captured by a French vedette to
the east of the battlefield—was brought to Napoleon bearing a dispatch from Blücher to Wellington which showed
that the troops visible on the heights of St. Lambert were
Bülow's corps, advancing from Wavre, and that the rest of
the Prussian army had spent the night around that town,
only thirteen miles away.

Napoleon, in other words, had been 'making pictures'—
the crime against which he had always warned his sub-
ordinates. He had made his dispositions to fight under conditions that did not exist. Instead of having only the English and their feeble auxiliaries to contend with, if he
proceeded with his attack he would have to face before
nightfall the intervention of another army. His attempt
to separate Wellington's and Blücher's forces had failed, at
least in any but the most temporary sense. He must either
withdraw—the prudent course—shift his offensive to the
west—as Wellington had anticipated when he placed a

reserve force at Hal—or break through the British lines in the next three hours. For after that he would have to contend against two foes.

Being a gambler, and being, both politically and strategically, in desperate need of an immediate victory, Napoleon decided to proceed with his frontal attack. It still seemed unthinkable to him that the breach he was about to blast in the British centre could fail to defeat Wellington, and, with him out of the way, Blücher could be dealt with in turn. Indeed, with Grouchy in his rear and his army committed to the muddy defiles between Wavre and Mont St. Jean, the old Prussian might end the day in an even worse disaster than Ligny. Napoleon, therefore, detached part of his reserve to delay the still distant Prussian advance and ordered the attack on the British to proceed.

The eighty-gun bombardment, which opened at one o'clock, fully came up to expectations. Twenty-four of the guns were Napoleon's great twelve-pounders, with a 2,000 yards' range. It took away the breath of Wellington's young recruits and militiamen, and surprised even Peninsular veterans by its intensity. Captain Mercer, commanding a reserve battery of horse artillery in a hollow several hundred yards in rear of the British right flank, found, even in that sheltered position, the shot and shell continually plunging around him. One shot completely carried away the lower part of the head of one of his horses. Fortunately the ground was still wet and many shells burst where they fell, while the round-shot, instead of hopping and ricocheting for half a mile or more, frequently became embedded in the mud.[27]

But though very alarming, owing to Wellington's skilful dispositions the bombardment did comparatively little harm except to a brigade of Belgians, whose commander, General Bylandt, misinterpreting his orders, had drawn it up, in the Continental manner, on the forward slope of the ridge. During its half-hour of bombardment in this exposed position it lost one man in four, and, had it not been hastily withdrawn to a less conspicuous position, its loss might

have been still greater. When, therefore, at half-past one,
D'Erlon in charge of the French right moved his corps
forward to the attack, with all the panoply and terror of a
Napoleonic offensive—drums beating at the head of dense
columns, bearded grenadiers marching four hundred
abreast shouting at the top of their voices, and clouds of
tirailleurs running and firing ahead—the customary conditions for success seemed to have been ensured. Four divisions of infantry—more than 16,000 men—each moving in
close column of battalions at a quarter of a mile's distance,
tramped down the slope and up the hill against the British
centre and left through clouds of sulphurous smoke. Behind came companies of sappers, ready to turn the farm of
Mont St. Jean beyond the British centre into a fortress as
soon as it was captured.

A hail of shot from the artillery on the crest greeted
them. But it did not halt the men who had conquered at
Wagram and Friedland. One column, supported by
cuirassiers, swept round La Haye Sainte, encircling it and
its German defenders and driving back the two companies
of the Rifles—the most formidable marksmen in Europe—
who were stationed in a sandpit on the opposite side of the
chaussée. Another column, to the east, forced the Dutch
out of Papelotte and La Haye and temporarily occupied
Smohain. In the centre about 8,000 men approached the
summit simultaneously. As they did so, Bylandt's Belgians
—raw troops who had endured to the limit of their capacity—fired one hysterical volley at the advancing, shouting
column and took to their heels, carrying away the gunners
of the reserve batteries behind. They never stopped till they
reached the forest of Soignes, where they remained for the
rest of the day.[28]

To Napoleon, watching from the knoll near La Belle
Alliance, it seemed as though, as at Ligny, his adversary's
centre was broken. But it was not a Netherlander or even a
Prussian army he had to dislodge, but a British. As the
French bore down on the gap they had opened, Picton
deployed Kempt's reserve brigade in their path. 'The
French came on in the old style,' recalled Wellington—

who was viewing their advance from his command-post beside an elm tree where the Charleroi road crossed the sunken lane—'and we drove them off in the old style.' The 28th, 32nd, 79th Highlanders and the 95th Rifles—all veterans of Spain—held their fire till the head of the column was only twenty yards away. Then, from their thin extended line, they poured in their disciplined rolling volleys, and, as the leading French files tried, too late, to deploy, charged with the bayonet. At that moment Picton was struck in the head by a bullet and killed.[29]

Farther to the east, D'Erlon's two other divisions reached the summit. Here, after its heavy losses at Quatre Bras, Pack's brigade—Royals, 44th, 42nd and 92nd Highlanders —could only muster 1,400 bayonets. Slowly, against odds, they began to give ground, while a brigade of French cavalry on their flank, having cut a Hanoverian battalion to pieces, swarmed on to the crest to the west of the Brussels-Charleroi *chaussée*.

At this point, Wellington, who had anticipated what was going to happen, intervened decisively. Forming the last infantry battalions behind the gap in his dented line into square, he ordered Lord Uxbridge to launch the Household Brigade of heavy cavalry at the intruders, he himself leading the Life Guards into line and sending them off with a brisk, 'Now, gentlemen, for the honour of the Household Troops!' Leading the brigade in person, Uxbridge drove the astonished French cuirassiers into the ranks of the infantry behind, who, seeing the big, scarlet-coated Life Guardsmen slashing at them, turned and joined in the flight. It was the charge at Salamanca over again. Simultaneously the Union Brigade—consisting of Royal Dragoons, Scots Greys and Inniskillings—swept down on another French column to the east of the *chaussée*. Within a few minutes the flower of D'Erlon's corps was flying across the plain with 2,000 British cavalry after it. 'Hundreds of the infantry threw themselves down and pretended to be dead,' wrote Kincaid, 'while the cavalry galloped over them and then got up and ran away; I never saw such a scene in all my life.' More than 4,000 were cut down or taken prisoner. Many did. not stop till they reached Genappe.

Unfortunately the pursuers did not stop either. The secret of cavalry is iron discipline. It was a secret that the British cavalry, though superlative in dash, physique and horsemanship, had never wholly mastered. According to Hamilton of Dalzell of the Scots Greys, the troopers had been served with rum before the charge. They followed the French into the heart of Napoleon's position, sabring the gunners of his great battery and riding on to the ridge of La Belle Alliance itself as though they were after a fox. Having charged in the first line, Uxbridge was unable either to stop them or to bring up reserve cavalry in support. When the French cuirassiers and lancers counter-attacked in superior strength, the scattered, breathless men and horses were powerless and became themselves the pursued. The flower of Wellington's cavalry—the striking-force of his tactical reserve—having saved his centre, was itself needlessly destroyed. Sir William Ponsonby was struck down at the head of the Union Brigade, and nearly half the personnel of the six splendid regiments which had smashed D'Erlon's columns was killed or taken prisoner. Vandeleur's Brigade, which gallantly tried to cover their retreat, also suffered severely. Those who got back to the British lines were too few to intervene with real effect in the battle again.[30]

.   .   .

But for this unexpected advantage, there would have seemed little object in Napoleon's continuing the battle. It was now three o'clock. Not only had one of his two corps of front-line infantry become heavily committed to an increasingly costly and still unsuccessful struggle in front of Hougoumont, but the British, contrary to expectation, had repulsed and shattered the other which, untouched at either Ligny or Quatre Bras, was to have breached and pinned down Wellington's centre until Lobau's reserve infantry, Ney's cavalry and, at the end of all, the Imperial

Guard, had destroyed him. Instead, Napoleon now found himself committed to an impending battle on a second front, to avert or postpone which he was forced to detach, under Lobau, the very reserve of infantry which was to have followed up D'Erlon's expected success. With the Prussians approaching from the other side, he dared not commit this now to a left-hook against the British centre, the vital approach to which was still untaken. Apart from the small portion of Reille's corps still uncommitted to the unending fight round Hougoumont, he had no infantry left for a new attack on the ridge except the twenty-four battalions of the Imperial Guard. And these, in view of the growing threat to his flank and the, to him, unexpected revelation of British defensive striking-power, he was not yet prepared to commit. For the Guard was the last card that stood between him and ruin. He kept it, 13,000 strong, the apple of his eye, unused beside him.

For about half an hour there was a pause in the battle, except at Hougoumont, where Jerome and Foy threw ever more troops into the inferno round the blazing but still defiant buildings. Wellington took advantage of the lull to readjust his dispositions. Pack's brigade took the place vacated by Bylandt's Netherlanders, Lambert's brigade came up from the second line to strengthen Picton's battered division, and two more companies of the King's German Legion were thrown into La Haye Sainte. The Prussians were taking far longer to arrive than the British commander had expected. There had been a delay in their start, aggravated by a fire in the narrow streets of Wavre and the fact that Bülow's as yet unused corps in the van had the farthest distance to march. After the rains, the cross-country lanes were almost impassable for transport, and Gneisenau, the Prussian Chief of Staff, was reluctant to attack Napoleon, with Grouchy's troops in his rear, until he knew for certain that Wellington was standing fast. Only Blücher's insistence—for the old man, oblivious of his injuries, was with Bülow's advanced-guard by midday—carried the tired and hungry troops forward through the soggy defiles of the Lasne and the dense woods which lay between it and the battlefield. 'I have promised Wellington,' he told them as they dragged the guns axle-deep through mire, 'you would not have me break my word!'

Meanwhile the French gunners had taken up their position again on the central ridge and, soon after three o'clock, reopened their fire. It was more intense than anything the oldest Peninsular veteran had experienced. The range was so accurate that almost every shot told, and after a quarter of an hour Wellington withdrew his infantry a hundred yards farther back from the crest. Under cover of the bombardment, La Haye Sainte in the centre was again surrounded. But Baring's handful of King's German Legionaries continued to hold the walls, and with Kempt's and Lambert's men standing firm on the plateau above, D'Erlon's mangled infantry refrained from pressing home their assault. They seemed to fear a renewal of the storm of cavalry which had struck their comrades.

Suddenly the battle took a novel and spectacular form. For, mistaking the partial withdrawal of Wellington's infantry for the beginning of a general retirement, Marshal Ney decided to take a short cut to victory by sweeping the ridge with heavy cavalry. Of these—the finest in the world —his master had almost as many as Wellington's British infantry. He therefore ordered forward 5,000 of them, including eight regiments of cuirassiers, drawing them up in the plain immediately to the west of the *chaussée* where the slope was easiest.

Wellington watched the splendid spectacle with amazement. It seemed unbelievable that the French would dare to assail a line of unbroken British infantry with cavalry alone. But such was plainly their intention, and, with his own heavy cavalry too weakened to counter-charge in strength, there was a danger that, if Napoleon was able to bring up infantry and guns behind them, the defenders, forced to remain in square, might be blasted out of existence by case-shot. The two divisions to the west of the Brussels road—the 3rd and 1st—were ordered to form battalion squares or oblongs[31] in chequer-wise pattern across the gently swelling, corn-covered plateau. They were aligned so that every face of every square had a field of fire free of the next. Until the attackers appeared over the crest, Wellington ordered the men to lie down. Behind the twenty squares his cavalry, including the remnants of the two British heavy brigades, were drawn up in support.

Between and a little in advance of the squares Wellington placed his guns, bringing up his last two reserve batteries of Horse Artillery to inflict the utmost damage on the advancing cavalry. 'Ah! that's the way I like to see horse artillery move,'[32] he said, as Mercer's men, on the order, 'Left limber up, and as fast as you can!' galloped into the inferno of smoke and heat on the plateau. As they did so, they heard a humming like the sound of myriads of beetles on a summer's evening; so thick was the hail of balls and bullets, wrote their commander, that it seemed dangerous to extend the arm lest it should be torn off. Their orders, in the event of the enemy charging home, were to run for shelter to the nearest square, taking the near wheel of each gun with them.

Mercer disregarded this order—one that could only have been given to gun detachments of the highest discipline and training—not because he doubted his battery's morale, but because he believed that the young Brunswickers in square on either side of him, who were falling fast, would take to their heels if they saw his men run. As soon as the French appeared out of the smoke a hundred yards away—a long line of cuirasses and helmets glittering like a gigantic wave on the crest of the rye—he ordered his six nine-pounders, doubly loaded with round-shot and case, to open fire. As the case poured into them, the leading ranks went down like grass before a skilled mower. Again and again, when the French charged, the same thing happened, and the Brunswickers who, before the battery's arrival, had stood like soulless logs in their agony and had only been kept at their posts by the gallantry of their officers, recovered heart.

Elsewhere, where the gunners obeyed Wellington's orders, the French cavalry, crowded in a dense mass into

the half-mile gap between Hougoumont and La Haye
Sainte, rode over the abandoned guns and swept round
the squares beyond. They did not gallop like English foxhunters, but came, as was their wont, at a slow, majestic
pace and in perfect formation, their horses shaking the
earth. As they appeared the British infantry rose at the
word of command, their muskets at the ready and their
bayonets bristling like gigantic *chevaux de frise*. If the
cavalry of the Empire were Atlantic breakers, the British
squares were the rocks of an iron coast. The men, many
of them rosy-faced youngsters from the plough, were much
impressed by the splendid appearance of the hordes of
legendary horsemen who suddenly encircled them, and
even more by their courage. But they were not intimidated
by them, as Ney had intended. As their experienced officers
and NCOs seemed to regard the newcomers as harmless,
in their stolid, unimaginative English way they did so too.
The cuirassiers and lancers made a great deal of noise and
glitter, brandishing their weapons like pantomime giants
and shouting '*Vive l'Empereur*,' but they seemed infinitely
preferable to the continuous hail of shot and shell which
had poured from the French batteries till they arrived on
the ridge.

Short of impaling their horses on the hedges of bayonets,
Ney's cavalry tried every device to break the squares.
Occasionally little groups of horsemen, led by frantic
officers, would dash for the face of one, firing off carbines
and pistols and hoping to draw sufficient fire to enable
their comrades behind to break in on a line of unloaded
muskets. But the British and Hanoverian squares preserved
perfect discipline, withholding their fire until they received
the word of command and then, with their volleys, bringing down everything before them. The loss of horses was
prodigious; the poor creatures lay dead or dying in hundreds, their riders, many of them wounded, making their
way in a continuous stream back down the hill, or sprawl-
ing in their heavy cuirasses in the mud, looking, as Wellington afterwards recalled, like overturned turtles.[33]

Whenever he judged that the intruders were sufficiently

worn down and wearied, Wellington endeavoured to push
them off the plateau with his cavalry, or, in default, by
edging forward his squares in échelon towards the abandoned guns. He did not hurry, for he was playing for time,
and he could not afford to let his light British and King's
German Legion cavalry encounter the heavier armed
cuirassiers until the latter were too exhausted and reduced
to retaliate. The foreign Horse which he had brought up
from the flanks and reserve to take the place of Ponsonby's
and Somerset's lost squadrons proved, most of it, worse
than useless, refusing repeated appeals from Uxbridge to
charge. One regiment of Hanoverian hussars, led by its
colonel,[34] fled as far as Brussels.

Even the British cavalry showed a reluctance at times to
charge home in the face of such overwhelming weight and
numbers, though several regiments, particularly the 13th
Light Dragoons and the 15th Hussars, behaved with the
greatest gallantry. The shock felt by men encountering for
the first time the sights and sounds of battle—and such a
battle—had in the nature of things a more paralysing effect
on cavalry than on infantry whose men in square had the
close support of officers and comrades. Once Uxbridge,
whose energy and initiative throughout this critical time
was beyond praise, was driven into exclaiming that he had
tried every brigade and could not get one to follow him,
and then, as he rode up to the 1st Foot Guards, 'Thank
God, I am with men who make me not ashamed of being
an Englishman.'[35] One of the officers recalled how, while
Wellington was sheltering in his square, the men were so
mortified at seeing the cuirassiers deliberately walking their
horses round them that they shouted, 'Where are our
cavalry? Why don't they come and pitch into these French
fellows?' Such resentment failed to take into account the
hopeless numerical inferiority of the Allied cavalry after
its earlier losses, and was based on an incomplete view of
the battlefield. All the hard-pressed infantrymen could see,
amid clouds of thick, eddying smoke, was the outer face of
the square on either side, and the hordes of encircling
French Horse. They could not realise that the very pre-

sence of the decimated English squadrons in their rear helped to sustain the wavering morale of the Netherlanders and Brunswickers, and that the memory of their earlier and heroic onslaught accounted for Napoleon's failure to follow up his cavalry with infantry and subject their squares to case-shot at close range.

Five times in two hours the French horsemen were driven from the plateau; five times, after rallying in the plain, they returned. Whenever they disappeared the British gunners ran out of the squares and reopened fire, while Napoleon's guns resumed their cannonade. Some time after five o'clock Ney brought up the last cavalry from the second line—Kellermann's two divisions of cuirassiers and the heavy squadrons of the Imperial Guard. At one moment more than 9,000 Horse assailed the ridge in a compact phalanx. This immense body was packed in the 800 yards' front between the *chaussée* and the British bastion at Hougoumont, where the ground was a morass piled with dead horses. The front ranks, including most of the senior officers, were completely wiped out by the English batteries, and the weary mounts could only proceed at a walk. Yet they still continued to return.

Throughout this time and during the bombardments which preceded each assault the British infantry patiently endured their fate. They seemed in their steady squares to be rooted to the ground. Though it would have been hazardous in the extreme to have manœuvred with some of the young British and Hanoverian Landwehr battalions, they showed themselves, under their fine officers and NCOs, as capable of standing fire as the oldest veterans. Theirs, as Harry Smith said, was no battle of science; it was a stand-up fight between two pugilists, milling away till one or the other was beaten. Inside each suffocating square, reeking with the smell of burnt cartridge and powder, it was like a hospital, the dead and dying strewing the ground. The sufferings of many of the wounded were indescribable; one rifleman had both legs shot off and both arms amputated, but continued to breathe as he lay amid his comrades. Few cried out in their pain, and, when they did so, their officers immediately quieted them;[36] it was a point of pride with Englishmen of all classes to take punishment without murmuring. Their stoicism was equalled by that of the French cavalry, who won the ungrudging admiration of the entire British army.[37]

Nor was less courage shown by the defenders of Hougoumont. The flank companies in the burnt-out mansion among the charred remains of their comrades, the Coldstream lining the hedge and garden wall, the 3rd Guards in the orchard, all lived that day up to the highest tradition of the Brigade of Guards. They had made up their minds to die sooner than yield. Three times the wood was taken and retaken; every tree was riddled with bullets, and in the orchard alone more than two thousand bodies were crowded together. 'You may depend upon it,' said Wellington, 'no troops could have held Hougoumont but British, and only the best of them.'

.   .   .

The British Commander-in-Chief neither avoided nor courted danger, but, knowing that his presence was necessary to keep his young soldiers to the sticking-point, he showed himself, placid and unconcerned, wherever the fire was hottest. Riding up and down his hard-pressed lines 'slowly and coolly,' as Lieutenant Wheatley of the King's German Legion twice saw him that afternoon, with an ever-dwindling staff and at one time without even a single aide, he seemed completely calm and oblivious of the storm of shot around him. Every now and then, with his raised telescope, he surveyed the battlefield, ready to anticipate the enemy's every movement. Whenever the French cavalry, swarming over the ridge, made it necessary, he withdrew into one of the squares. 'Wait a little longer, lads,' he called out to the men in one of them, as they begged to be allowed to avenge their sufferings with the bayonet, 'you shall have at them, presently.' Everywhere he infected men, near the limit of endurance, with courage and confidence.[38]

G

During the last hour of Ney's cavalry attacks the sound of Prussian guns had been audible on the British ridge in the lulls of firing, though few yet realised its import. By four o'clock, the two leading divisions of Bülow's corps had reached the western edge of Paris wood, just over two miles east of La Belle Alliance. Half an hour later, in view of the urgency of Wellington's messages, they went into action without waiting for their supports. Soon after five, when they had advanced to within a mile and a half of the Brussels road, Lobau counter-attacked and drove them back. But at six o'clock, two more Prussian divisions having emerged from the wood, Bülow again attacked, striking round Lobau's southern flank at Plancenoit, a village less than a mile from the French life-line.

The situation was growing grave in the extreme for Napoleon. His troops had been marching and fighting almost continuously for four days; their losses during the afternoon had been heavier than in any engagement of comparable scale in his career. Again and again they had seemed on the point of carrying the ridge and sweeping Wellington's international flotsam and jetsam down the Brussels road. Yet whenever the smoke cleared, the stubborn redcoats were seen to be still standing. The Prussian shot, already playing on the *chaussée*, brought home to the Emperor that, unless he could break Wellington's line in the remaining hours of daylight, his doom was certain.

Though, like his adversary, still in his middle forties, the Emperor had so far taken little active part in the direction of the assault. After a study of the battlefield in the early hours and the issue of orders for the attack, he had delegated tactical control to Ney. Exhausted by the exertions of the last three days and suffering from a severe attack of piles, he had spent part of the afternoon at his headquarters at Rossomme in what seemed to onlookers a coma, and had not even intervened to stay the impetuous Marshal's abuse of his cavalry. But he now roused himself, to snatch, as so often in the past, victory from defeat.

He had to fight on two fronts. To the south-east 30,000 Prussians were striking at his communications; to the north 20,000 Britons and as many or more Germans and Netherlanders were still barring the Brussels road. Despite his casualties he still had between 50,000 and 60,000 veteran troops, though of Grouchy's 33,000, wandering somewhere in space to the east,[39] there was no sign. To clear his flank and gain time for a further assault on the British, he dispatched eight Young Guard battalions of the Imperial Guard to reinforce Lobau and recover Plancenoit. Simultaneously he gave Ney peremptory orders to throw in infantry and capture La Haye Sainte.

Conscious that the crisis of the battle was at hand and that the interminable and futile attacks of the French cavalry must now be followed up by infantry, Wellington had already reorganised his line. Taking advantage of the lull after the last charge, he had brought up Clinton's division of Peninsular veterans from its place in reserve to a point at which, standing between the defenders of Hougoumont and Maitland's Guards, they could enfilade any attack on his right. Feeling that Hougoumont was now secure and that, as a result, no threat could develop from that quarter, he also summoned Chassé's Netherlanders from Braine L'Alleud and placed them in rear of his centre. Simultaneously, seeing that Ney's force was spent, he deployed his shrunken battalions from square, forming them four-deep instead of in the normal two-rank line so as to give extended fire-power against infantry while preserving sufficient solidity to repel what remained of the French cavalry.[40]

Soon after six Ney attacked in the centre with two columns of infantry and cavalry. They were driven back by a terrific fire from the British guns. But the French were fighting magnificently and with the recklessness of despair, and the young Prince of Orange, in charge of the defenders at this point, was without experience of command. Repeating a mistake made at Quatre Bras, he ordered one of Ompteda's battalions of the King's German Legion above La Haye Sainte to deploy in the presence of cavalry, with disastrous consequences. Their comrades inside the farmhouse were now down to their last round of

ammunition,[41] and at about six-thirty the key to the British
centre was captured. Baring's remaining forty men fought
their way back to the ridge with the bayonet. At about
the same time the eight battalions of the Young Guard,
sent to Lobau's aid, recovered Plancenoit.

This double success gave the French, at the eleventh
hour, a chance of victory. Throwing sharpshooters and
guns forward from the captured farm, they established
themselves on the ridge and opened a destructive fire on the
left of the 3rd Division and the right of the 5th. The
Prince of Orange, who had by now completely lost his
head, deployed another of Ompteda's battalions in the
presence of cavalry with the same disastrous result. A few
minutes later Ompteda was killed. His shattered brigade
and that of Kielmansegge's young Hanoverians had
reached the limit of their endurance and were on the
point of breaking. An immediate break through the British
centre was only averted by a timely charge of the 3rd
Hussars of the Legion and the gallantry of the 1st Battalion of the 95th Rifles, whose accurate fire from the
hedgerow to which they had fallen back from the adjacent
gravel-pit after the capture of La Haye Sainte, alone prevented the enemy field-guns from establishing themselves
on the summit and raking the defenders' entire line
from close range.

Had Napoleon been on the spot to exploit the opportunity, he might have turned the gap in the British centre
into a chasm. But when, still watching from La Belle
Alliance three-quarters of a mile away, he received Ney's
urgent appeal for more infantry, he only asked petulantly
whether the Marshal expected him to make them. At the
crisis of his gamble his moral courage faltered; he was not
yet ready to stake everything. And while the twelve remaining battalions of the Imperial Guard waited, unused,
Wellington, summoned from his position with the Guards
Division above Hougoumont, galloped to the spot, calling
up every remaining available unit.

The British Commander-in-Chief took the news of the
disaster to his centre with his habitual calm and decision.

Colonel Shaw Kennedy of the hard-pressed 3rd Division, General Alten's chief staff-officer who reported it to him, said that he received it 'with a degree of coolness and . . . with such precision and energy as to prove the most complete self-possession. . . . From the determined manner in which he spoke, it was evident that he had resolved to defend to the last extremity every inch of the position which he then held. His Grace's answer to my representation was, "I shall order Brunswick troops in reserve behind Maitland to the spot, and other troops besides. Go you and get all the German troops of the division to the spot that you can, and all guns that you can find." '[42] Then, sending for Vivian's light cavalry brigade from its reserve position behind Papelotte, as nearly all the Allied leaders in the centre had by now been killed or wounded he temporarily took over command there himself. Leading five young Brunswicker battalions into the full storm of the French batteries, he rallied them when they broke under that hurricane of shot and brought them steadily back into line. Swarms of *tirailleurs,* formed from D'Erlon's broken divisions, were now everywhere infiltrating the ridge, keeping the long-tried British squares under continuous fire at close range—a thing which would have been impossible had Uxbridge's heavy cavalry not suffered such disastrous losses through their inability to control their own triumphant charge earlier in the day. But the *tirailleurs* were driven back when Vivian, anticipating Wellington's orders and seeing a new force of Prussians moving up from the east, arrived on his own initiative from the left of the ridge. Simultaneously Uxbridge galloped off to fetch Vandeleur's 11th, 12th and 16th Light Dragoons, and Somerset, with the wreck of the Union Brigade extended in single rank to make the utmost show, instilled confidence and pressure from behind into Chassé's Netherlanders.

Once again a desperate situation had been saved by Wellington's action. But the losses of the battered 3rd Division were desperate. When Sir Colin Halkett, two-thirds of whose brigade had fallen, asked if it could be temporarily relieved, Wellington replied to his message,

'Tell him what he asks is impossible. He and I, and every Englishman on the field, must die on the spot which we occupy.'[43]

The bombardment had now reached a new degree of intensity as Napoleon brought up every available gun to reinforce his massed batteries. All along the Allied centre men were going down like ninepins; close by the cross-roads 450 of the 700 men of the 27th lay in square where they had fallen. In a neighbouring regiment—the 40th—both ensigns and fourteen sergeants had been killed or wounded round the tattered colours. The 5th Division, 5,000 strong when the battle started, seemed almost to have dwindled to a line of skirmishers. Kincaid with the Rifles began to wonder whether there had ever been a battle in which everyone on both sides had been killed.[44] The stream of wounded and fugitives towards the rear was so great that a Prussian aide-de-camp, who rode up from Ziethen's oncoming corps to investigate, returned with a report that the British were defeated and in retreat. No one knew what was happening outside his own immediate vicinity, for in the windless, oven-like, smoke-filled air visibility was reduced to a few yards.

Yet Wellington's grip on the battle never relaxed. Unlike his imperial adversary he was used to commanding comparatively small armies and to attending to every tactical detail himself. At one point, riding up to a square of the 1st Battalion of the Rifles which had lost its senior officers, he himself gave them the command, '95th, unfix your swords, left face and extend yourselves once more; we shall soon have them over the hill!' Then, according to the rifleman who recalled the incident, 'he rode away on our right, and how he escaped being shot, God only knows, for all that time the shot was flying like hailstones.'[45]

Lord Uxbridge, who had never before served under him, said after the battle that his coolness and decision in action surpassed anything he could have conceived. 'I thought I had heard enough of this man,' he told Lady Shelley, 'but he has far surpassed my expectations. It is not a man but a god.' 'Cool and indifferent at the beginning of battles,'

Sir Alexander Frazer, his artillery commander, wrote of him, 'when the moment of difficulty comes, intelligence flashes from the eyes of this wonderful man and he rises superior to all that can be imagined.'[46]

Almost every member of his staff had by now fallen, his Quartermaster, General de Lancey, and his leading aide, Colonel Canning—both killed by his side—his military secretary, Fitzroy Somerset, dangerously wounded, and his beloved Alexander Gordon, companion of every Peninsular campaign, with his thigh fatally shattered by a cannon-ball as he helped him rally the Brunswickers. Yet though he looked thoughtful and pale, he betrayed no sign of anxiety.[47] Once, when chatting with the commanding officer of a square in which he had taken shelter, he was heard to say, 'Oh, it will be all right; if the Prussians come up in time, we shall have a long peace.' But occasionally he looked at his watch.

'Hard pounding this, gentlemen,' he observed, 'but we will see who can pound the longest.' And when the smoke for a moment drifted away and the scanty lines of red were seen everywhere to be standing, a cheer went up from his tired countrymen that showed him to be justified. The hour for which he and they had endured so much was near. For streaming on to the east end of the battlefield from Smohain, driving the French from the environs of Papelotte and La Haye, where Bernhard of Saxe-Weimar's steady Nassauers had been holding their own all day, and filling in the two-mile gap between Bülow's men before Plancenoit and the left of the British line, came Ziethen's long-awaited Prussian corps. Recalled in the nick of time by General Müffling, who had galloped after it when, in the belief that the British were defeated, it had started to withdraw, its intervention—so long delayed—was far more decisive than Bülow's earlier, more distant attack on Plancenoit. As the Prussian batteries, adding their quota to the inferno on the ridge,[48] began to shell the ground near La Belle Alliance, Napoleon knew that the supreme crisis was at hand. Already from his right rear news had come that the Young Guard had been driven out of Plancenoit. The field was closing in as it had done at Leipzig, and the night was little more than an hour away.

Soon after seven, the Emperor took his final resolution. He sent two of the magnificent, untouched battalions of the Old Guard to recapture Plancenoit and prevent encirclement. Then, bidding his aides-de-camp announce that it was Grouchy, not the Prussians, who had arrived from the east, he ordered a general advance of all units. As its spearhead he brought forward the remaining battalions of the Imperial Guard, keeping only three as a last reserve. With the former he descended the plain, marching at their head towards the British ridge. As he did so the French guns again increased their tempo.

Fresh from its triumph at Ligny two nights before, the Guard advanced with a deeply impressive *élan*. Its men were conscious that they bore the destinies of the world. Such was their tremendous prestige that the two veteran battalions who had been sent to recapture Plancenoit did so in twenty minutes without firing a shot and in the face of 25,000 Prussians. Those advancing against the British were inspired by the personal presence of Napoleon. At the foot of the slope, in a sheltered hollow, he halted to let them pass, throwing open his greatcoat to display his medals and repeatedly crying out, '*A Bruxelles, mes enfants! à Bruxelles!*' They answered with shouts of '*Vive l'Empereur!*' and pressed forward with solemn tread and shouldered arms. In front of each regiment rode a general, Marshal Ney—'*le rougeaud*'—with powder-blackened face and tattered uniform, directing all. Cavalry moved on their flanks, and in the intervals between the battalions came field-pieces loaded with case-shot. Ahead went a cloud of sharpshooters. Simultaneously, closely observed by Wellington through his telescope, what remained of Reille's three divisions moved up for a new assault on Hougoumont, while to the east of the Brussels *chaussée* D'Erlon's regrouped corps massed for one last blow against the battered British left centre. Everything Napoleon possessed was being staked on a final culminating bid for victory.

The Guard went up the hill in two columns, the one

moving obliquely up a spur from the Brussels road towards the centre of the British right, the other using, so far as Wellington's dispositions admitted, the sheltered ground between La Belle Alliance and Hougoumont. True to the tactical conception which had dominated the earlier attacks, the frontal blow was to be clinched by a left hook. But with Hougoumont firmly held and Du Plat's Hanoverians and Adam's brigade of Light Infantry deployed by the Duke across the hollow way between it and the ridge, the front on which the attackers could operate was narrower than ever. And, with his unerring tactical sense, Wellington was waiting at the very spot at which his adversary's main knock-out blow was aimed : on the right of the Guards Division where it touched the left battalion —the 2nd 95th—of Adam's brigade. Warned of the imminent approach of the Imperial Guard by a deserting royalist colonel, as well as by what he had seen through his field-glass before the marching columns disappeared into the declivity below the ridge and by the ominous, ever-nearing throbbing of the imperial drums, he had ordered his men to lie down in the corn until the French appeared; their long vigil of endurance, he told them, would soon be over.

Until the columns reached the summit Wellington's artillerymen, serving their exposed guns on the ridge till the last possible moment, drove swathes of death through them. In the general darkness and confusion, and because of the fire from the guns on the ridge, the leading battalions of the first column struck the British line at two points : where Halkett's battered brigade of the 3rd Division was drawn up in front of Chassé's Netherlanders, and immediately to the west where Wellington was waiting with Maitland's 1st Guards. As the huge bearskins loomed suddenly out of the swirling mist and smoke, the Commander-in-Chief's voice rang out, 'Now, Maitland, now's your time,' followed by the order—taken up by officers and the sergeants along the ranks—'Stand up, Guards! Make ready! Fire!' Then the British sprang to their feet in the corn and, enfilading the advancing files from either

side, poured from their extended lines a tremendous and
shattering volley, following it up by the familiar rolling
fire by platoons and half companies which had broken so
many French columns. The 'Immortals' tried to deploy
but too late, and most of their leading officers were swept
down. Then, while they were still in confusion, the British
Guards charged.

But though the Imperial Guard recoiled, it did not yet
break. Both parts of the main column re-formed and
opened fire on the oncoming British, their field-guns supporting them with case. To the east the remnants of the
33rd and 69th were driven back by a smaller column and
almost broke, but were rallied by Halkett and by Wellington himself, who galloped quickly to the scene. A Dutch
battery, behaving with great coolness and gallantry, raked
the French column, and Chassé's Belgians, 3,000 strong,
kept in position by Vivian's shepherding cavalry in their
rear, came up in support. Gradually the attackers, isolated
and without support behind them, began to give ground.
Meanwhile those opposed to the 1st Guards, though driven
back for some distance, had also rallied. Maitland ordered
his Guardsmen back, but his voice could not be heard above
the firing, and some of them, mistaking his intention, tried
to form square. In the confusion the two British battalions
withdrew in some disorder, only to re-form at the word of
command, with flawless and habitual steadiness, on regain-
ing their original position.

But before the battle between the rival Guards could be
resumed, it was decided by the action of the most experienced regiment on the British side. Wellington always
maintained that, if he had had at Waterloo the army with
which he crossed the Pyrenees, he would have attacked
Napoleon without waiting for the Prussians : 'I should have
swept him off the face of the earth,' he said, 'in two hours.'[49]
The first battalion of the 52nd, commanded by John
Colborne, afterwards Lord Seaton, had served in John
Moore's original Light Brigade; Colborne himself was
Moore's finest living pupil. It had gone into action at
Waterloo with more than a thousand bayonets, half of

them veterans of the Spanish War, being one of the very few British battalions which were up to strength—'a regiment,' wrote Napier of its Peninsular exploits, 'never surpassed in arms since arms were first borne by men.' Owing to the skilful way in which Colborne had placed and handled it during the French cavalry charges and the long hours of bombardment, its casualties had been extraordinarily light.

As the second and westernmost column of the Imperial Guard after passing by Hougoumont pressed up the slope towards Maitland's unbroken line, the drummers beating the *hummadum, dummadum, dum,* of the *pas de charge,* Colborne, who was stationed in the centre of Adam's brigade to the right of the Guards, took a sudden decision. Without orders either from the Duke or any superior officer, he moved his battalion forward out of the line for a distance of three hundred yards, and then, as it drew level with the leading company of the advancing French column, wheeled it to the left as though on parade, with the order, 'Right shoulders forward.' He thus laid it on the flank of the French. By doing so he took the risk both of leaving a gap in the line behind and of having his men cut to pieces by cavalry—a fate he had experienced when, as one of Stewart's brigade commanders, he had moved up the hill at Albuera.

The reward of his daring was decisive. The Imperial Guard, taken by surprise, halted and poured a volley into the 52nd which brought down a hundred and forty of its men. But the British reply of this grave Roman battalion was decisive. It seemed as though every bullet found its mark. So heavy were the casualties in the dense column that the Imperial Guard did not wait for the 52nd to charge. It faltered, broke and fled. As it did so, the 52nd resumed its advance eastwards across, and at right angles to, the British front, with the two other battalions of Adam's brigade—the 95th and 71st—moving up on Wellington's instructions on either flank and firing devastating volley after volley into the recoiling veterans' ranks. A few hundred yards on, this magnificent brigade, so care-

fully husbanded for this decisive moment, encountered another French column re-forming, and dealt it the same
treatment and with the same results.

Then, as with cries of *'La Garde recule!'* the disordered
assailants of that impregnable ridge fell back once more,
Wellington was seen to raise his hat high in the air and
wave it three times towards the enemy. With the instinct
of genius, he realised that the moment for which he and
his men had waited had at last come. 'Oh, damn it!' he
was heard to say, 'In for a penny, in for a pound!' One
who was with him told Lady Shelley afterwards that the
expression of his face at that moment was almost super-
human. Then, hat still raised high, he galloped eastwards
along the ridge from one tattered, enduring regiment to
another. 'Who commands here?' he shouted to Harry
Smith, Lambert's brigade major. 'Generals Kempt and
Lambert, my Lord.' 'Desire them to form column of companies and move on immediately.' 'In what direction, my
Lord?' 'Right ahead, to be sure.'[50] And when, uncertain
whether to proceed farther in its daring march across the
flank of the discomfited attackers, the 52nd halted for
instructions, the Commander-in-Chief, spurring down to
it, called out, 'Well done! Go on, Colborne, go on! Don't
give them time to rally! They won't stand!'

It was now nearly dusk. But, as the French cannonade
ceased and the smoke began to drift from the ridge, the
setting sun, breaking through the low clouds of that long
day, cast a ray of light along the glinting British line,
motionless no more, and on the accoutrements of the
defeated columns in the plain. The whole French army
was suddenly dissolving with the landscape: entire regiments leaving their arms piled and taking to their heels.
From the east the Prussians were pouring in a great flood
across the battlefield, and to the south, where the Old and
Young Guard were still fighting fiercely to keep Napoleon's
life-line open, Bülow's men had swept through Plancenoit
and were approaching the *chaussée*. 'I have seen nothing
like that moment,' wrote Frazer of the Artillery, 'the sky
literally darkened with smoke, the sun just going down and

which till then had not for some hours broken through the gloom of a dull day, the indescribable shouts of thousands where it was impossible to distinguish between friends and foe.'

In that final advance, with scattered units of British and French cavalry appearing out of the darkening gloom in charge and counter-charge, and little groups of French gunners and a few unbroken squares of the Old Guard fighting to give their Emperor time to escape, Lord Uxbridge, riding forward by the Duke's side, had his leg shattered by a shell. 'By God! I've lost my leg,' he said. 'Have you, by God!' replied his chief as he dismounted and helped him to the ground. Then, as with stoic grandeur Uxbridge let himself be carried away, the Duke rode on, following the receding fight. Most of the British regiments were so exhausted that they halted in the plain. Only the cavalry and Adam's brigade, harrying the last retreating squares of the Imperial Guard, proceeded through the heart of what had once been the French position. 'We are getting into enclosed ground and your life is too valuable to be thrown away,' urged one of Wellington's entourage. 'Never mind,' he answered, 'let them fire away. The battle's won; my life is of no consequence now.'[51]

As Ziethen's Prussian cavalry from the east and Vivian's and Vandeleur's British from the north met at La Belle Alliance, the union of the armies, fought for so fiercely during three days and nights, was consummated. Somewhere between nine and ten o'clock the two men whose good faith, constancy and resolution had made it possible, met on the spot where Napoleon had launched his attack. They were both on horseback, but the old Prussian embraced and kissed his English friend, exclaiming, *'Mein lieber Kamerad,'* and then, *'Quelle affaire!'* which, as Wellington observed, was about all the French he knew.

Then, having agreed on plans for the pursuit, in weariness and darkness Wellington turned his tired horse towards Waterloo and the ridge he had so long defended. He rode in silence across a battlefield in which 15,000 men of his own army, including a third of the British troops engaged, and more than 30,000 Frenchmen lay dead, dying or wounded. The sound of gunfire had ceased, but, to the south, trumpets could be faintly heard as the Prussian cavalry took up the pursuit of their inexorable enemies. As their infantry, many of whom had marched fifty miles in the past two days, debouched from Plancenoit into the Charleroi highway, where the 52nd, with its tattered colours, was halted by the roadside, they broke into slow time and their bands played 'God Save the King.'[52]

* * *

It was eleven o'clock before the victor dismounted outside the inn at Waterloo. As he patted the horse which had borne him so patiently all day, Copenhagen made his commentary on the terrible battle through which he had passed by suddenly lashing out and breaking free.[53] Inside the inn Wellington bent over the prostrate form of Colonel Gordon, the faithful aide-de-camp who had been with him ever since he sailed for Portugal in 1809 and whose leg had been amputated three hours earlier. 'Thank God you are safe,' Gordon whispered, as his life began to ebb. But the Duke, hoping for his recovery, ordered him to be carried to his own bed.

There were forty or fifty persons gathered for supper in the crowded inn, including several high-ranking prisoners, among them General Lobau and General Cambronne of the Imperial Guard who was to go down to history with the false legend of having defied surrender with the words, '*La Vielle Garde—qui meurt mais ne se rend pas.*'[54] But though Wellington ordered them to be given some supper, as traitors to the King to whom they had sworn allegiance he declined to let them remain, saying, '*Messieurs, j'en suis bien fâché, mais je ne puis pas avoid l'honneur de vous recevoir jusq'à ce que vous avez fait votre paix avec Sa Majesté Trés-Chrétienne.*' His own table had been laid, as always in a campaign, for his personal staff, but there were only Alava and one or two others to share it with him. Whenever the door opened, he looked up in hope, but no more came to that silent feast of ghosts. Presently he held up his hands and said to Alava, 'The hand of Almighty God has been upon me this day.' Then he raised his glass and gave a single toast : 'To the memory of the Peninsular War !' immediately afterwards he lay down on a pallet on the floor and, exhausted, fell asleep.

Soon after 3 a.m. he was awoken by his surgeon, Dr. Hume, who told him that Gordon was dying. He rose at once and went to him, but found him already dead. As the doctor, taking his proffered hand, read the list of those whose deaths had been reported during the night, he felt tears on his hand and, looking up, saw them coursing down the Duke's battle-grimed face. 'Well, thank God I don't know what it is to lose a battle,' he said when Hume had finished. 'But nothing can be more painful than to gain one with the loss of so many friends.'[55]

Then he rose, washed and dressed and sat down for an hour to begin his Waterloo dispatch to the Secretary of State. 'It gives me great satisfaction,' he began, 'to assure your Lordship that the army never, upon any occasion, conducted itself better. The Division of Guards, under Lieut-General Cooke, who is severely wounded, Major-General Maitland and Major-General Byng, set an example which was followed by all; and there is no officer nor description of troops that did not behave well. . . .' But though his dispatch dwelt on the army's losses, there was little in it about victory and glory, and it was so laconic that, when it was published in London, the American Minister, Quincy Adams, at first believed it came from a defeated general whose army had been annihilated.[56]

So many of the staff and general officers had been killed or wounded that, with their places to fill and urgent orders to be given for the pursuit of the French, at 5 a.m. the Duke, with his dispatch unfinished, mounted his horse and rode to Brussels. Here all the bells were ringing and the reprieved people shouting in the streets.[57] Sitting at the open window of his hotel room, Wellington resumed his task. There was a crowd outside, including Thomas Creevey who recorded for posterity what happened. 'Upon recognising me, he immediately beckoned to me with his finger to come up. . . . The first thing I did was to put my hand out and congratulate him upon his victory. He made a variety of observations in his short, natural, blunt way, but with the greatest gravity all the time, and without the least approach to anything like triumph or joy. "It has been a damned serious business," he said, "Blücher and I have lost 30,000 men. It has been a damned nice thing—the nearest run thing you ever saw in your life. Blücher lost 14,000 on Friday night, and got so damnably licked I could not find him on Saturday morning; so I was obliged to fall back to keep up communications with him." Then, as he walked about, he praised greatly those Guards who kept the farm (meaning Hougoumont) against the repeated attacks of the French; and then he praised all our troops, uttering repeated expressions of astonishment at our men's courage. He repeated so often its being *so nice a thing—so nearly run a thing*, that I asked him if the French had fought better than he had ever seen them do before. "No," he said, "they have always fought the same since I first saw them at Vimiero." Then he said, "By God! I don't think it would have done if I had not been there." '58

As well as his dispatches the Duke wrote that day to those whose near relations had served on his staff and fallen. 'I cannot express to you,' he assured Lord Aberdeen, brother of his beloved Alexander Gordon, 'the regret and sorrow with which I look around me and contemplate the loss which I have sustained, particularly in your brother. The glory resulting from such actions, so dearly bought, is no consolation to me, and I cannot suggest it is any to you. . . . But I hope that this last one has been so decisive . . . that our exertions and our individual losses will be rewarded by the early attainment of our just object. It is then that the glory of the actions in which our friends and relations have fallen will be some consolation for their loss.'59 In a similar letter to the Duke of Beaufort about Lord Fitzroy Somerset, he wrote, 'The losses I have sustained have quite broken me down and I have no feeling for the advantages we have acquired.' 'The Duke,' Georgina Capel reported from Brussels—a city now become a hospital 'crowded with wounded wretches and with wagons filled with dead and dying'—'was never known to be in such low spirits as he was in consequence of the blood shed at Waterloo.' 'It was the most desperate business I ever was in,' he told his brother, William. 'I never took so much trouble about any battle, and never was so near being beat. Our loss is immense, particularly in that best of all instruments, British Infantry. I never saw the Infantry behave so well.'[60]

Three weeks after the battle, when his victorious troops had entered Paris, the Duke spoke again of his feelings to his friend, Lady Shelley. 'I hope to God,' he said, 'that I have fought my last battle. It is a bad thing to be always fighting. While in the thick of it I am too much occupied to feel anything; but it is wretched just after. It is quite impossible to think of glory. Both mind and feelings are exhausted. I am wretched even at the moment of victory, and I always say that, next to a battle lost, the greatest misery is a battle gained. Not only do you lose those dear friends with whom you have been living, but you are forced to leave the wounded behind you. To be sure, one tries to do the best for them, but how little that is ! At such moments every feeling in your breast is deadened. I am now just beginning to regain my natural spirits, but I never wish for any more fighting.'[61]

His wish was granted.

CHAPTER SEVEN

THE RISING IN THE NORTH,
1842
Dark Satanic Mills

> 'We have game laws, corn laws, cotton fac-
> tories, Spitalfields, the tillers of the land paid by
> poor rates, and the remainder of the population
> mechanised into engines for the manufactory
> of new rich men; yea the machinery of the
> wealth of the nation made up of the wretched-
> ness, disease and depravity of those who should
> constitute the strength of the nation.'
>
> *S. T. Coleridge.*

In May, 1842, four men—Southwood Smith a doctor,
Thomas Tooke an economist, and R. J. Saunders and
Leonard Horner, factory inspectors—published a document
which profoundly troubled the conscience of England. It
was called the First Report of the Children's Employment
Commission. It dealt with the conditions of labour of
children and young persons working in coal mines. The
commission had been set up two years before by Lord
Melbourne's government, largely through the pertinacity of
Lord Ashley (the future Earl of Shaftesbury), an incon-
veniently well-connected young Tory[1] of strong evangelical
tendencies who had taken up the cause of the north-
country factory operatives with an enthusiasm which
seemed to some of his contemporaries to border on the
hysterical.

Everybody knew that the conditions of life and labour
in the new factory towns of the north and midlands, until
now a remote, barren and little visited part of the country,
were of a rough and primitive character. There had always
been rough and primitive Englishmen, and in these smoky
and unsavoury districts they were undoubtedly on the increase. It was part of the price that had to be paid for the
nation's growing wealth. But the revelations of the Commissioners' pages took the country by surprise.

From this document it appeared that the employment of children of seven or eight years old in coal mines was almost universal. In some pits they began work at a still earlier age : a case was even recorded of a child of three. Some were employed as 'trappers,' others for pushing or drawing coal trucks along the pit tunnels. A trapper, who operated the ventilation doors on which the safety of the mines depended, would often spend as many as sixteen hours a day crouching in solitude in a small dark hole. 'Although this employment scarcely deserves the name of labour,' ran the Commission's report, 'yet as the children engaged in it are commonly excluded from light and are always without companions, it would, were it not for the passing and repassing of the coal carriages, amount to solitary confinement of the worst order.'

Those who drew the trucks were 'harnessed like dogs in a go-cart' and crawled on all-fours down passages in some places only eighteen inches high. Other children worked at the pumps in the under-bottom of the pits, standing ankle deep in water for twelve hours. One who was cited, only six years of age, carried or dragged half a hundredweight every day up a distance equivalent to the height of St. Paul's Cathedral.

What struck the conscience of early Victorian England with especial horror was the fact that girls as well as boys were employed in these tasks. Naked to the waist, and with chains drawn between their legs, the future mothers of Englishmen crawled on all-fours down tunnels under the earth drawing Egyptian burdens. Women by the age of 30 were old and infirm cripples. Such labour, degrading all who engaged in it, was often accompanied by debauchery and sickening cruelty : one witness before the Commission described how he had seen a boy beaten with a pick-axe. Lord Ashley in a speech in the Commons mentioned another whose master was in the habit of thrashing him with a stick through which a nail had been driven : the child's back and loins were beaten to a jelly, his arm was broken and his head covered with the mark of old wounds. To add to its horrors the Report was illustrated with pictures.

Here was something never contemplated by Church and State. 'We in England,' wrote a leading journal, 'have put ourselves forward in every possible way that could savour of ostentation as champions of the whole human race; and we are now, on our own showing, exhibited to the world as empty braggarts and shallow pretenders to virtues which we do not possess. . . . We have listened to the cries of the slave afar off, but we have shut our ears to the moaning of the slave at our feet.' When Ashley, striking while the iron was hot, rose in the Commons a month later to introduce a Bill excluding all women and girls from the pits and boys under thirteen, he found himself almost a national hero.

●　　　　　＊　　　　　＊

Yet there was nothing new in what the Report revealed or Ashley described : these things had been going on for years. They had been defended, as they were even defended on this occasion, with all conscientiousness by many honourable men in positions of responsibility on the ground that they were the unavoidable result of the laws of supply and demand. Since the publication of the economist Malthus' treatises, serious minds had been haunted by a fear that the staggering increase of population rendered possible by the advance of machinery and medical science would outgrow the earth's productive capacity and culminate in famine. They were equally possessed of the belief, so brilliantly propounded by Adam Smith more than half a century before and revered by every living economist, that the wealth of men and nations depended on the unimpeded operation of economic law. 'It is not from the benevolence of the butcher, the brewer or the baker,' he wrote, 'that we expect our dinner, but from their regard to their own self interest. We address ourselves, not to their humanity, but to their self-love, and never talk to them of our necessities, but of their advantage.' Only by leaving every man free to pursue his own interest could production in such a revolutionary age keep pace with the rise in consumption. The more the population increased and the greater the consequent suffering of the poor, the more incumbent it became on those who governed to refrain from any interference with economic processes. For it could only end in calamity: The most one could hope for, in the view of the professors of 'the dismal science,' was that the poor should be fed at all. Hardships suffered by them in the course of obtaining food were in reality blessings, since without them they and all mankind would starve.

This belief was widely held by humane and enlightened reformers who were passionately anxious to eradicate ancient abuses, of which there were many, and to mitigate human suffering. The English individualists who subscribed with such uncritical zeal to the doctrine of *laissez-faire* in economic matters were among the world's greatest humanitarians. They led a reluctant mankind in every philanthropic crusade : by their unflagging efforts they had abolished slavery in the British dominions, removed from the statute book the barbarous laws which condemned men to the pillory and women to the lash, reduced from more than a hundred and fifty to six the crimes punishable by death and rendered illegal the cruel sports of cock-fighting and bull-baiting. These humanitarians rigidly opposed the infliction of all needless pain except in the factories and mines of England. For here, in their view, it could not be avoided.

This melancholy and fatalistic attitude towards industrial suffering was bound up with the high hopes which had been formed of human nature by the idealists of the eighteenth century. It was this that made it so formidable. The age of reason saw the birth of a belief that challenged the older notion of revealed religion and morality. By the light of the untrammelled mind, man would be able to attain to perfection. Only two things were necessary : that he should strictly observe natural law and be freed from every antiquated legal shackle, superstition and custom that prevented him from following his will according to the light of his own reason. The emancipation of the individual reason was the key to a new era of happiness and perfection. Man was born free : he had only to rid himself of his chains to enter into his heritage.

In France this theory, first preached by philosophers and later accepted as a social truism, had resulted in the storming of the Bastille, the Declaration of the Rights of Man and the Revolutionary and Napoleonic armies. In sober commercial England it had taken a more prosaic form. Expounded for more than half a century by a rich and respectable philanthropist of genius, the promotion of 'the greatest happiness of the greatest number' had become the polite faith of nine 'enlightened' English reformers out of ten. It was Jeremy Bentham's belief that that happiness could most readily be realised by the free exercise on the part of every individual of enlightened self-interest. Complete freedom of contract was the very core of the utilitarian creed. Any denial of it by the State could only delay and perhaps defeat the beneficent purposes of Providence.

A theory, running counter to the whole course of English social history, was thus employed both by members of the government and by manufacturers, as well as by academic economists, to justify almost any suffering or inhumanity. Employers and employed must be left free to make whatever bargains they chose : legislative interference could only make confusion worse confounded. Nine years before the Report of 1842, when Ashley had been struggling to get a Bill through Parliament limiting the hours of children in textile mills to ten a day, he was opposed on the ground that the measure would hamstring one-sixth of the nation's producing power and, by weakening British industry in competition abroad, react fatally on the wages and employment of the adult worker. Even so humane a man as Lord Althorp, then leader of the Commons, argued it would make famine inevitable. Cobbett's commonsense remark that the House had discovered that the stay and bulwark of England lay, not as was hitherto supposed in her navy, maritime commerce or colonies, but in the labour of 30,000 little factory girls, was regarded as perverse nonsense.

For the English, being bad theorists, though masters of

practice and adaptation, overlooked the fatal error in the logic of *laissez-faire*, which accorded so readily with their own stubborn hatred of tyranny and love of independence. That liberty was a sacred blessing never to be lightly infringed and that every man should be free were propositions which appealed to their deepest instincts. What in their passion for liberty they failed to see was that men were not rendered free merely because they ought to be, or by the removal of artificial legal restrictions on trade and contract. A child, a cripple, a pregnant woman, an epileptic or a neurasthenic was not free but was the slave of circumstances over which he or she had no control. The theory that the economic price for services and commodities could only be determined by the unimpeded bargaining of buyer and seller assumed a different aspect when the buyer was a rich man in no hurry to buy and the seller a hungry wretch with a sick wife and family. Unfortunately the English could not grasp this in theory : it was only after they had been brought face to face with its cruel and degrading consequences that they reacted against it. Even then, they failed to detect the cause of the effect they deplored.

That the ruling classes were so slow to perceive the evil that was sapping the nation's health and unity was due to a combination of causes unique in history. The social changes wrought by the English inventions of the eighteenth and early nineteenth century—themselves the product of a glorious vitality, ingenuity and disciplined activity of mind —were so far-reaching that men already absorbed by the problems of an ancient, vigorous and intricate society had some excuse for not grasping their significance. For they happened with bewildering rapidity. They took place in remote and little frequented parts of the country which, having formally been scantily populated, were without parliamentary representation. And at first they only affected an insignificant minority. At the beginning of the century factory and mine-workers formed only a small fraction of the population. The speed at which their numbers increased upset all normal calculations of statecraft.

But the chief cause for the failure of the English government—aggravated as it was by the prevailing *laissez-faire*
theory—was the overwhelming pressure of external events.
From the outbreak of the French Revolution—itself following only six years after the disastrous war with the American colonies—to the fall of Napoleon, England had no
time for reflection. It was in circumstances of continual
peril and while facing a dangerous revolutionary theory
abroad and bewildering changes at home that the hideous
problem, which came to be called the Condition-of-
England question, arose in the new manufacturing areas.
What the menace of Communist ideology and aggression is
to-day, that of French Jacobinism seemed to our stubborn
forefathers as they fought for their threatened homes and
the liberties of Europe. To them every sign of discontent
was a symptom of revolutionary terror and the most legitimate criticism the blackest treason. With all the obstinacy
of Englishmen in time of duress, the rulers of George III's
England clamped down the hatches of the ship of state
against change. For more than a quarter of a century reform was driven under ground and a new population,
growing up amid unprecedented social phenomena, was
deprived of leadership. Humane and kindly men, at their
wits' ends how to feed a besieged island and taught by the
economists that in such matters sentiment would prove
fatal, accepted as inevitable the spectacle of women with
blackened faces and tears coursing down their cheeks as
they dragged their loads up pit ladders, of work-dizzy cotton
spinners mangled in the shafts of unfenced machinery, of
workhouse children rented by frugal-minded overseers to
rough north-country millowners who treated them like
beasts of burden. They treated them worse, for while only
a fool would maltreat his horse, a manufacturer could
always replace crippled or prematurely senile human
workers by further supplies of cheap labour that cost him
nothing but their keep. An American cotton planter who
bought and bred his own slaves had an interest in being
careful of his 'Labour.' A Lancashire cotton manufacturer
only hired his; his responsibility for it began and ended at

the factory gates.[2] He was merely concerned with paying as little for it and getting as much out of it as possible. And this was precisely what the economists—the 'feelosophers' of Cobbett's indignant phrase—told him to do. Selfishness had been elevated by the theorists of the study into a public virtue.

There were many manufacturers whose consciences were repelled by these methods of conducting business. But not only were they told by those learned in such matters that to question economic law was folly, but the competition of rivals who had no such scruples about underpaying and overworking their wretched employees compelled them under pain of bankruptcy to do the same. A kind of Gresham's law operated to debase the standard of the best employer to that of the lowest. Among the small mill-owners—and even in capitalist Lancashire the unit of employment was still by modern standards very small—were many of humble origin who had achieved wealth by their talent for using their elbows. Though men often of splendid vigour, courage and independence, they were without the ruling tradition of responsibility and *noblesse oblige*, and the professors of economic science told them that such scruples were in any case antiquated and useless. They had one main concern, to get rich, and by every legitimate method available. As is often the way with servants turned master, they tended to confuse discipline with terror. Their own manners and habits were rough and brutal,[3] and they saw no reason to soften them in their relations with employees.

Machinery gave them their chance. Every new invention by simplifying the processes of manufacture and multiplying the rate of output increased their opportunities for growing rich. They took them with all the boisterous energy of their race. All that was needed by the new 'manufacturer,' working not by his own hand but by machine and proxy, was capital enough to buy or hire a roomful of power-looms, a resolve to keep his expenses and consequently his prices down against all rivals and a plentiful supply of cheap labour. The machine took the place of the domestic craftsman whose hereditary skill it rendered useless, whose price it undercut and whose ancient markets it captured. If continued unemployment did not drive him to lower his wage demands, women and children could be hired for the factories at half or a third of his price. So could filthy, barefooted Irish paupers who were always ready to leave their own overcrowded and half-starving island at almost any wage. They were shipped into Liverpool and Glasgow in tens of thousands to feed the mills. By a curious nemesis, their ways of life—little better than those of the pigsty—still further depressed the wages and social standards of England and Scotland.

.   .   .

The first great surge of invention affected the textile trade and principally the manufacture of cotton goods. It was in the humid valleys of south Lancashire that the factory system appeared. The earliest cotton mills, worked by water-power though later by steam, were largely operated by apprentice pauper children from the urban slums who, consigned by the Guardians to the millowners in cartloads, were housed or rather packed in barrack-like 'prentice houses (where they slept in shifts) and kept more or less continuously at work until they either died or reached an age at which their labour ceased to be profitable. The working hours of one mill in 1815 were from 5 a.m. till 8 p.m. with half an hour's grace for breakfast and dinner. There were no Saturday half-holidays, and Sundays were partly devoted to cleaning the machinery. One instance is recorded of unwanted children being taken when the mill was idle to a neighbouring common and turned loose to shift for themselves.[4]

The early factory reformers—a little minority of humane men, several of them millowners like the first Sir Robert Peel—concentrated their efforts on regulating the worst abuses of indentured child labour in the cotton mills. Later they were able to extend their tentative reforms to what was ironically termed 'free' child-labour and to other branches of manufacture. But they received small encouragement from the bulk of their well-to-do country-men who in a stay-at-home age were not given to trips to smoky and remotely situated factory towns and were un-able to imagine what they had not seen. The isolation of the industrial areas before the coming of the railways created a deep gulf between one part of the nation and the other. The only reforms philanthropists could smuggle on to the Statute Book were of the most rudimentary kind, such as the prohibition of the employment of children under nine in cotton mills and the limitation of hours of labour for young persons under sixteen to twelve a day. Even these were avoided in practice. The Factories' Inquiry Commission of 1833 showed that many manufac-turers were still employing children of six and seven and that the hours of labour were sometimes as high as sixteen a day. Flogging was regarded as a necessary part of the process of production. Harassed parents, with their eye on the family budget, accepted all this as inevitable and even desirable : many fathers acted as sub-contractors for the employment of their own children.

Nor did the reforms, such as they were, keep pace with the growth of the system. The victims of the factory—at first only an insignificant fraction of the population—in-creased by leaps and bounds. Every year new inventions widened the scope of machinery, offered new oppor-tunities for growing rich and forced more hungry crafts-men to seek employment for their wives and children in the factory towns. What had hitherto been a localised evil became a national one.

During the period of transition from cottage to factory labour, the course of nature was reversed. The bread-winner was left idle in the home, the wife and her little ones driven by want to the mill. In 1833 the cotton mills employed about 60,000 adult males, 65,000 adult females, and 84,000 young persons of whom half were boys and girls of under fourteen. By 1844, of 420,000 operatives less than a quarter were men over eighteen and 242,000 were women and girls.

The result was appalling. A wife who worked twelve or thirteen hours a day in a factory had no time to give to her children who grew up, in Engels' tragic words, like wild weeds. Put out to nurse with some half-savage creature for a few pence a week until old enough to become wage-earners, they learnt nothing from their mothers of the arts of domestic life and little of its charities. Even immediately after confinement women were forced out of sheer necessity to return to the mills. Lord Ashley made English gentlemen in the House of Commons listen to evidence that revealed their misery : 'H. W. has three children, goes away Monday morning at five o'clock and comes back Saturday evening : has so much to do for the children then that she cannot get to bed before three o'clock in the morning; often wet through to the skin, and obliged to work in that state. She said : "My breasts have given me the most frightful pain, and I have been dripping wet with milk." '

The effect on the children can be imagined. The home to which they returned at night, often too weary even to eat, was an untended hovel. The machines to which they hurried back before dawn never tired as they did. In the country which had abolished slavery and was vigorously opposing the slave trade in every corner of the world, 'strappers' were kept to flog drowsy factory children lest they dropped asleep at their work, and groups of pallid mites could be seen supporting each other home as they dragged their limbs up the dark cobbled lanes of the Lancashire and Yorkshire valleys.

Many were crippled for life : few grew to mature and healthy manhood or womanhood. Long, monotonous and unnatural working positions resulted in permanent curvature of the limbs. Whole families went about with crooked legs or twisted shoulders. Knees bent inwards and backwards, ankles were thickened and deformed and spinal columns pressed forward or to one side. Every street had its company of cripples, of prematurely aged and arthritic youths bent double and limping, of hag-like girls with deformed backs and hips. Constitutions were permanently enfeebled : long hours in hot, damp, crowded rooms and foul and vitiated air left debilitated bodies and listless minds. The factory population of Lancashire and the West Riding was discoloured and stunted and seemed more like some ill-fated race of pigmies than normal human beings. A Leeds surgeon testified that but for the constant new recruits from healthy country stock, the race of mill-hands would soon be wholly degenerate.

On no one did the tragedy of factory life fall more heavily than on the old craftsmen class of northern England—the finest artisans in the world. Accustomed to independence, to the regulation of their own hours of labour, to a solid standard of comfort and to the environment of the countryside, they found themselves through causes beyond their ken deprived of their wonted markets, undersold by cheap machine-made wares and finally driven in desperation into the close air and foetid lanes of the new towns where their wives and children could sell their labour. The bottom had fallen out of their world. In a letter to Oastler, the factory reformer, a Yorkshire workman described how a fellow artisan, tramping Lancashire in search of work, had come across an old acquaintance of his in a cellar in St. Helens.

'There sat poor Jack near the fire, and what did he, think you? why he sat and mended his wife's stockings with the bodkin; and as soon as he saw his old friend at the doorpost he tried to hide them. But Joe had seen it, and said : "Jack, what the devil art thou doing? Where is the missus? Why, is that thy work?" and poor Jack was ashamed, and said : "No, I know this is not my work, but my poor missus is i' the factory; she has to leave at half-past five and works till eight at night, and then she is so knocked up that she cannot do aught when she gets home, so I have to do everything for her what I can, for I have no work, nor had any for more nor three years, and I shall never have any more work while I live;" and then he wept a big tear. Jack again said : "there is work enough for women folks and childer hereabouts, but none for men; thou mayest sooner find a hundred pound on the road than work for men—but I should never have believed that either thou or any one else would have seen me mending my wife's stockings, for it is bad work. But she can hardly stand on her feet; I am afraid she will be laid up, and then I don't know what is to become of us, for it's a good bit that she had been the man in the house and I the woman; it is bad work, Joe;" and he cried bitterly. . . . Now when Joe heard this, he told me that he had cursed and damned the factories, and the masters, and the Government, with all the curses that he had learned while he was in the factory from a child.'[5]

When such simple Englishmen, feeling themselves cheated and lost, turned for relief to their rulers they received little comfort. It had formerly been regarded as part of the duty of society to ensure at the expense of its principal beneficiaries a 'fair wage' to every Englishman willing to labour. But a cold and alien philosophy now ruled the conduct of those in power. A Realm of England that denied the validity of its own authority announced that it could no longer help the People of England to preserve their traditional rights and status. Those who were submerged in the factory towns responded by forgetting that they had any part in the tradition of the realm. There was nothing to remind them that they had.

The new spirit informed the Poor Law which was enacted in 1834 to remedy the disastrous effects of the well-intentioned but makeshift system—known as Speenhamland—of subsidising wages out of rates. It bore the cold impress of the mathematical mind. It was based on the principle that the smaller the burden placed by the relief of poverty on the taxpayer the greater the country's wealth. Itself a contradiction of the strict letter of that economic law, it adhered as closely to it as was compatible with the traditional and obstinate English dislike of allowing a man to die of hunger. Outdoor relief, with all its kindly charities, was sternly discouraged : in its place the Workhouse, built with sombre economy by the administrative Unions of parishes formed under the new Act, offered to the needy poor the maximum of deterrent with the minimum of subsistence.

It was this austere form of charity that was doled out to the dispossessed weaver, the hungry handcraftsman deprived of his employment and the agricultural labourer who had simultaneously lost his grazing rights on the common and the supplementary earnings of the traditional home industries which the machines had destroyed. To men and women nursed in a kindlier tradition it seemed an outrage that old folk who had laboured all their lives and had become destitute through no fault of their own should be torn from their homes, separated from each other's company and herded in sexes into prison-like institutions.

For the economists did not see Labour as a body of men and women with individual needs and rights but only as a statistical abstraction. Labour was a commodity of value on which the man of Capital, with whom all initiative lay, could draw as the state of the market demanded. And as that market—a world one—was at the mercy of accident and fluctuated unpredictably, a 'reserve' of labour was indispensable. In exceptionally good times the whole 'reserve' could be quickly absorbed by productive industry : in normal or bad ones, it must remain unemployed and subsist on poor relief or beggary.[6] Engels writing in 1844, reckoned the surplus in England and Wales at a million and a half or about a tenth of the entire population.

The economic justification of all this was that the factories were giving to the country a wealth she had never before possessed and bringing within the purchasing power of the poor articles which had hitherto been available only to princes. The evils which were inseparable from that system were merely transitional; the nation had only to be patient, to refrain from palliative and wasteful measures and observe the laws of supply and demand, and all would be well. The general body of the middle class accepted this comforting proposition. To any one with capital the mechanical multiplication of productive processes offered un-

precedented opportunities : never had there been such a
chance for the far-seeing investor. The same processes by
cheapening the price and multiplying the quantity of
goods must surely benefit labour too. The march of progress was irresistible. 'Our fields,' declared Macaulay, voic-
ing the buoyant sentiment of his class, 'are cultivated with
a skill unknown elsewhere, with a skill which has extracted
rich harvests from moors and morasses. Our houses are
filled with conveniences which the kings of former times
might have envied. Our bridges, our canals, our roads, our
modes of communication fill every stranger with wonder.
Nowhere are manufactures carried to such perfection. Nowhere does man exercise such a dominion over matter.'

The spirit of the age—that is, of the readers and writers
of books, newspapers and journals—was preoccupied with
the getting of material wealth and a purely mechanical
organisation of society. It preferred a quantitative to a
qualitative ideal of production. It was opposed to that
older and more catholic conception in which rural and
traditional England still lingered. It was pragmatic,
vigorous and vocal. The other England was passive and
unthinking. The few who set its ancient and forgotten
philosophy against the spirit of the age were dismissed by
the intellectuals as dreamers and mischievous meddlers.

That those few included some of the profoundest minds
of the time was not realised. No one heeded Coleridge's
warning that the price of neglecting human health, breeding and character for the sake of profits would have to be
paid with heavy interest in the future. 'You talk,' he wrote,
'about making this article cheaper by reducing its price in
the market from 8d. to 6d. But suppose in so doing, you
have rendered your country weaker against a foreign foe;
suppose you have demoralised thousands of your fellow-
countrymen and have sown discontent between one class
of society and another, your article is tolerably dear, I
take it, after all.' Persons were not 'things.' The latter
found their level, as the economists maintained, but after
starvation, loss of home and employment, 'neither in body
nor in soul does man find his level.' Man was not an un-

changing and measurable commodity but a variable and creative creature intensely sensitive not only to his immediate environment but to that of his progenitors from whom he inherited many of his attributes.

The wealth and power of Britain to which the economists and their middle-class disciples loved to draw attention was not merely the result of machinery and the laws of supply and demand. It was based on the skill, discipline, industry and social cohesion of the British people—qualities which they had derived from generations of healthy living and sound social organisation. It was these invisible assets that enabled British manufacturers to sell their goods in every corner of the world. To destroy them by ignoring human rights and needs for the sake of an excessive and impatient expansion of material wealth was to deprive coming generations of the very advantages they had enjoyed and exploited. Such improvidence could only end in killing the goose that laid the golden eggs. The early Forsytes for all their private integrity and frugality never comprehended this, and, unknowingly, committed waste on the national estate.

.   .   .

The new England they built was housed not so much in towns as in barracks. These were grouped round the new factories, on the least expensive and therefore most congested model attainable. Unrestrained individualism was the order of the day. Since the rate of profits was not affected if their inhabitants died prematurely no consideration was paid to matters of sanitation and health. The dwellings which housed the factory population were run up by small jerry builders and local carpenters, who like the millowners were out for the maximum of profit with the minimum of responsibility. They were erected back to back and on the cheapest available site, in many cases marshes. There was no ventilation and no drainage. The intervals between the houses which passed for streets were unpaved and often followed the line of streams serving a conduit for excrement.

H

The appearance of such towns was dark and forbidding.
Many years had now passed since the first factories
appeared among the northern hills. Now the tall chimneys
and gaunt mills had been multiplied a hundredfold, and
armies of grimy, grey-slated houses had encamped around
them. Overhead hung a perpetual pall of smoke so that
their inhabitants groped to their work as in a fog. There
were no parks or trees : nothing to remind men of the green
fields from which they came or to break the squalid monotony of the houses and factories. From the open drains and
ditches that flowed beneath the shade of sulphurous chimneys and between pestilential hovels arose a foetid smell.
The only symbols of normal human society were the gin
shops. Here on the rare days of leisure the entire population would repair, men, women and children, to suck themselves into insensibility on 'Cream of the Valley' or Godfrey's Cordial.

In a terrible passage in one of his novels of the 'forties,
Disraeli described such a town. 'Wodgate had the appearance of a vast squalid suburb. As you advanced, leaving
behind you long lines of little dingy tenements, with infants
lying about the road, you expected every moment to emerge
into some streets, and encounter buildings bearing some
correspondence, in their size and comfort, to the considerable population swarming and busied around you. Nothing
of the kind. There were no public buildings of any sort; no
churches, chapels, town-hall, institute, theatre; and the
principal streets in the heart of the town in which were
situated the coarse and grimy shops . . . were equally
narrow, and if possible more dirty. At every fourth or fifth
house, alleys seldom above a yard wide, and streaming
with filth, opened out of the street. . . . Here, during the
days of business, the sound of the hammer and the file
never ceased, amid gutters of abomination, and piles of
foulness, and stagnant pools of filth; reservoirs of leprosy
and plague, whose exhalations were sufficient to taint the
atmosphere of the whole of the kingdom and fill the
country with fever and pestilence.'

Reality was more terrible than art. Disraeli did not exaggerate but, out of deference to Victorian proprieties, toned down the horror of his picture. The official reports of the Royal Health of Towns Commission of 1845 were more graphic for they were more exact. In 442 dwellings examined in Preston, 2,400 people slept in 852 beds. In 84 cases four shared a bed, in 28 five, in 13 six, in 3 seven, and in 1 eight. The cellar populations of Manchester and Liverpool, nearly 18,000 in the former and more in the latter, were without any means of removing night-soil from the habitations. Even for those who lived above ground water-closets were unknown and the privies, shared in common by hundreds, were generally without doors. A doctor in his report on the Lancashire towns testified :

'I have known instances where the wall of a dwelling-house has been constantly wet with foetid fluid which has filtered through from a midden and poisoned the air with its intolerable stench : and the family was never free from sickness during the six months they endured the nuisance. Instances in which foetid air finds its way into the next dwelling-house are not infrequent. I know an instance (and I believe there are many such), where it is impossible to keep food without its being tainted for even a single night in the cupboards on the side of the house next the public necessary, and where the foetor is offensively perceptible always and oppressive in the morning before the door is opened. In this instance the woman of the house told me she had never been well since she came to it, and the only reason she gave for her living in it was, the house was 6d. a week cheaper than others free from the nuisance.'

Such horrors, intolerable to modern minds, must be judged in proper proportion : it was only the unprecedented rapidity and extent of their growth which made them seem terrible to contemporaries. There had always been filthy slums in the small, semi-rural cities of the older England; nobody had dreamt of regulating them. Nor was sanitary carelessness confined to the poor of the new towns. Even at royal Windsor the footmen in the pantry suffered perpetually from sore throats until 1844 when more than fifty unemptied cesspits were discovered under the castle. A people still rustic regarded bad drains as a joke in the same category as high cheese and 'old grouse in gunroom,' and even welcomed their stench as a useful warning of bad weather. But those of the better-to-do classes who had to pass through the new factory towns found the nuisance there beyond a joke. It had become, as Disraeli later reminded the House of Commons, not a matter of sewage but a question of life and death.

In Little Ireland, Ancoats, Engels, seeking material for his great work on the proletariat of south Lancashire, described the standing pools, full of refuse, offal and sickening filth, which poisoned the atmosphere of the densely populated valley of the Medlock. Here 'a horde of ragged women and children swarm about, as filthy as the swine that thrive upon the garbage heaps and in the puddles. . . . The race that lives in these ruinous cottages behind broken windows mended with oilskin, sprung doors and rotten door-posts, or in dark wet cellars in measureless filth and stench . . . must really have reached the lowest stage of humanity. . . . In each of these pens, containing at most two rooms, a garret and perhaps a cellar, on the average twenty human beings live. . . . For each one hundred and twenty persons, one usually inaccessible privy is provided; and in spite of all the preachings of the physicians, in spite of the excitement into which the cholera epidemic plunged the sanitary police by reason of the condition of Little Ireland, in spite of everything, in this year of grace, 1844, it is in almost the same state as in 1831.[8]

But Engels encountered worse. Groping along the maze of narrow covered passages which led from the streets of the old town of Manchester into the yards and alleys that lined the south bank of the Irk, he found a courtyard at whose entrance there stood a doorless privy so dirty that the inhabitants could only pass in and out of the court by wading through stagnant pools of excrement. In this district, where one group of thirty hovels housing three hundred and eighty people boasted not even a single privy, the joint founder of modern Communism obtained his famous view of the Irk from Ducie Bridge :

> 'The view from this bridge, mercifully concealed from mortals of small stature by a parapet as high as a man, is characteristic for the whole district. At the bottom flows, or rather stagnates, the Irk, a narrow, coal-black, foul-smelling stream full of debris and refuse which it deposits on the shallower right bank. In dry weather, a long string of the most disgusting, blackish-green, slime pools are left standing on this bank, from the depths of which bubbles of miasmatic gas constantly arise and give forth a stench unendurable even on the bridge forty or fifty feet above the surface of the stream. . . . It may be easily imagined, therefore, what sort of residue the stream deposits. Below the bridge you look upon the piles of debris, the refuse, filth, and offal from the courts on the steep left bank; here each house is packed close behind its neighbour and a piece of each is visible, all black, smoky, crumbling, ancient, with broken panes and window frames. . . . Here the background embraces the pauper burial-ground, the station of the Liverpool and Leeds Railway, and in the rear of this, the Workhouse, the "Poor-Law Bastille" of Manchester, which, like a citadel, looks threateningly down from behind its high walls and parapets on the hilltop upon the working people's quarter below.'⁹

To comprehend the dual nature of early nineteenth century Britain and the legacy of discontent and social division we still inherit from its tragic dualism, this picture drawn by Engels from Ducie Bridge must be set against Wordsworth's sonnet written on its fellow English bridge at Westminster.

As Engels justly asked, how could people who were compelled to live in such pigsties, and who were dependent for their water supply on this pestilential stream, live natural and human lives or bring up their children as anything but savages? And what kind of posterity was England, in her feverish search for wealth, breeding to preserve

and enjoy that wealth? It was a question to which economists gave no answer.

There were more urgent ones to answer which concerned not posterity but the present. If reflection could not
teach the intellect that men who inhabited the same country
were dependent on one another, germs could. Typhus and
putrid fever took a less individualist view of man's nature
than the economists. The microbes of infection never
acknowledged the law that every man could find and
maintain his own separate level. Asiatic cholera in 1831
and typhus in 1837 and 1843 from their strongholds in the
industrial towns defied every effort of hastily improvised
sanitary police and chloride of lime to dislodge them and
threatened to devastate the whole country.

·   ·   ·

There were other warnings that a nation could not neglect
a substantial part of its population without endangering
its safety. A sullen and savage proletariat, growing in numbers, was turning against the rest of the community, its
symbols and traditions. Carlyle, with his poet's sensitive-
ness, felt from the seclusion of his Chelsea study the im-
minence of some terrible explosion among the northern
workers. 'Black, mutinous discontent devours them. . . .
English commerce, with its world-wide, convulsive fluctua-
tions, with its immeasurable Proteus steam demon, makes
all paths uncertain for them, all life a bewilderment;
society, steadfastness, peaceable continuance, the first blessings of man are not theirs. This world is for them no
home, but a dingy prison-house, of reckless unthrift, rebellion, rancour, indignation against themselves and against
all men. . . .'[10]

In such a soil the orator of social revolution and the
agitator could look for speedy returns. In 1837, the year of
Victoria's accession, a People's Charter was put forward
by a small group of radical members of Parliament, dissent-
ing ministers and Irish and Cornish orators. It demanded
the immediate transfer of electoral power from the middle-

class electorate of 1832 to the numerically superior labouring class through universal franchise, the ballot, annual parliaments, the abolition of the property qualification, payment of members and equal electoral districts.

The Charter, which was submitted to mass meetings in Birmingham and London in the following year, caught on like wildfire in the industrial towns. The agitation soon assumed an alarming aspect. At meetings arms were called for by excited Celtic orators, and forests of oak saplings were brandished by grimy sons of toil. Stories were whispered about the country of how the master workmen of Birmingham—the savage "bishops" of heathen Midland tradition—were manufacturing pikes which, smuggled out in the aprons of Staffordshire chain and nail makers, were being sold to honest revolutionaries at 1/8 a piece or 2/6 polished. Men spoke of kidnapping the wives and children of the aristocracy and carrying them into the northern towns as hostages, of the secret manufacture of shells and hand-grenades and caltrops for strewing in the path of the hated yeomanry. Newcastle was to be reduced to ashes : 'If the magistrates *Peterloo* us,' the cry went round, 'we will *Moscow* England.' In 1839 the principal town of Monmouthshire was attacked by miners with muskets and pitchforks. Here and in riots at Birmingham many lost their lives.

The ruling class ignored the movement. The violence of its spokesmen[11] rendered it ridiculous in the eyes of responsible persons. The House of Commons, with its hatred of exaggeration, refused to receive its petitions. During the debate on one, purporting to bear the signatures of millions of operatives, the House was half empty : though a Tory back-bencher, who one day as Prime Minister was to take more than one step towards the fulfilment of the People's Charter, contended that the rights of labour were as sacred as those of property. Those within the movement who advocated violence were correspondingly strengthened. For it seemed that the rulers of England had no interest in the sufferings of its disinherited people.

The climax came in 1842, the year which saw the publication of the Report on the employment of children in the coal mines. One of those prolonged and periodic depressions that attended industrialisation had culminated in almost unbearable hardship in the midlands and north : factories were closing and the families of the operatives starving. Through the previous winter stories had been reaching the breakfast tables of the well-to-do and respectable of the sufferings of their human brethren in such remote places as Bolton and Paisley. The growth of the newspaper-reading habit and the introduction of the penny post were beginning to open the eyes of the middle class to what was happening in other parts of the country. That year the first illustrated weekly appeared in London and the pages of its earliest issues were full of sombre pictures of the distress of the manufacturing districts.

In the spring Sir Robert Peel's Conservative government, faced by a serious budget deficit, resorted to its revolutionary device (for peacetime) of an income tax of sevenpence in the pound on all incomes of over £150 a year. At Buckingham Palace that May a Bal Masqué was held in the hope of stimulating trade. The Queen, who was dressed as Queen Philippa, accompanied by Prince Albert in the costume of the chivalrous Edward III, wore a pendant stomacher valued at £60,000. Several nobles, inspired by the Gothic revival, commissioned suits of full armour for the occasion. Another hired £10,000 worth of jewellery for the night from Storr and Mortimer. Under the soft glare of five hundred and thirty gas jets the spectacle continued till long after three in the morning. A few days later, as the Queen returned down Constitution Hill from her afternoon drive in Hyde Park, a crazy youth tried to assassinate her with a pocket pistol. As he was seized by the police he was heard to cry out : 'Damn the Queen; why should she be such an expense to the nation !'[12]

Meanwhile the news from the north grew worse. At Burnley the Guardians, with a quarter of the population destitute, were forced to appeal to the government for help. Here the weavers were working for 7½d. a day. Idlers with faces haggard with famine stood in the streets, their eyes wearing the fierce and uneasy expression of despair. A doctor who visited the town in June found in eighty-three houses, selected at hazard, no furniture but old boxes, stone boulders (for chairs) and beds of straw and sacking. The whole population was living on oatmeal, water and skimmed milk.

Revolution was in the air. The workers were talking openly of burning down the mills in order to enforce a nation-wide strike. In Colne and Bolton hands were clenched, teeth set and fearful curses uttered. Haggard orators bade starving audiences take cheer, for soon 'Captain Swing' would rule the manufacturing districts. At a Chartist gathering on Enfield moor near Blackburn, a speaker announced that the industrial north would soon be marching on Buckingham Palace; if the Queen refused the Charter, every man would know what to do.[18]

Across St. George's Channel, Ireland—herself the mother of many an English factory operative—starved and rioted. In Ennis the mob attacked the flour mills; at Cork, growing weary of a diet of old cabbage leaves, it stormed the potato markets. Dear corn—popularly believed to be the price of the time-honoured Corn Laws which protected the landowner at the expense of the poor—the new machines and the middle-class franchise were alike indicted by bitter and angry men as the cause of their sufferings. As the uneasy parliamentary session of the summer of 1842 drew to a close, the authorities reinforced the troops in the industrial areas.

The first rumblings of the storm came from Staffordshire. Here towards the end of July the colliers, following a reduction of their wages to 2/6 a day, turned out and, marching on every works in the neighbourhood, compelled their comrades to do likewise. Those who refused were flung into the canals, plugs were hammered out of the boilers and furnaces extinguished. The word went round that all labour was to cease until the Charter had become the law of the land. The markets in the towns of the western midlands were deserted and every workhouse besieged by vast queues of gaunt women and children and idle men.

The Lord Lieutenant, sitting with the magistrates at the Dartmouth Hotel, West Bromwich, called out the county yeomary. The 3rd Dragoon Guards, stationed in Walsall, endeavoured to restore order. Shopkeepers and farmers were enrolled as special constables, and the old England was pitted against the new. But in the industrial areas the dispossessed had the advantage of numbers and they were desperate. At Wolverhampton strikers surrounded the workhouse and established virtual mob-law. Farther north a procession of 6,000 workmen surged down on collieries, ironworks and potteries until every chimney in the district had ceased to smoke. There was little physical violence for only in a few places was there any resistance. Under threat of crowbar and torch, the owners of bakeries, groceries and public houses distributed provisions with the best face they could. Bills appeared on the walls calling the 'Toiling Slaves' to monster demonstrations: others, issued by alarmed authorities, threatened transportation to those who destroyed machinery or used intimidation.

Such was the position as the parliamentary session of 1842 drew to a close and Ministers, who doubted their ability to keep the peace for more than a few days longer, prepared after the imperturbable manner of England for the customary Cabinet fish dinner at the Crown and Sceptre tavern, Greenwich. In the seaports there were signs of a slight improvement in trade. But the reports which poured in from every manufacturing district continued menacing. The whole population was in a state of intense excitement. It was difficult to say whether the cause was hunger, wage reductions, Chartism or the popular demand for cheap bread and repeal of the Corn Laws.

The explosion came on August 4th at Staleybridge, where the employees of Messrs. Bayley's mill had received notice of a further reduction in wages. The strikers, as though acting on prearranged orders, turned out the workers at every factory in Ashton and Oldham. Next morning they marched on Manchester. For a few noisy hours the main body was held up by a small detachment of police and troops at Holt Town. But other rioters swarming out from the streets on either flank, the authorities were forced to fall back leaving factories and provision shops at their mercy. At Messrs. Birley's mill, where momentary resistance was encountered, the roof was stormed, every window broken, and two policemen and an onlooker killed. On Saturday, 6th, while Sir Robert and his fellow Ministers were embarking at Hungerford Pier on the *Prince of Wales* steam-packet for their outing at Greenwich, riots were raging in every district of Manchester. Police stations were demolished and more officers killed.

The great 'Turn Out,' long threatened by heady orators and whispered among the people, had come at last. The workers were on the march. On Sunday the rioting spread to Stockport and other parts of Cheshire. Mills were attacked, bakeries looted and the police pelted with stones. At Preston the mob attacked the military, and several lost their lives. In the Potteries some colliers arrested by the police were rescued by their fellow miners who subsequently stormed the Burslem Town Hall, burnt its records and rate books, and sacked the George Inn and the principal shops. Afterwards the town looked as though an invading army had passed through it.

The scene of the insurrection would not have been England had its grim and starving landscape not been lightened by flashes of humour. At one place where a band of marauding Amazons from the cotton mills threatened to burn down a farm, the farmer turned the tables by loosing his bull. In another—it was at Wigan—the local miners insisted on keeping guard round Lord Crawford's park against their fellow strikers so that, as one of them put it, the old Lord could drink his port in peace.[14]

Work throughout the industrial north was now at a complete standstill. In Manchester all the shops were shuttered and the streets thronged with thousands of workmen who besieged the sidewalks demanding money and food from passers-by. Similar scenes were enacted in almost every industrial town from Leicester to Tyneside, and in western

Scotland. At Stoke-on-Trent the mob gutted the Court of Requests, the Police Station and the larger houses; at Leeds the Chief of Police was seriously wounded, and fatal casualties occurred at Salford, Blackburn and Halifax. The wildest rumours circulated : that in Manchester the police had been cut to pieces with volleys of brickbats; that the redcoats, welcomed by the hungry populace as brothers, had risen against their officers; that the Queen who had 'set her face against gals working in mills' was ready to grant the Charter and open the ports to cheap corn.

The alarm of the well-to-do classes in the adjacent rural areas was by now intense. In the factory towns of Lancashire 6,000 millowners and shopkeepers enrolled as special constables to defend their menaced interests. The Government decided to act with vigour. In every northern and midland county the yeomanry were called out, and farmers' sons sharpened sabres on the grindstone at the village smithy before riding off to patrol the grimy streets of a world they did not understand. Tall-hatted magistrates rode beside them ready to mumble through the Riot Act and loose the force that had triumphed at Peterloo over the urban savagery their own neglect had created.

On Saturday, August 13th, there was fierce rioting in Rochdale, Todmorden, Bury, Macclesfield, Bolton, Stockport, Burslem and Hanley. At the latter place 5,000 strikers marched on a neighbouring country mansion and left it blazing. Hordes of rough-looking men in fur caps carrying clubs and faggots patrolled the squalid unpaved roads around the idle mills; others attempted to hold up the mail and tear up the permanent way on the Manchester-Leeds railway. Next morning, though Sunday, the Cabinet met and issued urgent orders to the Guards and the Artillery at Woolwich to hold themselves in readiness for Manchester. That evening as the 3rd battalion of the Grenadiers debouched with band playing through the gates of St. George's Barracks into Trafalgar Square, vast numbers of working men and boys closed in and tried to obstruct its progress. In Regent Street the crowd became so menacing that the order was given to fix bayonets; all the way to Euston Square Station, which was packed with police, hisses and groans continued. The 34th Foot, summoned in haste from Portsmouth, was also continuously hooted on its march across London.

By the evening of the 16th, Manchester was held by three regular infantry battalions, the 1st Royal Dragoons and artillery detachments with howitzers and six-pounders. A few miles away the streets of Bolton were patrolled by companies of the 72nd Highlanders. Other troops poured in by the new railroads with such rapidity that the rebellion quickly began to lose its dangerous appearance. All that week the magistrates and police, protected by the military, were busy arresting ring-leaders and detachments of rioters, and every main road and railway was watched by mounted constables and dragoons.

After that the insurrection crumbled. Further resort to force was useless. Hunger did the rest. Anger and hectic excitement gave place to weakness and despair. The shops were guarded and, with the mills closed, even the miserable wages of the past year of want ceased. The poor rates in every Lancashire town soared as pale, famished multitudes besieged the workhouses, and ruined householders, unable to pay their rent, abandoned their homes. In November Engels saw gaunt, listless men at every street corner in Manchester, and whole streets of houses in Stockport standing empty.

· · ·

Gradually the factories reopened and a defeated people crept back to work. The insurrection had failed. Yet, like the Report on the employment of children in coal mines, it had done something to awaken the conscience of England. It had added to pity fear, and, as is the way with the English in times of trial, a sober resolve to remove the cause of the evil. So long as the rioting continued, worthy and peace-loving folk set their faces resolutely against the rioters. But when it was over they took counsel of their consciences.[15]

Many, particularly the manufacturers and the new middle class, who had nothing to gain by the protection of agriculture and much by the cheapening of provisions, laid the blame on the Corn Laws. Others, like the country land-owners, condemned the inhumanity of the millowners, who retaliated by pointing to the low wages and neglected hovels of the agricultural workers in the southern counties. As Ashley, the factory reformer, knew to his misery, none were worse than those on the Dorset estate of his father, Lord Shaftesbury. The economists and the statesmen who subscribed to their theories continued to reiterate the importance of non-interference with the laws of supply and demand.

But with the general thinking public the view gained ground that there were limits to the efficacy of *laissez-faire*, where public health and the employment of children were concerned. Sanitary reform and factory regulation began for the first time to be taken seriously. Early in 1843 Ashley was able to carry without opposition an address to the Crown for the diffusion of moral and religious education among the working classes. In the following year a new Factory Bill became law limiting the hours of children under sixteen to six and a half a day and establishing further regulations for the fencing of machinery and the inspection of industrial premises. In the same year a commission on the Health of Towns was appointed. Its Report written by Edwin Chadwick revealed that of fifty large towns examined, only six had a good water supply and not one an adequate drainage system.

Public opinion was by now far ahead of parliamentary action. During the middle and latter 'forties the novels of Dickens, Disraeli and Charles Kingsley, the pamphlets of Carlyle and the poems of Elizabeth Barrett Browning educated the reading classes in the Condition of the People question and stimulated their desire for social reform. Intelligent England had become conscious of the new towns. Even Tennyson turned from his dreams of a remote chivalry to confront the inescapable problem of his age :

'Slowly comes a hungry people, as a lion creeping nigher,
Glares at one that nods and winks behind a slowly
   dying fire.'

The thought of a new generation was crystallised in Ashley's unanswerable question, 'Let me ask the House, what
was it gave birth to Jack Cade? Was it not that the people
were writhing under oppressions which they were not able
to bear? It was because the Government refused to redress
their grievances that the people took the law into their
own hands.'

So, inspired by pity and purged by the fear of some new
and more terrible arising, the conscience and common sense
of England addressed themselves to the redress of great
wrongs. They received little direction from the responsible
rulers of the nation who were blinded by a theory.[16] The
urge for social reform was spontaneous and its first fruits
were mainly voluntary and unofficial. It took the form of
numberless remedial activities of a private or only semi-
public nature, from feverish church building and the foundation of industrial schools for the waifs and strays of the
urban slums to the 'poor peopling' which became so
fashionable an occupation for well-to-do young ladies in
the late 'forties : it was in this work that Florence Nightin-
gale began her life of voluntary service. All over England
and Scotland isolated individuals began to tackle self-
imposed tasks, each striving to cleanse his or her own small
local corner of the Augean stable. Such were provincial
doctors who faced fever and vested interest in a tireless
campaign against insanitary conditions, devoted clergymen
and non-conformist ministers, city missionaries and tem-
perance workers, and young men and women of comfortable circumstances—often evangelicals or quakers—who
gave up their leisure hours to teach in ragged schools or to
organise clubs, sports and benefit-societies for their poorer
neighbours. In this way, not for the first time in England's
history, the destruction wrought by her own tumultuous
vitality was redeemed in part by the operation of her own
generous conscience.

But the evil was deeply rooted, and the remedy, for all the energy and enthusiasm behind it, so ill-co-ordinated and tardy that those who prophesied revolution and social chaos[17] might have been proved right had it not been for one over-riding factor. The social maladies which provoked revolt were not destroyed, though they were henceforward slowly but steadily mitigated. On the other hand, while diminishing in intensity, they continued to grow in extent through further urbanisation. Revolution was avoided by extending the area of exploitation. But the very factor which most hastened that process ended the isolation of the industrial areas from the rest of the community. The railways had already been decisive in the suppression of the rebellion: an express train had brought a critical appeal for help from Preston to Manchester, and the Guards had been transferred from London to Lancashire in the course of a single night. Rapid internal communication and a new habit of travel, born of cheap transport, was within a few years to transform England and give her a new unity and orientation.

CHAPTER EIGHT

THE SUMMER OF DUNKIRK 1940

"This was their finest hour."

Churchill

The days between May 29 and June 3, 1940, proved a turning point in history. They marked the first check in Germany's triumphant march towards world dominion.

In one sense Dunkirk, like Corunna, was a tactical British victory, and, as such, has tended to obscure the events that preceded it. In another it was the greatest military disaster in our history. An army of more than a quarter of a million men, a force far larger than any commanded by Wellington or Marlborough, with practically the country's entire available field equipment, was surrounded and penned in a narrowing corridor to the sea with no apparent choice but surrender or death.

The fault was not primarily that of the army but of its allies, who had been defeated on either flank. But in a larger sense the great disaster of May 1940 was as much the responsibility of Britain as of any other nation. It marked the apparent collapse of all the values which an easy-going parliamentary democracy had stood for in the years between the wars. It marked equally the apparent triumph and material vindication of Hitler's barbaric revolution and of the cruel and ancient tyrannies he had enthroned. Right based on mere good intentions, it was proved, could not stand in the field against evil based on might. At that moment the miracle occurred. It did not reverse the verdict of the 'Battle of the Bulge,' but redeemed it. It was like a rainbow at the climax of some terrible storm. In the midst of it, long columns of men, tormented, utterly weary and in deadly peril, were seen going down unperturbed to the water's edge.

Their only means of escape were a single port blasted

by enemy bombs and shells, and a line of exposed beaches with shelving shores from which evacuation would have been impossible in anything but a dead calm. They stood there in long patient queues, as though waiting for the last bus home, or sheltered in impromptu holes excavated in the sand, while overhead dive-bombers roared and screamed, and fantastic air battles were fought out in the midst of immense pillars of drifting smoke and fountains of water.

After the traditional fashion of their race in the hour of crisis, the waiting men showed no sign of panic or despair; nor, it would seem, of any visible emotion at all. They merely waited with a kind of dogged faith, and presently their faith was justified. Guarded by lean, crowded destroyers, hundreds of little boats came out of England and bore them away. By some strange magic of courage and improvisation these hundreds of thousands of men were taken on board and borne out of the reach of the dragon's fiery breath and closing jaws. For five days and nights the miracle continued, until no one remained on the beaches at all save the dead. The living came back out of the delirium of modern war to the quiet and ordinariness of England; to neat railway carriages and smiling policemen, and girls holding up cups of tea; and there they lived to fight another day.

For a few days England breathed again, and the free world with her. Then the terrible surge of German victory was renewed. The newspapers were filled with pictures of tanks, motorised guns and trucks, packed with proud, fanatic-looking young Germans, glowing with health and vigour and passing in seemingly endless procession through the streets of cowed French and Belgian towns; of great black bombers and troop-carriers with hooked crosses swarming overhead in droves, of the horror and devastation wrought wherever they swooped; and of pitiful starving refugees flying through the rubble before the terror that nothing could stay. There were photographs of Hitler smiling in triumph in the midst of his staff, of General Giraud being borne away to captivity among clicking, staring Nazis; of grim-jawed parachutists, ready to drop out of the clouds, as they had done in Holland, and shoot down all who dared resist. For those who were not Germans the world was being taught there was only one virtue —instant and unconditional surrender; for those who delayed, only one fate—certain and imminent destruction.

Under that knowledge France, for two generations the military Colossus of Europe, crumpled, broke and yielded, while every road to the south-west was blocked with fugitives, and the Panzer surge swept unresisted into the Rhône valley. The men of Bordeaux, after Premier Reynaud's last, vain, despairing appeal to an unarmed America, made their abject surrender. In the eyes of the overwhelming majority of mankind, there seemed nothing else for them to do.

The world prepared itself for the inevitable. The last Americans hurried home across the Atlantic; the anxious Russians pretended not to be interested and talked of the end of an unnecessary capitalist, imperialist war; and those within the European prison house who were not already slaves queued up to kiss the conqueror's chains. From Bordeaux and Budapest, from Bucharest and Sofia, from Madrid and Helsinki, in top-boots and medals, in Homburgs and summer suitings, the respectable of a fallen Christendom made the pilgrimage to Berchtesgaden. There, amid the clicking priesthood of the jackboot and hip-revolver, they made their obeisance and paid the first instalment of Danegeld. And looking over their shoulders they waited for the proud, rich, helpless island State, which had led Europe into the illusion of government by debate and agreed rules, to follow their example. The cheats and thugs had won. The time had come for the mugs to pay up.

But the voice which came out of England at that moment was neither repentant nor submissive. It was not the voice of the hypocrite saying acceptable things before sacrifice, nor of the humbug temporising to save his face. It was the voice of a man angry, defiant and utterly resolved; or rather of forty-seven millions looking in a single direction, and that direction seawards, and intoning in their hearts the words which one of them spoke for all. 'We shall defend our island whatever the cost may be. We shall fight on the beaches; we shall fight on the landing-grounds; we shall fight in the fields and in the streets; we shall fight in the hills; and we shall never surrender.'

It sounded to the world the wildest extravagance. For, outside the British Empire and the White House in Washington, there was scarcely anybody to whom such words at such an hour made sense. The *Herrenvolk*, who were too busy counting their gains and herding their prisoners into pens to listen, announced them to be the drivel of a 'broken down drunkard in the pay of impotent moneylenders,' and contemptuously offered the English peace in a global concentration camp.

Churchill and the doomed islanders did not hear. With the minimum of fuss and chatter and the maximum of speed, they were girding on their armour. They were no longer interested in either Hitler's beguilements or threats. They had long ceased to believe in the former, and they had now ceased to notice the latter. They knew that he could and would do his worst; but they were not thinking about what he could do, but about what they could do. With all the terrible concentration of their race, they were resuming a craft which they thought they had abandoned for ever. In the words of their leader, they meant to make war, and persevere in making war, until the other side had had enough.

The miracle of Dunkirk was twofold. It not only restored a British army: it revived the nation's soul. It made the islanders realise themselves, to know, under God, of what they were capable, and resolve to do it. Their arms, save at sea, were negligible. Their military equipment had mostly been fashioned for the troglodyte campaigns of 1917, and the bulk of it had been lost at Dunkirk, their vital trade routes were outflanked from Biscay to the North Cape, their shores were threatened with invasion and their cities with destruction. But since there was now no one but themselves to save the truths and decencies in which they believed, and they could not conceive of a world without them, there was no longer any question in their minds as to what they had to do. Doubts, divisions and sloth, blindness and fear, fell away from them at that hour like the mists of morning at the rising sun. Britain was herself again.

This was the real miracle of Dunkirk. The genius of the Navy, the dogged patience of the men on the beaches and the calm of the summer seas had wrought the conceivable out of the inconceivable. Yet from it had sprung something still more wonderful than the evacuation under the Luftwaffe's nose of 300,000 men in yachts and paddle steamers. The England of the Peace Pledge Union and the dole queue had been changed in a flash of summer lightning into the England of Nelson and Alfred :

'Greed and fraud, unabashed, unawed,
May strive to sting thee at heel in vain,
Craft and fear and mistrust may leer
And mourn and murmur and plead and plain;
Thou art Thou, and thy sunbright brow
Is hers that blasted the strength of Spain.'

No one who lived in England through that wonderful summer of 1940 is ever likely to forget it. The light that beat down on her meadows, shining with emerald loveliness, was scarcely of this world. The streets of her cities, soon to be torn and shattered, were bathed in a calm serene sunshine; and in forge and factory, field and mine, her people worked with a fierce, unresting, yet quiet intensity, as they had never worked before. In every village men dragged out primæval carts that might have barred the way of Napoleon's Grand Army, and, wreathing them in farmyard wire, placed them across the roads. Signposts were taken down, trenches and gun emplacements dug in fields, and in city and country millions of citizens strove to make themselves soldiers. Factory hands and retired ambassadors, greybeards and boys in their teens, middle-aged men holding themselves taut, after twenty years of easy living, in memory of their former prowess in war, paraded side by side in working clothes with armlets lettered 'L.D.V.' Many

of them wore medals; they had little else. Many made arms
during the daytime which they learnt to use in anticipation
at night. By doing the utmost that they could, they reckoned, with the sober patience of their kind, they would
'whiles do mair.'

For—and this was part of the miracle of Dunkirk—the
British people were already thinking, not of averting defeat,
but of earning victory. Like Pitt when Napoleon's Grand
Army was waiting to cross the Channel, they were concen-
trating not on saving themselves, but on delivering Europe.
In doing so they were instinctively following the historic
path of their salvation. For a small island, moored off the
coast of a Continent, cannot indefinitely survive when the
whole of the latter is mobilised against her. Before a cowed
Europe can be consolidated by her foes Britain must take
the offensive or perish. Never in her history had victory
seemed more remote or improbable than in 1940. Yet at the
very hour when, in the midst of unparalleled disasters, he
offered his countrymen 'blood, toil, tears and sweat,'
Churchill defined her goal. 'You ask,' he said, 'what is our
aim? I can answer in one word : Victory—victory at all
costs, victory in spite of all terror, victory however hard
and long the road may be; for without victory there is no
survival.'

Already, with empty arsenals and housewives mobilising
their pots and pans to make enough fighter planes to save
London from the fate of Warsaw, Britain was planning the
four-engine bomber programme to wipe out the cities of
the Ruhr. With invasion hourly expected, she was sending
out her only armoured division on the long sea passage
round the Cape of Good Hope to guard the Nile Valley
and lay the foundations of future offensives. Her own
preservation was seen only as a means to the greater end
of saving mankind.

Meanwhile, the angry Germans, slowly and incredulously
realising that the British would not make peace, prepared
with Teuton thoroughness to smash them to pulp. The
men of Bordeaux, who had good reason to know the might
and ruthless power of Germany, supposed that the island

State which had withstood Napoleon would have its 'neck
wrung in a few weeks like a chicken.' The swastika rose
over the Channel Islands; Mussolini's legions, outnumber-
ing Wavell's Middle East Forces by ten to one, marched
into Egypt; the Japanese sharpened their swords at the
gates of Hong Kong; and the victorious, greycoated hordes
danced and revelled in the streets of a dazed and ravished
Paris preparatory to a final triumph amid the burning
villages of the Weald and the smouldering debris of
London. All the while the long procession of barges floated
down the rivers and canals of Europe towards the Channel
ports, the endless columns of grey and steel moved to their
appointed places, and the great black laden aeroplanes
gathered in their thousands on the airfields of Northern
France, Belgium, Holland and Norway. And as the world
watched, the world suddenly realised, with a thrill of
wonder and awe, that England was going to fight.

Scarcely anyone imagined she could survive such a con-
test. Even in America, where so many generous hearts bled
for her, where the Nazis were generally hated and where
British agents, aided by every device open to a far-sighted
President, were desperately buying up machine and tommy-
guns, the general belief was that Britain and Europe were
alike finished. Yet all over the world backs bowed to slavery
stiffened instinctively at the sight of the British mongoose
poised to spring, with every hair taut and bristling as it
faced the giant Teuton cobra.

That was the rallying-hour of freedom, and from every
country brave men who had fled to England—Poles and
Czechs, Frenchmen and Norwegians, Dutchmen and
Belgians and Jews—stood side by side with the islanders
and their faithful kinsfolk from overseas, unshaken, un-
seduced, unterrified. For though Europe had relapsed into
barbaric darkness, a light had been lit that summer which
could not be put out; or rather an ancient flame long
secretly tended had been revived.

Already on the Kentish aerodromes, as the sirens began
their low wail over the London streets, the few who were
to save the many were preparing for battle, and the Spit-

fires were warming up. Already in the cities tens of thousands of men and women, dedicated to death, calmly
awaited the hour when hell would descend out of the
skies to blast their homes and pulp and tear their bodies.
The Battle for Britain and of the world's deliverance had
begun. The love of the British people for their native land
—long derided by intellectuals as a barbarous and antiquated superstition—their faith in their enduring destiny
and their stubborn refusal to admit the possibility of defeat
had given mankind another chance.

'Hitler knows,' their leader told them, 'he will have to
break us in this island or lose the war. If we can stand up
to him, all Europe may be free, and the life of the world
may move forward into broad sunlit uplands. But if we fail,
then the whole world, including the United States, including all that we have known and cared for, will sink into
the abyss of a new Dark Age, made more sinister, and
perhaps more protracted, by the lights of perverted science.
Let us therefore brace ourselves to our duties, and so bear
ourselves that, if the British Empire and its Commonwealth
last for a thousand years, men will still say, "This was their
finest hour." '

NOTES

CHAPTER ONE

1. The man who led the archers, and who died three years later during the Black Death, lies in his armour of alabaster, his hands crossed in prayer and a lion at his feet, in the Despenser tomb in Tewkesbury abbey whose glorious vaulting posterity owes to his and his wife's munificence.

2. His effigy, still coloured in faded Garter blue, can be seen in Tewkesbury abbey. He married the widow of Hugh Despenser, hero of the Blanchetaque crossing.

CHAPTER TWO

1. T. Walsingham, *Historia Anglicana* II, 32.

2. He had been caught at Lakenheath as he was trying to cross the Brandon, a country woman having recognised him and pushed the ferry boat into mid-stream so that he should not escape his pursuers, who executed him on the spot.

3. *The Anonimalle Chronicle* (ed. V. H. Galbraith).

4. Froissart's estimate of 1500 hanged or beheaded, like most of his figures, seems wildly inaccurate. In his detailed but unfinished study of the rising, André Réville made a list—admittedly incomplete—of a hundred and ten persons who suffered the supreme penalty. André Réville, *Le Soulèvement des Travailleurs d'Angleterre en 1381.*

CHAPTER THREE

1. The minister, Mr. Benjamin Wesley, was a great-grandfather of John Wesley.

2. Fourteen years later, as Bishop of London, he was to prove that his courage was as great in the day of worldly success as in that of adversity, by remaining at his post during the plague, and at the end of his long and useful life his last blessings were to rest on the rising stones of Wren's St. Paul's.

CHAPTER FOUR

1. '. . . they being the finest that ever I saw in my life, that is the truth of it'. *D.* June 19th, 1666.

2. 'Up betimes and shaved myself after a week's growth, but Lord! how ugly I was yesterday, and how fine today!' *D.* Sept. 17th, 1666.

CHAPTER FIVE

1. *Recollections of Rifleman Harris*, 71. See also *Boothby, under England's Flag*, 185-6 *et passim*; *Service Adventures and Experiences of Captain Blakeney*, 22-4, 27-9; A. L. F. Schaumann, *On the Road with Wellington*, 11-63; *Journal of a Soldier of the Seventy-First Regiment*, 50-1; *Oxfordshire Light Infantry Chronicle* (1902), 226.

2. Schaumann, 92-3. 'I blush for our men,' wrote a Scot who shared their sufferings. 'I would blame them, too; alas! how can I, when I think upon their dreadful situation, fatigued and wet, shivering, perishing with cold?—no fuel to be got, not even straw to lie upon. Can men in such a situation admire the beauties of art?' *Journal of a Soldier*, 55.

3. Blakeney 49-51; *Journal of a Soldier*, 58-61; Harris, 96; Schaumann, 107-111, 128; A. M. Delavoye, *Life of Lord Lynedoch*, 293; *Diary of Sir John Moore* (ed. J. M. Maurice), 378-84; Cope, *History of the Rifle Brigade*, 36, 104.

CHAPTER SIX

1. 'There they go, shaking their blankets again,' said the old soldiers. Leeke I, 11; *Near Observer*, 2-4; Becke, 49-50; Bessborough, 240-1; Costello, 190; *Creevey Papers*, I, 223, 226-7, 229-30, 232; Lynedoch, 756; D'Arblay, III, 341-2, 347-8; Frazer, 520-4, 529-30, 536, 544, 572; Jackson, 6, 14-18; Kincaid, 153-6; Mercer, 1, 47, 53-5; 103-4, 156-7, 198-202, 217-19, 230-9, 242-3, 284; Siborne, 3, 23; Simpson, 16-17; Smith, I, 226.

2. Weller, *Waterloo*, 42-4; Fraser, 267; Ellesmere, 193-4; Greville, I, 82.

3. Weller, *Waterloo*, 45-9; Glover, 196-8; Ellesmere, 185-6, 194-9, 224-7, 237; Becke, 49-52.

4. 'I told them so myself, but of course in different terms. I said to them, "Everbody knows their own army best; but, if I were to fight with mine here, I should expect to be beat." . . . They were dotted in this way—all their bodies along the slope of a hill, so that no cannon-ball missed its effect upon them; they had also undertaken to defend two villages that were too far off, only within reach of cannon-shot. Now here is a general rule. Never attempt to defend a village that is not within reach of musketry.' Stanhope, 109. See also Ellesmere, 127, 186.

5. Retailing this conversation to George Chad nine years later, Wellington observed, 'By God, if I had come up five minutes later, the battle was lost.' Chad. 7.

6. There are excellent detailed accounts of Quatre Bras in Jac Weller's *Wellington at Waterloo*, Elizabeth Longford's *Wellington, The Years of the Sword*, Volume X of Fortescue's *History of the British Army*, and A. F. Becke's *Napoleon and Waterloo*.

7. Hamilton of Dalzell MS., 46-8, 77. See Weller, *Waterloo*, 53-77; Simmons, 364; Stanhope, 244; Tomkinson, 286-8; Ellesmere, 230-1; Anglesey, 128-32; Howarth, 20.

8. 'If the Prussians are beat, which I think is very probable,' he told the Duke of Richmond on the night of the ball, 'that is the spot'—pointing on the map—'where we must lick those fellows.' Lady Shelley, I, 171. For a first-hand confirmation of this story, see Granville, II, 538. See also Mercer, I, 194.

9. See Fraser, 265, 268, 270.

10. 'It is not true that I could not have retreated. I could have got into the wood and I would have defied the Devil to drive me out.' Arbuthnot, I, 235. See also Cotton, 303; Fraser, 264.

11. Lynedoch, 764; Ellesmere, 216-18; Fortescue, 238, 243-7; Gomm, 363-4; Jackson, 10; Kincaid, 325, 329; Mercer, I, 93-4, 197-8, 281.

12. Stanhope, 221.

13. When someone mentioned to Wellington that Lord Uxbridge had the reputation of running away with everybody he could, he replied, 'I'll take good care he don't run away with me.' In this anecdote, Fraser adds, he was compelled to soften 'the vigorous vernacular of the Duke.' Fraser, 186. See also Frazer, 520. Anglesey, 119-24.

14. 'The real truth was that our cavalry never had much to do before this sanguinary battle; and the officers were, and always have been, very inferior to that of the infantry, being generally composed of country gentlemen's sons from the hunting counties of England. Such persons have no particular inclination for fighting but enter the Army as a genteel business, the oldest son being the squire, the second the parson, the next the dragoon.' *Hamilton of Dalzell* MS., 80. See also Kincaid, 161; Stanley, 105; Tomkinson, 296, 318.

15. 'I thought at first that they had all been wounded, but on finding how the case stood, I could not help telling them that theirs was now the better situation to verify the old proverb, "The uglier, the better the soldier." ' Kincaid, 334.

16. 'Mein Gott,' said Blücher, after inspecting Mercer's battery, 'dere is not von 'orse in diss batterie wich is not goot for Veldt Marshal.' Mercer, I, 217.

17. To Earl Bathurst, May 4th 1815.

18. 'It was my business to be prepared for all events.' *Gascoyne Heiress*. See also Stanhope, 280; Ellesmere, 104-5, 183, 234; Fortescue, X, 351, 355; Fraser, 264-5, 269-70; Greville, I, 82-3; Tomkinson, 297; Glover, 200.

19. Fraser, 2-3.

20. See also James, 200; Weller, 82; Longford, 444.

21. Brett-James, 308-9.

22. 'I never get wet when I can help it.' *Croker Papers*, II, 311.

23. Smith, I, 270; Stanhope, I, 220; H. M. C. Bathurst; Bessborough, 242; Frazer, 546; Kincaid, 338; Smith, I, 268; Gronow, I, 68-9; Leeke, 187; Gomm, 363-4; *Hamilton of Dalzell* MS., 49-50; Jackson, 7-8.

24. Foy, 278-9, 345.

25. Weller, *Waterloo*, 88; Hooper, 189; Longford.

26. Stanhope, 47. See also Ellesmere, 105-6; Frazer, 556; Gronow, I, 198-9; Greville (suppl.), I, 83; Cotton, 51-7; Kennedy, 89-92; Houssaye, 187-9; Morris, 229-32.

27. Becke, 168; Cotton, 87-8; Fortescue X, 360; Houssaye, 203; James, 223; Kennedy, 107; Kincaid, 341; Mercer, I, 294-6; Siborne, 327-8; Tomkinson, 297, 303.

28. 'I peeped into the skirts of the forest, and truly felt astonished; entire companies seemed there, with regularly piled arms, fires blazing under cooking kettles, while the men lay about smoking as coolly as if no enemy were within a day's march. . . . General Müffling—Wellington's Prussian liaison officer—in his account of Waterloo, estimates the runaways hidden in the forest at 10,000.' Jackson, 47.

29. Becke, 195-7; Belloc, 171-3; Fortescue X, 360-4; Gomm, 351, 358-9; Gronow, I, 188; Horsburgh, 249-51; Houssaye, 193-6; Jackson, 47, 88-92; James, 223, 228-9; Kennedy, 107-12; Kincaid, 344-6; *Random Shots*, 206, 273; Siborne, 19; Simmons, 365, 367; Smith, I, 270-1, 277; Stanhope, 221; James, 228-35; Cotton, 59-62; Weller, *Waterloo*, 95-100; Howarth, 83-93.

30. Lynedoch, 760, 762-3; Fortescue, X, 365-7; Gomm, 351; Gronow, I, 78-80, 195-6, 204; II, 3; *Hamilton of Dalzell* MS., 50-3, 70-1, 77-8; Haydon, I, 311; Houssaye, 197-20; Kennedy, 110-11; Kincaid, 345; Picton, 78-80; Lady Shelley, I, 173-4, 183; Siborne, 7-10, 16-17, 43-4, 72, 77, 81-2; Tomkinson, 300, 304; Howarth, 93-102; Becke, 197-8; Weller, *Waterloo* 102-5.

31. The unusual but convenient formation chosen by young Captain Shaw Kennedy, a pupil of Moore and Craufurd, who was acting as chief-of-staff to Alten's third division. Kennedy, 98-102.

32. Mercer, I, 313.

33. Someone once asked him whether the French cuirassiers had not come up very well at Quatre Bras. 'Yes,' he replied, 'and they went down very well too.' See also Becke, 202-9; *Croker Papers*, I, 330; Lynedoch, 759; Ellesmere, 98-9, 240; Fortescue, X, 370-6; Fraser, 558-9; Frazer, 559; Gomm, 373; Gronow, I, 69-73, 190-1; Houssaye, 204-14; Jackson, 48-51; Kennedy, 19, 20, 115-16; Mercer, I, 310-11; Picton, 81-2, 85-6; Siborne, 1-12; Tomkinson, 305.

34. 'The Aide-de-Camp . . . seeing that the Hanoverian would not advance, said, "As you do not attend to the order given, I have another from the Duke of Wellington which is *that you fall back to the rear of the army*." This the Hanoverian readily complied with, saying it was very considerate of the Duke when engaged in so

much action to think of his corps with so much care. Accordingly this corps retreated, and it was from them that a report reached Brussels that the French had gained the victory.' Farington, VIII, 19-20. See also *Hamilton of Dalzell* MS., 73; Frazer, 560-1; Siborne, 14, 18-19; Stanhope, 221; Tomkinson, 296.

35. From a copy of a letter of Captain (later General) Horace Churchill of June 24th 1815, communicated by Brigadier C. E. Hudson, VC, CB, DSO, MC. 'All that Churchill says in censure,' wrote Napier of this letter, 'was the common talk of the Army at the time.' See *Hamilton of Dalzell* MS., for a cavalryman's criticism, and Gronow, I, 73; Tomkinson, 318. Lord Uxbridge afterwards wrote in glowing terms of the conduct of the British cavalry as a whole. Siborne, 12, 16-17.

36. 'The rear man made a considerable outcry on being wounded, but on one of the officers saying kindly to him, "O man, don't make a noise," he instantly recollected himself and was quiet. This was the only noise . . . which I heard from any wounded man during the battle.' Leeke, I, 33.

37. 'Never was such devotion witnessed as the French cuirassiers. . . . I could not help exclaiming when the mêlée was going on, "By God, those fellows deserve Bonaparte, they fight so nobly for him." ' MS. letter of Horace Churchill, June 24th 1815.

38. 'Not a private in the ranks but felt that the Duke of Wellington—the man of Wealth, Rank and Success with the world at his feet—was jeopardising his life to at least the same degree as the poor outcast who had become a soldier from starvation.' Fraser, 252-3. See also D'Arblay, VII, 134; Lennox, *Three Years with the Duke*, 114-115.

39. Unknown to him they were at that moment fiercely attacking the Prussian rearguard at Wavre twelve miles away.

40. Becke, 211; Ellesmere, 207-9; Fortescue, X, 372, 378; Tomkinson, 308; Weller, *Waterloo*, 106-7, 111-12.

41. Through a failure on the Prince of Orange's part, and ultimately on Wellington's, to make adequate provision in time. 'The Duke lamented the loss of La Haye Sainte from the fault of the officer commanding there, but immediately correcting himself, "No, in fact it was my fault, for I ought to have looked into it myself." ' Stanhope, 245-6, 220. See also Ellesmere, 104, 208-9; Fortescue, 381-3; Kennedy, 122-3, 174-5; Siborne, 32-3; Tomkinson, 305.

42. Kennedy, 128. See also Weller, *Waterloo*, 119-24.

43. Clinton, 421.

44. Kincaid, 352. See also Ellesmere, 172-3; Fortescue, X, 396-7; Frazer, 139, 189, 219; Gomm, 359-60, 366; Gronow, I, 212; Basil Jackson,, 75-6; *Autobiography of Sergeant Lawrence*, 239; Simmons, 375; Tomkinson, 308.

45. Booth, *Waterloo*, II, 275 (Letter of Rifleman Lewis), cit. Glover, 274.

46. *Spencer and Waterloo*, 114-15; Lady Shelley, I, 106; Frazer, 560.

47. Broughton, I, 103; Castlereagh, X, 383; Ellesmere, 172-3; Farington, VIII, 32; Frazer, 263, 276; Gronow, I, 69-70; Guedalla, 275-6; *Hamilton of Dalzell* MS., 56-60; Kennedy, 126-9, 176; Picton, 88-9, 106; Jackson, 42-4; Smith, I, 271; Stanhope, 183; Longford, 471-3; Weller, *Waterloo*, 121-4; Becke, 216-19; Muriel Wellesley, 370.

48. Mercer's battery was almost cut to pieces by their fire. See also Mercer, I, 325-30; Siborne, 21-2.

49. Fraser, 38; Ellesmere, 106, 163; Kincaid, 356.

50. 'I never saw his Grace so animated,' Smith, I, 272-3. See also Becke, 222-30; Longford, 478-80; Weller, *Waterloo*, 149-50; Howarth, 182-3; Cotton, 125-35, 305-6; Ellesmere, 183-4; Fortescue, X, 391-2; Gomm, 361-2, 367-73; Gronow, I, 73, 89-90; Housaye, 221-32; Jackson, 69-70; Kennedy, 140-50; Leeke, I, *passim;* Moorsom 256-65; Robinson, 611-14; Siborne, *passim;* Tomkinson, 311-15; Chesney, 210-13.

51. Longford, 81.

52. Leeke, 67; Moorsom, 267; Jackson, 57-9; Tomkinson, 315; Gronow, I, 200; Simpson, 129; Stanhope, 245; Picton, 98; Gomm, 370-1, 375-6.

53. It took a groom half an hour to catch him. 'There may have been many faster horses,' Wellington said of him, 'no doubt many handsomer, but for bottom and endurance I never saw his fellow.' Longford, 484.

54. ' "Never, certainly," said the Duke, "was anything so absurd as ascribing that saying to Cambronne." ' Stanhope, 172. See also *Idem*, 245. 'There is not a word of truth in all this bombast. I have fought the French as often as anybody, and . . . I never saw them behave ill except at the end of the battle of Waterloo. Whole battalions ran away and left their arms piled, and as for Cambronne, he surrendered without a wound.' Strathfieldsaye, March 31st 1820. Chad, 2; Ellesmere, 111.

55. Longford, 485; Stanhope, 84.

56. *Dispatches*, XII, 484; Stanhope, 145.

57. 'What a contrast to six hours' plunder by the French which Napoleon had promised.' Spencer Madan to Dr. Madan, June 19th 1815. *Spencer and Waterloo*, 108.

58. *Creevey Papers*, I, 23-67.

59. *Dispatches*, XII, 488.

60. To the Hon. William Wellesley-Pole. Wellesley-Pole, 35.

61. Lady Shelley, I, 102.

CHAPTER SEVEN

1. He was Palmerston's son-in-law.

2. 'A man may assemble five hundred workmen one week and dismiss them the next, without having any further connection with them than to receive a week's work for a week's wages, nor any further solicitude about their future fate than if they were so many old shuttles.' *Sir W. Scott, Familiar Letters, Vol. II, 19th May, 1820.* The practice still seemed shocking to any one nursed in the older social system.

3. In the early years of the nineteenth century the publican of a famous Manchester tavern patronised by the town's leading manufacturers used to expel his customers at closing time with the help of a lash. A. F. Fremantle, *England in the Nineteenth Century*, 42.

4. The proprietors denied that the children were 'turned adrift'; they were merely 'set at liberty.' 'To be sure, they would not be well off; they would have to beg their way or something of that sort.' *Report on Children in Manufactures, 1816 (Peel's Committee, 288-93, cit.* J. L. & H. Hammond, *The Town Labourer, 148-9).*

5. Engels, *145-6.*

6. ' "At the gates of all the London docks," says the Rev. W. Champney, preacher of the East End, "hundreds of the poor appear every morning in winter before daybreak, in the hope of getting a day's work. They await the opening of the gates; and, when the youngest and strongest and best known have been engaged, hundreds, cast down by disappointed hope, go back to their wretched homes." When these people find no work and will not rebel against society, what remains for them but to beg? And surely no one can wonder at the great army of beggars, most of them able-bodied men, with whom the police carries on perpetual war.' F. Engels, *The Condition of the Working Class in England iv, 1844,* 86-7.

7. Dr. Lyon Playfair, *Health of Towns Commission, I. Report on the State of Large Towns in Lancashire, 1845.*

8. Engels, *60.*

9. Engels, *49-50.*

10. T. Carlyle, *Chartism.*

11. Feargus O'Connor, the Chartist leader, who claimed to be descended from the Irish Kings, thus addressed his followers in Palace Yard, Westminster. 'It was said the working classes were dirty fellows, and that among them they could not get six hundred and fifty-eight who were fit to sit in the House of Commons. Indeed! He would soon alter that. He would pick out that number from the present meeting, and the first he chose he would take down to Mr. Hawes's soap factory; then he would take them

where they should reform their tailors' bills; he would next take them to the hairdresser and perfumer, where they should be anointed with the fashionable stink; and having done that by way of preparation, he would quickly take them into the House of Commons, when they would be the best six hundred and fifty-eight that ever sat within its walls.'

12. *Illustrated London News*, I, 67.

13. Another speaker on Pendlehill referred to the Queen as a dawdling useless thing.' (*Annual Register, June, 1842.*)

14. Communicated by the present Earl of Crawford and Balcarres.

15. 'It is certainly a very dismal matter for reflection, and well worthy of the consideration of the profoundest political philosophers, that the possession of such a Constitution, all our wealth, industry, ingenuity, peace, and that superiority in wisdom and virtue which we so confidently claim, are not sufficient to prevent the existence of a large mountain of human misery, of one stratum in society in the most deplorable state, both moral and physical, to which mankind can be reduced, and that all our advantages do not secure us against the occurrence of evils and mischiefs so great as to threaten a mighty social and political convulsion.' *Greville Memoirs, Part II, Vol. II, 119-20.*

16. In later years men like Sir James Graham, the Home Secretary, and John Roebuck, the Radical economist, admitted that they had been wrong in their fear that the limitation of hours of labour would ruin the country.

17. Engels expected a further and probably decisive revolutionary crisis in 1847, or at latest 1853. *The Condition of the Working Class in England, 296.*